1·21·97

D0890222

Henry E. Huntington's
LIBRARY of LIBRARIES

HENRY E. HUNTINGTON'S
LIBRARY *of* LIBRARIES

by Donald C. Dickinson

HENRY E. HUNTINGTON LIBRARY
and ART GALLERY - San Marino

HUNTINGTON LIBRARY • SAN MARINO, CALIFORNIA

Library of Congress Cataloging-in-Publication Data
Dickinson, Donald C.
Henry E. Huntington's library of libraries / by Donald C. Dickinson
   p. cm. Includes bibliographical references and index.
   ISBN 0-87328-153-5
1. Huntington, Henry Edwards, 1850–1927. 2. Henry E. Huntington
Library and Art Gallery. 3. Rare books—Collectors and collecting—
United States—History—20th century. 4. Art—Collectors and
collecting—United States—History—20th century. 5. Capitalists
and financiers—United States—Biography. 6. Book collectors—
United States—Biography. I. Title.
Z989.H95D53 1995   95-10396
002'.074' 092—dc2 [B]   CIP

HUNTINGTON LIBRARY PRESS
1151 Oxford Road, San Marino, California 91108

FOR SEVEN WONDERFUL WOMEN

Colleen
and our daughters
Ann, Jean, Ellen, Mary, Katie, Sheila

Readers and collectors all

CONTENTS

Henry Huntington chose ten devices representing important printers and publishers of the fifteenth and sixteenth centuries to be used in the design for the bronze doors to his library. The printers' marks were incorporated in the corners of the larger and central panels.

The library doors are pictured on the dust jacket of this volume, and the devices are featured in the chapter headings and on the endpapers. The descriptions below were adapted from *Printers' and Publishers' Devices in England and Scotland 1485–1640,* by Ronald B. McKerrow (London, 1913).

← Mercury's hat and caduceus with two cornucopias and seascape, a design used by several printers, including Hatfield, Bishop, and Barker. By 1594 it was the device of Eliot's Court.

Richard Tottel's device, with his → monogram and name in full, of a hand holding a star within an architectural frame containing the words *Cum priuilegio.*

← Rebus of Richard Grafton, with *Suscipite incitum verbum &c. Iaco . I:*

Mark of William Caxton, with → his initials. Although it appeared first in a book printed in Paris, the mark was probably cut in England.

The mark of John Day, a framed → device of Christ rising from the tomb with a palm branch in his hand.

The arms of the city of Geneva. → Rowland Hall worked at Geneva from 1559 to 1560 and used the arms as his sign in 1562 and 1563.

← Device of Lucretia with *Lucretia Romana* and *Thomas Bertheletus,* used by Berthelet.

Device of the sun in glory, → with *Sol oriens mundo,* used by Edward Whitchurch from about 1545 to 1553.

← St. John the Evangelist with eagle, the sign of Robert Wyer. The spelling "Wyre" was also used by the printer.

A device of a pavior paving, with → the motto, "Thou shalt labor till thou returne to duste" and the initials "T. P." above the frame. The device was probably used by Thomas Pavier.

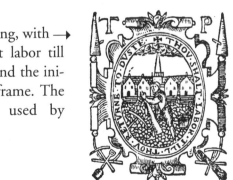

List of Illustrations

Acknowledgments

A number of people and institutions supported work on this study of Henry Edwards Huntington as a book collector. I am grateful to the University of Arizona for granting me a sabbatical leave during the fall term of 1987, when I began work in the archival collections at the Huntington Library. A fellowship from the Andrew W. Mellon Foundation and a grant from the College of Social and Behavioral Sciences of the University of Arizona provided further assistance.

I am deeply indebted to a number of individuals associated with the Huntington Library. Edwin H. Carpenter, long-time staff member, read and reread the entire manuscript and made countless helpful suggestions. I was fortunate to have had conversations with two of Huntington's grandchildren, Edwards H. Metcalf and Harriet Doerr. Many members of the Huntington staff provided invaluable assistance. Thomas Lange, curator of early printed books and bindings, gave both suggestions and encouragement. William Frank, Alan H. Jutzi, Karen Kearns, Brita Mack, Harriet McLoone, Virginia Renner, James Thorpe, Robert R. Wark, Daniel Woodward, and Mary Wright provided help of many kinds. A number of research scholars working at the library, especially Robert N. Essick and William B. Fredericks, took the time to discuss Huntington's collecting activities with me. The index to the book was prepared by Carol B. Pearson, who also shared her knowledge of cataloging and of the institution's history.

Parts of the text, in different form, appeared as "Mr. Huntington and Mr. Smith," and "Mr. Huntington and Mr. Brigham" (*Book Collector,* vol. 37, no. 3, and vol. 42, no. 4, respectively); and as "Huntington and Robert Hoe: An Overland Book Trail from New York to California" (*AB Bookman's Weekly,* vol. 21, no. 6). I would like to thank the original publishers for permission to use this material.

I greatly appreciate the assistance given me by the staff of the Huntington Library Press, including Peggy Park Bernal, director, Susan Green, editor, and Karen Harms, designer.

Donald C. Dickinson

INTRODUCTION

Beginning with the colonial period and continuing down through the 1880s, private book collecting in America was dominated by genteel amateurs. Collectors such as Thomas Prince (1687–1758), William Byrd (1674–1744), James Logan (1674–1751), George Brinley (1817–75), James Lenox (1800–1880), Robert Hoe (1839–1909), and Beverly Chew (1850–1924) were well educated, affluent, and secure in positions of responsibility in business, law, politics, or the ministry. They enjoyed their stately homes, art collections, and well-stocked libraries. For most of them, collecting was an exhilarating hobby, one to be pursued in the spirit of gentlemanly competitiveness. Although there was little thought of financial gain by means of collecting, they enjoyed finding bargains that others had overlooked. Without being scholarly, many of them took a serious interest in developing their book collections. They rummaged in book stores, attended auctions, and studied book catalogs in order to obtain the finest copies available. They understood the importance and appreciated the beauty of early printings, association copies, fine bindings, and illustrated limited editions. The libraries they formed often represented the efforts of a lifetime. In the end, the collector would will his library, along with other household goods, to his heirs or, if they were not interested, turn it over to the auction houses. These practices had been employed by collectors in Great Britain, Europe, and Asia for generations, and until 1900, American collectors simply followed in their footsteps.

During the last decades of the nineteenth century, rapid industrial development in America brought about many social changes. The new breed of business entrepreneurs who led this development made vast fortunes in railroading, manufacturing, and banking. As their wealth became established they brought a new viewpoint to collecting and connoisseurship in America. Efficient, cool-headed, and purposeful, they understood the importance of decisive action, consolidation, and closure. Instead of spending their time browsing in bookshops looking for choice titles, they employed book dealers to buy up private libraries en bloc. Unlike the genteel amateur who simply passed his books along to the family, many of the new collectors set up endowments and boards of trustees to make sure that their collections would have continued support and would be available for the use of scholars. In the early decades of the twentieth century, Henry E. Huntington perhaps best exemplified the new perspective that these American entrepreneurs brought to book collecting.

After making a fortune in the railroad industry, Huntington set out to build a rare book and manuscript library. He succeeded in gathering his unequaled collections over a period of only fifteen years, a result not only of personal determination and unlimited means but of fortunate timing. As Huntington began to develop a serious interest in rare books, a number of important private collections came on the market. In 1911, working with the formidable New York dealer George D. Smith, Huntington obtained the entire Elihu D. Church library and some of the most spectacular items from the Robert Hoe collection. Huntington recognized the unusual opportunity the sale of these libraries presented and, with his businessman's decisiveness, immediately acquired the rarities for his own. As other major collections became available over the next fifteen years, Huntington responded with equal decisiveness. Between 1911 and the time of his death in 1927 Huntington dominated the book markets of New York and London.

Huntington's motives for collecting on the grand scale changed over time: he began by gathering a trove of sumptuous volumes to satisfy his own tastes and ended by endowing a research library for scholars. Throughout, his determination to obtain the best and the unique controlled the direction of his buying. He brought this desire to excel with him from his career in railroading, along with a straightforward and competitive view of the way excellence was achieved. He knew how to drive a hard bargain; take the advice of experts; combine small units into larger profitable units; and put profits back into the business.

In his effort to gather distinguished collections, Huntington was aided by a group of trained librarians headed by George Watson Cole and a number of sophisticated book dealers, most prominently George D. Smith, A. S. W. Rosenbach, and Charles Sessler. These men provided Huntington with the expertise he needed to acquire and organize his collections. Still, Huntington kept a firm hand on all the activities involved in the growth and development of the library. He had the final word on purchases, even when small amounts of money were involved and even, in later years, when his health began to fail. He felt, as he once said, like a trustee who had been given the responsibility to care for great masterworks of literature and art—riches that were entrusted to him temporarily but that someday would be turned over to the public. It was not a responsibility to be taken lightly.

Huntington was a builder. He created a vast business empire in Southern California and used his fortune to establish a renowned book and manuscript collection. The Henry E. Huntington Library as it stands today, a center for humanistic research, is a testament to both his careful planning and his generosity.

Chapter 1

ONEONTA AND BEYOND
1850–1900

 On the evening of 24 April 1911, four hundred book collectors and dealers gathered at the sumptuous Clarence Hyde mansion on Madison Avenue and Fortieth Street in New York City to take part in the auction of the Robert Hoe library. Of all the rarities listed in the Anderson Auction Company's sale catalog, lot 269, *Biblia Sacra Latina,* the Gutenberg Bible, thought to be the first book printed in the West from movable type, caused the most speculation. Up to that time the largest amount of money given for a printed book at auction had been $22,750, the price Bernard Quaritch paid in 1884 for a copy of the Mainz Psalter. Experts felt certain that a new record would be set at the Hoe sale. When the famous two-volume folio, bound in leather-covered oak boards and printed on vellum, was brought forward, George D. Smith—dubbed "the Napoleon of booksellers" for his brash, assertive manner—opened the bidding at $10,000.[1] Other dealers quickly moved the figure up to $20,000 and then to $30,000. Finally the field narrowed to Smith and Joseph Widener, a wealthy Philadelphia collector representing his father. After Widener bid $49,000 Smith signaled $50,000, and the contest was over. As the hammer fell there was "a burst of general applause followed by cries throughout the room 'The

buyer? Who is the buyer?'" With a word of permission from Smith the auctioneer announced that the new owner of the Gutenberg Bible was Henry E. Huntington. At that point "the applause was renewed with great heartiness."[2]

Despite the acclaim that followed the announcement, few present that night knew much about the stocky sixty-one-year-old man with the carefully trimmed military moustache and the dignified demeanor.[3] Some perhaps associated his name with railroad development and realized he was the nephew of Collis P. Huntington (1821–1900), the Central Pacific rail magnate. Others may have remembered that two weeks earlier he had purchased the choice Elihu D. Church library of Americana and English literature for a figure reputed to be in the neighborhood of one million dollars. Because of Huntington's reticence, few knew more than that. Only the most prescient could have guessed that over the next fifteen years he would dominate all the important book auctions in London and New York and eventually become known as the founder of one of the greatest private research libraries in the world.

Huntington had the good fortune to grow up in the midst of a closely knit, hardworking, churchgoing family. He was born the fourth child of Solon and Harriet Saunders Huntington in Oneonta, New York, on 27 February 1850.[4] Located near the headwaters of the Susquehanna River in hilly country halfway between Albany and Binghamton, Oneonta was at that time a dairying and lumbering center of nineteen hundred inhabitants. Solon Huntington was an enterprising small businessman who ran a general merchandise store, had a share in a carriage factory, and from time to time bought and sold farm property. He had come to New York from the family homestead in central Connecticut, where the first Huntingtons had emigrated from England in the middle of the seventeenth century. In 1840, shortly before moving to Oneonta, he had married Harriet Saunders, the daughter of Sally (Edwards) Saunders—a descendant of the American theologian Jonathan Edwards—and Dr. Henry Saunders, a prominent physician of the Burnt Hills area in Saratoga County. The young couple must have had some savings because soon after they arrived in Oneonta they were able to buy an attractive eight-bedroom house on the town's main street. Little is known about Solon's interests outside of his work, but one story from Harriet's girlhood is significant in light of her son's interest in book collecting. As a young

woman Harriet showed a "marked individuality" and wanted a better education than that provided by the local schools. She was thwarted in this by her
father who, like many of his contemporaries, opposed higher education for
women. She made up for this disappointment by reading everything she
could find in her father's extensive library, a collection that included not only
medical texts but classic works in literature, history, and biography. She continued to enjoy books throughout her life and passed that enthusiasm along
to her children.[5]

Henry Edwards, named for his great-grandfather on his mother's side,
soon became "Edwards," or "Ed," to his family and friends. Until he was seventeen he attended the two-story wood-frame private school on Grove Street
and learned his lessons from such standard texts as Clark's Grammar,
Thompson's Arithmetic, and Colton's Geography. Opportunities for further
education were not plentiful and most young men and women went to work
immediately on completing the elementary or secondary grades. For a boy in
rural New York in the 1850s and '60s, work for wages usually meant helping
on a farm or, as in Huntington's case, clerking in a store. In addition, young
people shared in the home chores—chopping wood, preparing meals, and
tending to the garden. Country boys were expected to be up early in the
morning, and leisure time was relatively unknown. What amusements did
exist were simple and inexpensive: sledding, in the winter, on Chestnut Street
hill, and in warm weather swimming in the Schenevus Creek. The social
highlights of the year centered around the Fourth of July, circus days, and
church meetings. The Huntingtons were loyal members of the Presbyterian
church and many of their activities followed the church calendar. Little is
known of Edwards's early years, but the work ethic was clearly an important
factor in his development.

In the autumn of 1870 Huntington decided to test his independence
beyond the borders of Oneonta. For several months he lived with his sister
and her husband in Cohoes, New York, paying for his room and board by
working as a clerk in his brother-in-law's dry goods store. In February 1870
he moved to New York City and took a room at 71 Henry Street in Brooklyn.
Although jobs were scarce he found one as a porter, sweeping floors and
stocking shelves with Sargent and Company, a hardware manufacturing firm
on Beekman Street. It could have been a lonely time for a young man away

from home for the first time, but Uncle Collis, now an established railway executive with a residence and a business office in New York, provided frequent invitations for dinner and other family social events. Edwards attended church and Sunday school at the Plymouth Congregational Church in Brooklyn, where he often heard the renowned orator Henry Ward Beecher deliver his witty sermons. In letters home he described his work, the room he was staying in, the church, and his weekend visits with Collis. Money was a persistent problem. On his salary of three dollars a week he could barely pay for room and board. In one or two emergencies, he accepted a small amount of money from Collis but declined when larger amounts were offered. In July he wrote to his mother:

> Uncle Collis has given me some money and wants to give me more, but I didn't accept as I think a man of my age should be independent.[6]

It has been said that young Huntington was fortunate in his choice of relatives, a jibe that suggests his success in railroading came directly and only from his close association with his uncle. It is true that Collis helped him get a start, but Edwards quickly made his own way through personal determination and hard work. By 1870 Collis—characterized by the historian Oscar Lewis as "cold, crafty, hard and frequently dishonest"[7]—was one of the most powerful men in the rapidly developing American railroad system. He, along with Charles Crocker, Mark Hopkins, and Leland Stanford, "The Big Four," had provided the vision and the financial backing for the development of the western portion of the first transcontinental railroad— a linking of the Central Pacific and the Union Pacific that took place at Promontory Point, Utah, in May 1869. With the successful completion of the overland route, Collis looked east and seized the ownership of the floundering Chesapeake, Ohio and South Western. Among the many problems he faced in extending the C & O line was the high cost of railroad ties. He shrewdly resolved the difficulty by buying a sawmill in St. Albans, West Virginia, and making his own. The mill needed a manager and Collis knew the right person for the job. In the spring of 1871 he asked his energetic young nephew to leave the hardware store in New York and take the post in St. Albans for a salary of $150 a month plus travel expenses.

FIG. 1. Henry Huntington about 1873.

Huntington's assignment was to negotiate contracts for lumber supplies and keep the mill running day and night.

Life as a mill manager offered unexpected challenges. In 1872 Huntington proudly told his mother how, through his efforts, disaster was averted when a flood on the Coal River endangered the mill's supply of timber.

> Everyone here said it was impossible for me to save a stick of my timber, but I showed them different before I got through—I got but nine hours sleep from Sunday morning to Thursday night but

I did save all my timber and the inhabitants say that it is something
that has never been done before.[8]

Such crises were not the rule, and Huntington found many everyday satis-
factions on the job. By instituting practical labor-saving techniques he was
able to double production and cut costs. In 1873, he and a co-worker, Stanley
Franchot, combined their savings and bought the mill from Collis. When
Franchot decided to move to another job, Huntington took over the entire
contract and became sole owner—an early sign of his independent nature.
During this period he married Collis's niece, Mary Alice Prentice, of
Sacramento, California, bought a small house in St. Albans, and settled into
a pleasant round of domestic activities.

With a modest but regular income he began to gather a home library. He
bought standard sets of the literary works of Ruskin, Dickens, Scott, Whittier,
and Lowell, and the historical writings of Parton and Bancroft. It was a surprisingly large collection for a young working man and must have been a matter of considerable pride. Unfortunately Huntington lost his first library in
negotiations involving the mill. It was a matter of business before pleasure: he
needed to raise all the money he could to buy out Franchot, and the books,
valued at $1,800, became an important part of the settlement.[9] Meanwhile,
Solon Huntington's business affairs back in Oneonta had grown to such an
extent that he needed his son's help. In the spring of 1876 the young mill
owner sold his St. Albans holdings and with his wife and their infant son
Howard returned to the rolling hill-country of central New York state. For the
next five years Huntington devoted himself to the family business.

In 1881 Collis, always a keen judge of talent, saw an opportunity to lure his
nephew back into railroading. The task of rebuilding the Chesapeake, Ohio and
South Western track between Trimble, Tennessee, and Covington, Kentucky,
required a construction boss who could manage the men and get the job done
quickly. It was obvious to Collis that his nephew was the right
person for the job, and Huntington was happy to make the move. He and his wife
packed up the family, now two daughters and a son, and returned to the south.

Once there, he found the hours long and the job arduous. In a letter to his
mother, Huntington spoke of the satisfaction he felt in filling a tall order, as
well as the admiration he felt for his uncle.

I received an encouraging letter from uncle Collis about my work here which was very gratifying to me. I have never worked harder than I have on this work nor had more to contend with and I cannot tell you how gratified I am to know that he appreciates it and I feel fully repaid for my labour.[10]

Huntington's colleagues also recognized his ability. At a testimonial dinner held many years after completion of the C & O project, one speaker declared:

I wish to express my best wishes for the good health and happiness of my dear good friend and Boss, Mr. Huntington, for whom I worked twenty-three years since as the Principal Assistant Engineer of Construction. He is the one you should be proud of. I am proud to be able to say I worked for him three years without being fired. But I did not work half as hard as did Mr. Huntington. He never stopped working.[11]

In 1885, after Huntington had completed his assignment with the C & O, Collis asked him to take on an even more difficult task, the reorganization of the floundering Kentucky Central Railroad. The assignment was to see the line through a receivership procedure and to get it back on a productive basis. By the fall of 1891 Huntington, first serving as superintendent and then as vice president and general manager, had negotiated the receivership successfully and brought the Kentucky Central to a respectable level of solvency. As a result of these negotiations he achieved recognition in the industry for his own management skills—not as in the past, simply for his relationship to Collis. He had been tested at several levels and in each case proved his ability.

Huntington's next assignment carried him to the far west. Collis, who was spending more and more time in New York and Washington, D. C., needed a reliable manager in California. In 1892 he asked his nephew to move to San Francisco to take on the varied responsibilities of a newly created position, "First Assistant to the President" of the Southern Pacific. Huntington accepted and by spring of that year was in charge of the SP office on the corner of Post and Montgomery streets. His growing family, now three daughters and a son, lived for nearly a year at the Hotel Richelieu and later moved into a pleasantly appointed three-story, twenty-four-room house at 2840 Jackson Street.

The city to which Huntington came was very different from any place he had lived until then. With a population of 298,997, San Francisco was the seventh largest urban area in the United States. The rapid growth stimulated by the discovery of gold in 1849 and silver in the 1860s had leveled off, but newcomers arrived in a steady stream, attracted by a salubrious coastal climate and a romanticized vision of the good life—available in abundance, so it was thought, in the city on the bay. Huntington was enthusiastic about everything California had to offer, particularly the fine summer weather. In June 1892 he wrote to his mother:

> When I read of the hot weather in the east, I am glad to be in California for you know how the hot weather [affects] me, and there has been hardly a day this summer that I have gone to the office without a light overcoat.[12]

But there were many delights beyond the pleasantly cool days. Up on Nob Hill one could see mansions bedecked with observation towers and surrounded by carefully landscaped patios and gardens. The eleven-story Crocker Building, designed by the New York architect Arthur Page Brown, dominated the downtown area and suggested the business potential of the city. In nearby Palo Alto, Leland Stanford Junior University, with its first president David Starr Jordan, was beginning to supply intellectual leadership for the state; while across the bay in Berkeley similar forces were at work on the campus of the new University of California. By 1890 writers such as Bret Harte, Joaquin Miller, Gelett Burgess, and Frank Norris had established a lively literary tradition. Newspapers and journals ranged from the conservative to the fiercely experimental. Intellectual life was supported by such organizations as the California Academy of Sciences, the San Francisco Art Association, and the Historical and Meteorological Society. Hotels and restaurants thrived and musical performances catered to every taste. The Mercantile Library and the Mechanics Library supplied books and journals for their members while the San Francisco Public Library, founded in 1879, offered free services to all. From 1849, when John H. Still established his shop "on the Plaza," San Franciscans also had access to a wide variety of new and used books. By the middle of the 1890s Adolph Bourgoin, Frank Thompson, William Doxey, Patrick Healy, and Paul Elder offered large stocks of books and journals. Only a few eastern cities could rival San Francisco's cosmopolitan intellectual environment.

To all of this Huntington brought a keen mind and an observant eye. Although his duties with the SP kept him busy he found time to visit bookshops, especially those in the vicinity of his office. Increased responsibilities had brought financial rewards, so that he could now afford to buy books without reserving them for collateral. For the first time in his life he not only had the means to purchase books but, through the city's well-developed book trade, he had access to a wide and inviting selection.

Shortly after moving to San Francisco Huntington started to buy books from William Doxey, a knowledgeable dealer who established his first small shop on Grant Avenue near Post, then moved to 631 Market Street under the Palace Hotel. For a number of years Doxey sponsored *The Lark*, a well-known literary journal edited by Gelett Burgess, and the dealer's books were advertised and sold at "The Sign of the Lark." His clientele, attracted by a fine stock of imported books, included many of the wealthiest people of the city. The book dealer was known to have "business ability and an excellent knowledge of good books and fine bindings."[13] He also had a refreshingly direct approach to sales. In a note to Huntington he urged immediate action.

> My dear Sir
>
> If you would like to secure a set of Balzac the edition de luxe <u>this afternoon</u> I will give you a good bargain. I do but have two sets left.
>
> Yours very truly
> Wm. Doxey

For $150, discounted from $200, Huntington became the owner of the forty-volume deluxe set. Two months later Doxey was back with a more general offer. He wrote Huntington,

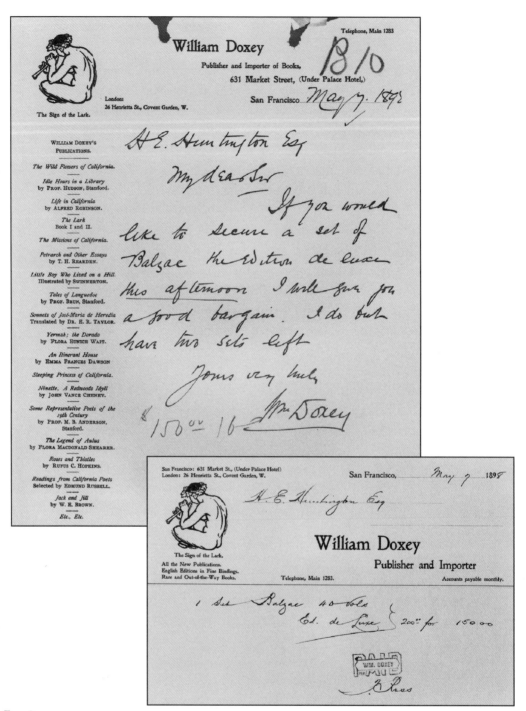

FIG. 2

William Doxey, the knowledgeable San Francisco book dealer, sponsored *The Lark,* a well-known literary journal, and advertised and sold his books at "The Sign of the Lark." The Balzac set mentioned in the letter reflects Huntington's early collecting interests. When he turned toward Anglo-American materials, modern literature in foreign languages was eliminated from the collection.

My dear Sir:

I am very desirous of making a sale today, and if there are any books I could sell you I would give you a good bargain—I should be glad if you could drop in at lunchtime.[14]

By 1895 Huntington had become one of Doxey's best customers. Among his earliest purchases, according to a book bill of that year, were a three-volume set of the *Poems* of James Whitcomb Riley ($3.75), Ranke's *History of the Popes* ($20), Lappenberg's *History of England under the Anglo-Saxon Kings* ($10), *Masterpieces of French Art* ($25), Mackenzie's *Voyages* ($5), and Cable's *Old Creole Days* ($1.25). He also bought books when business took him east. When he was in New York he often stopped in at Henry Miller's store at 122 Nassau Street, between Ann and Beekman. Miller advertised himself as a "Bookseller and Importer" and according to his billing forms offered "Book binding as a specialty." There is no record to indicate how Huntington got started buying from Miller, but the Beekman Street area was certainly familiar to him from his days working nearby in Sargent's hardware store. It is not difficult to imagine a connection going back to that time. Between 1892 and 1898 Huntington bought regularly from Miller, acquiring a variety of standard literary and historical sets. In 1896, for example, he spent $1,018 for the complete works of Robert Southey, Thomas Love Peacock, Walter Savage Landor, and William Shakespeare. At the same time he bought Bancroft's *History of the United States* and Green's *Conquest of England*. In view of Huntington's strong preference for English and American authors, it is surprising that in 1896 Miller sold him a fifteen-volume set of the writings of the French historian François Guizot. With the exception of a few orders placed with New York subscription agents and an occasional purchase from the San Francisco dealer Paul Elder, Doxey and Miller handled most of Huntington's orders from 1885 to 1900. An undated note from Doxey to Huntington listing seven different books on the discovery of America indicates the collector's early interest in that subject.[15] Marion Huntington remembered the books in her father's San Francisco library as being well bound and nicely printed but not rare.

I do not think at that time father's books consisted of any 1st editions or rare books. I was an inveterate reader and browsed through every set from Thomas Love Peacock to Douglas Gerrold so that I am fairly familiar with the material. He was fond of good paper, good bindings, but I doubt if they were in any way rare. For the most part they were the standard American and English authors.[16]

As Huntington began to buy books and other appurtenances of gracious living, he followed a path already taken by his uncle. By the middle of the 1880s Collis, who had always scorned frivolities and prided himself on personal austerity, had undergone a dramatic change. In 1884, almost immediately after his first wife died, he married Arabella Yarrington, a Southern beauty with aristocratic aspirations. Under Arabella's tutelage, Collis began to invest heavily in real estate—a palatial home on San Francisco's Nob Hill, a country estate at Throgg's Neck overlooking Long Island Sound, a huge Fifth Avenue mansion, and an elaborate "camp" on Racquette Lake in the central Adirondack mountain region of northern New York state. On trips to Europe he and Arabella bought paintings, bronzes, sculpture, fine china, and furniture by the carload. He even indulged himself with a few modest philanthropies: a chapel for the town of Harwinton, Connecticut, where he was born; and two library buildings, one for Westchester, Long Island, and another for Tuskegee Institute in Alabama. In 1897 he gave the University of California, in Berkeley, a collection of books and manuscripts about California history. This sudden, nearly chaotic, surge of spending in the the last few years of Collis's life could hardly have escaped Henry Huntington's attention. To the younger man, just starting to enjoy the benefits of wealth, it must have seemed a pity that his hardworking uncle, whom he idolized, had so little indulged himself for most of his life. Wouldn't it be better, Huntington mused, to enjoy some of the finer things while one still had a reserve of good health and energy?

By 1900, at the age of seventy-nine, Collis had started to slow down. In early August he left New York City to spend a month at Pine Knot Camp on Racquette Lake. On 14 August, after a pleasant evening with friends, he suffered a sudden heart attack and died.

Along with their son, Archer, and Arabella, Henry received a large portion of the estate. In Henry's case the amount of stock and other assets came to approximately fifteen million dollars. The question of replacing Collis as president of the Southern Pacific, however, was another matter. Powerful fac-

FIG. 3
Arabella Huntington sometime in the 1890s, when she and Collis lived in San Francisco.

tions within the organization, long jealous of the close relationship between uncle and nephew, eliminated Huntington from contention. Although it was a disappointment Huntington did not feel himself without options. If he couldn't run the SP, Huntington reasoned, at least he would make a substantial amount of money from his holdings. In 1901 he sold his stock to E. H. Harriman of the Union Pacific, ending a thirty-year period of family domination of the Southern Pacific. This did not mean, however, that Huntington intended to remove himself from the rail business. Where Collis had built his empire with intercontinental rail lines, Henry decided to build his around urban transportation. From his earliest days in San Francisco, Huntington had shared in the management of the Market Street Railroad, one of the city's first interurban transportation systems. With this background and a keen sense of the opportunities waiting to be developed in Southern California, Huntington gradually moved the center of his operations to Los Angeles.

The rapid growth of Southern California at the turn of the century forms a unique chapter in American social history. The population of Los Angeles doubled, from 50,000 to 100,000, in the last two decades of the nineteenth century and rose to 319,000 by 1910. Midwesterners weary of snow and freezing temperatures were lured by attractive chamber of commerce brochures that promised orange blossoms and a relaxed style of seaside living. If the brochures were to be believed, employers in the Los Angeles area were ready to provide steady jobs and good wages. Lush farmland would make it easy to grow all kinds of vegetables as well as exotic fruits and nuts. The message was irresistible. Families started coming in the 1880s and by the early 1900s the trickle had become a flood.

The discovery of oil within the city limits in 1892 brought instant wealth to a few and dreams of prosperity to many. Equally important to the local economy was the development of a deep-water harbor south of the city at San Pedro. By the end of the first decade of the twentieth century Los Angeles would challenge San Francisco and San Diego as a center for international trade. Those who owned the land, built houses, and supplied services made huge profits. But along with the expansion came growing pains. Downtown Los Angeles in 1900 was, according to Kevin Starr, "an eclectic, patchwork sort of place, combining elements of the Spanish Southwest and the American Midwest."[17] Many competing values and cultures were at work and none could claim dominance.

Although Los Angeles was a raw and untamed place at the turn of the century, there were stirrings of better things to come. Traveling opera companies occasionally stopped in the city, Morosco's Burbank Theatre supplied regular bills of music and drama, and by 1898 the Los Angeles Symphony had started to give regular concerts. In the West Adams neighborhood and in such enclaves as Fremont Place and Hancock Park the wealthy began to build mansions surrounded by park-like grounds. The Jonathan Club offered the same kind of privileged retreat to Southern California gentlemen as the Bohemian Club provided to their counterparts in San Francisco. The beaches were popular with people from all levels of society, as were the restaurants and hotels that developed around them. Suburbs, with row on row of modest bungalows, soon spread out for miles around the hub of downtown Los Angeles. Newspaper advertisements invited city dwellers to consider the advantages of country living. Brick and frame homes just one and a half miles

FIG. 4
Cover of a fifteen-page booklet describing the attractions of Los Angeles as a summer resort along with its year-round comforts. The text boasts that Los Angeles has "more automobiles in proportion to population than any other city in the United States."

from the city limits and directly on the electric trainlines could be had for four thousand dollars or less. Unfortunately such necessary elements as ample water supply, transportation, schools, and hospitals were often lacking.

The timing of Huntington's arrival on the Los Angeles scene could hardly have been better. With his experience managing the Market Street rail system and with the backing of his considerable fortune, he was able to provide Los Angeles with a successful transportation system linking downtown with the expanding suburbs. Many of the other amenities of suburban living simply followed the path of Huntington's rail lines.

As early as 1897 Huntington, along with the banker I. W. Hellman and a few San Francisco investors, started to acquire small rail lines such as the Temple Street Cable Railway and the Pasadena and Mt. Lowe Railway. In November 1901, with Huntington as president, the group incorporated as the Pacific Electric Railway Company. Two years later Huntington expanded his holdings with the purchase of the Los Angeles Traction Company and its subsidiary the California Pacific, properties owned briefly by another Los Angeles businessman and budding book collector, William Andrews Clark, Jr. Through a series of careful land purchases Huntington obtained rights-of-way for new lines and promptly forged links to the outlying areas of Long Beach, Alhambra, Newport, Santa Ana, Glendale, Covina, Monrovia, and Sierra Madre. He also bought water, electric, and power companies, thus insuring his control over utilities throughout the suburban Los Angeles area. The claims made in an advertisement in a 1906 issue of the *Los Angeles Times* show how closely the suburban rail lines and the real estate market worked together:

IT MEANS GREAT THINGS—ONLY DRAWBACK REMOVED
TRANSPORTATION NOW ASSURED

RECENT WEST SIXTH RAIL DEVELOPMENT
LEAVES NO ROOM FOR DOUBT

BUY NOW
WILSHIRE HARVARD HEIGHTS HOMES[18]

According to historian Glenn Dumke:

Few districts in the United States owe as much of their character to local transportation systems as does southern California . . . Throughout the history of these early organizations [electric rail lines] there runs one name—the name of Henry E. Huntington.

He it was who gathered the threads together and wove the master fabric, the Pacific Electric system.[19]

Huntington seldom discussed his plans for the Los Angeles area but when he did it was with the utmost enthusiasm. In 1904 he wrote to a friend:

Barring the accidents against which none of us poor mortals can provide, the work which I have undertaken in Southern California is not going to be checked in any way as long as I have confidence in the future of that section, and I have any quantity of that now, and expect to go on acquiring more and more faith as the years roll by.[20]

By the turn of the century, supported by a burgeoning transportation system, Los Angeles began to take on a new character; no longer a provincial outpost dominated by a few ranchers and traders, it quickly became an independent and thriving metropolis. Huntington was one of the chief architects of that change.

At the same time that Huntington was building the Los Angeles urban rail network he also assumed management responsibilities for the Newport News Shipyards in Virginia and the Mills Building in New York. This meant a pressing schedule of six months on the East Coast and six months in California. Family relationships suffered. Looking back on this period Clara, one of Huntington's daughters, wrote with some regret, "For my own part, I see how the few have to be sacrificed for the benefit of the greater number, meaning that we rarely saw father, and his ambitions, his dreams and plans that would have been interesting to hear about, we just didn't."[21] After 1900 Huntington and his wife lived apart. She continued to maintain a home for herself and the children in San Francisco while he moved into a suite of rooms at the Jonathan Club in Los Angeles. In New York he took rooms at the Metropolitan Club on Fifth Avenue and Sixtieth Street.

At age fifty Huntington had come to a turning point. He had worked his way up in the railroading industry and inherited a great fortune. Now he was ready to invest that fortune along with his railroading experience in the future of Southern California. While deeply involved in business he was also able to look ahead to a time when he could devote more energy to his collections and to the pleasures of his ranch in California.

Huntington had started to collect standard literary and historical works in St. Albans and San Francisco, and he continued to pursue those interests in Los Angeles. During the last decade of the nineteenth century he had bought books in ever-increasing numbers but was in fact doing little more than acquiring what could fairly be called a traditional gentleman's library. His interest in specific collecting fields and in rarities would develop more systematically over the next ten years.

Chapter 2

A Few Shelves of Sumptuous Books
1900–1910

Huntington's appetite for books increased dramatical-
ly between 1900 and 1910. Not only had he acquired
the financial resources to indulge his tastes but in
New York had access to one of the finest antiquarian book markets in the
world. Further, on his ranch in San Marino, ten miles northeast of Los
Angeles, he was building a palatial home where there would be ample space
for a large library. Myron Hunt, the architect, had specific instructions from
Huntington along those lines. As Hunt later recalled:

> He had recently been accumulating a number of books and the
> house was primarily to furnish him with a large room to be the
> library, and of course, there would have to be a dining room, and
> the necessary servants [*sic*] quarters and a few bedrooms.[1]

Those who wished to buy antiquarian books in the New York market had
two options: they could browse from shop to shop and visit the auction
rooms—a pleasant but time-consuming process—or they could identify certain dealers who understood the fluctuations of the city's book market and
commission them as agents. Early in his collecting career Huntington decid-

ed to rely on the advice of a few trusted experts. The first person to work closely with him in that capacity was Isaac Mendoza. By 1900, Mendoza was known as the proprietor of one of New York City's largest antiquarian bookshops. It was said that once you entered his seven-story gas-lit shop, known as the "Old Ann Street Book Store," it was impossible to leave without buying something from the half-million-volume stock.[2] In spite of his reputation, Mendoza met with considerable resistance the first time he tried to sell books to Huntington. Early in January 1904, the bookseller had obtained the private library of Charles A. Morrogh, a retired stockbroker with a taste for fine illustrated volumes and first editions. Although Mendoza had not met Huntington, he had heard enough about the Californian's collecting tastes to think that the Morrogh books might appeal to him. Mendoza's initial visit to Huntington's office at 25 Broad Street, however, was far from promising. As he recalled in later years:

> I called on Mr. Huntington at 25 Broad Street, and on entering the outer office was met by Mr. Graham, his Secretary, who on being told my business, emphatically informed me that Mr. Huntington "had no books, and wanted no books."[3]

Undaunted, Mendoza asked for an appointment for the following morning and was somewhat grudgingly granted one. His reception on the second visit was more encouraging. According to the bookseller,

> Mr. Huntington received me cordially, asked my business, which was stated briefly, for I could see he was very busily occupied (a large stack of mail lay before him unopened)—He immediately became interested, inquired where the Library was on exhibition, and strangely enough did not at once inquire the price. . . . Mr. Huntington then called Mr. Graham to his room, saying "he was going out and would return shortly." Accompanying me (for he was intent upon examining the Library) we repaired to the store. Casually examining the Library, he expressed a desire to see the most valuable items, which were pointed out without further ado. He asked about Cruikshank, the Kelmscott Press items, . . . their desirability and importance to a collector, after which he inquired the

price, which was $15,000. This quotation was eminently satisfacto-
ry, for he said, he would take the collection. It was all done so quickly, it was hardly believable, but Mr. Huntington was an individual
who appreciated good things, and made up his mind instantly that
this Library was worth purchasing. . . . I selected for him, the most
important books in the Library, and calling here daily for several
weeks, he would engage a hansom cab, put the items in two or three
leather bags, and take them to the [Metropolitan] Club.[4]

The Morrogh purchase brought Huntington slightly over one thousand
titles, many of them notable for the quality of their design and printing.
Among the items he obtained were fifty-seven volumes illustrated by George
Cruikshank and fifty-four printed by William Morris at the Kelmscott Press,
a solid base for his interest in the book arts. In addition the Morrogh collection contained representative examples of the work of notable English
draughtsmen, such as Hablot Knight Browne, Henry Alken, John Leech, and
Thomas Rowlandson. These choice volumes were encased in sumptuous
tooled-leather bindings by Rivière or Zaehnsdorf and many were printed in
limited editions on handmade paper. All together, the Morrogh books gave
Huntington his first showcase collection.[5]

In 1904 Mendoza cemented his relationship with Huntington by selling
him two other private libraries, one from a Mrs. Roberts of Brooklyn and the
other from the widow of the collector John A. Morschhauser. While both collections featured multivolume sets of the works of popular literary figures of
the nineteenth century, the Morschhauser books, with many volumes encased
in inlaid bindings and embellished with hand-colored plates, drawings, and
etchings, were the more distinguished. As Mendoza remembered,

> Mr. Huntington and I became very friendly, he had the utmost
> confidence in my judgment, and almost daily I advised him on the
> values of books, and the desirability of possessing certain items,
> with other bibliographical information which would be necessary
> for one forming a private library.[6]

Four years later, in 1908, Huntington paid Mendoza $9,000 for the John A.
Stow collection, two thousand volumes of literary and historical interest. In

addition to the complete works of such major authors as Dickens, Hawthorne, Longfellow, Dumas, and Gibbon, the Stow library held some literary sets in French and German. At this early date, Huntington had a rather narrow view of the collection; it was principally for his own use, a reflection of his own interests. Since he found it hard to understand why any collector would keep books he couldn't read,[7] he disposed of the foreign language sets as quickly as possible.[8]

While Huntington was buying complete libraries from Mendoza, he was adding individual items and sets from a variety of other suppliers. The subscription departments of such New York publishing firms as Dodd, Mead, and Company, Houghton Mifflin, Brentano's, and Putnam's all counted him as a good customer. Whether the purchase was a single inexpensive volume or an elaborate set running to hundreds of dollars, Huntington expected a fair return for his money. In 1905 he wrote the Dodd, Mead firm,

> Msrs. Dodd, Mead
>
> In looking over a set of Trollope in my library I have discovered that one of the volumes is, so to speak, a dummy. My book is one of a set published in 1892 . . . in cloth and entitled "The Warden." It contains the Introduction, then the first 8 pages of Chapter First repeated over and over again for a third of the thickness of the book, all the rest of the pages being blank. Of course this spoils my set and I would ask you if you cannot give me a perfect volume in exchange for this one.[9]

It is easy to imagine someone in Dodd, Mead's front office acting as quickly as possible to improve Huntington's imperfect set.

In addition to his purchases from important New York publishers, Huntington acquired a number of volumes from the Grolier Society, a commercial firm specializing in subscription sets. In 1905, for example, that company sold him books totaling $7,300, including a twenty-nine-volume set of the Connoisseur Edition of *Beaux and Belles of England* bound in morocco with deckle-edge, watermarked paper and illustrated with two hundred etchings and mezzotints ($319), a Bible bound in pigskin and oak ($210), and a set of Sir Walter Scott in fifty-one volumes ($1,125). In another expensive purchase, this time from the New York firm of Manzi, Joyant and Company, Huntington made an exception to his characteristic Anglophilia. For $1,000, he bought one of the ten copies of the "Aquarelle Edition" of Pierre de Nolhac's *Nattier: Painter to the Court of Louis XV*, which was embellished with three suites of hand-colored illustrations, one on wove paper, one on Japon vellum, and the third on white India. The decisive reason for the purchase of this elegant edition, aside from its rarity, may have been that the the text was in English. Other purchases fell in line with Huntington's developing interests in English history and literature. In 1904, for example, he bought a dozen books of English poetry from John Skinner's bookshop in Albany, New York. One item on the billing, John Stow's 1561 "black letter" edition of the works of Chaucer, secured for $100, stands apart from the others both in price and in importance. This edition with its handsome woodcuts provided an early indication of the library's prominence as a center of Chaucer studies.

Although 1906 was a rather uneventful year for Huntington as a book collector, it was a crucial time in his personal life. For six years he had lived apart from his wife. Early in March the courts formalized the separation by granting Mrs. Huntington an uncontested divorce on the grounds of desertion. The settlement provided her with a million-dollar trust fund, an annual allotment of forty thousand dollars, and permanent ownership of the San Francisco property. Later that summer another family link was severed when Huntington's mother died, in San Francisco, at the age of eighty-five. Huntington and his mother had always been close. After his father died he had helped her settle the estate and organize her investments. She, in turn, was his ever-understanding confidante, and his regular letters to her—about his successes on the job, church attendance, and the growth of the grandchildren—show his affection and attachment. Her death brought him a measure of grief he had not experienced before.

Early in his career Huntington had discovered that work was the most effective antidote for personal problems. From his office in the seven-story Pacific Electric Building at Main and Sixth streets in Los Angeles he supervised the steady expansion of his Southern California interurban rail system and its affiliated land and power companies. The legal and financial problems associated with these enterprises required long and complicated negotiations, but to all of these matters Huntington brought determination and a sure confidence in the future of Southern California. In November 1905, when an interviewer asked him if there were any clouds on the California horizon, Huntington replied:

> No, not one. The whole future looks bright. People are coming here in increased numbers every year. The city has doubled itself in the last five years. I have not the slightest doubt that we will have a million inhabitants inside twenty years or less. Yes, sooner. There is no reason why we shouldn't have them. We will have half a million, I expect, by 1910 or soon after.

When asked if the trolley lines were keeping up with the city's growth, Huntington answered that they were "keeping a little ahead" and then added one of the homilies he had learned from Collis, "You can't do things unless you are ahead of the other fellow."[10] Huntington understood the situation perfectly. Los Angeles was a city in a hurry and he was ready to match that mood.

By 1905, Huntington's rail lines were bringing the fledgling communities of Southern California closer to one another, and the California Dream closer to reality. Already his tracks stretched to Glendale, Glendora, Pasadena, Whittier, and Santa Monica, and in a few years would reach Pomona, San Bernardino, Riverside, and Redlands. According to Los Angeles historian Harris Newmark, Huntington's development of the Los Angeles interurban system was "the crowning work of his life."[11]

The impact on the Southern California economy was unmistakable. In October 1906, a distinguished group of one hundred fifty businessmen, bankers, and city officials gathered at the Hotel Maryland in Pasadena to pay honor to the man referred to in one newspaper account as "The Trolley King." It was an impressive affair, with huge bouquets of pink roses (Huntington's favorite) on the tables, a quartet, and ice cream desserts made in the shape of miniature trolley cars. The menu, printed for the occasion, included a brief biography, a carbon photograph of Huntington, and a hand-painted map of the railroad lines. The text described Huntington's early years in the rail industry, and concluded:

> Today Henry E. Huntington stands in the very front rank of electric railway builders and operators and to him is given credit for

the new and flourishing life of that large section of California which his railway lines serve.

After the leisurely dinner, Dr. Robert J. Burdette, the master of ceremonies, rose and offered a lengthy toast to the guest of honor, concluding with a wish for "long life, long lines, and long leases!"[12] This brought the guests to their feet for a rousing rendition of "For He's a Jolly Good Fellow." When the room quieted Huntington rose, smiled at the crowd, said "Gentlemen, I thank you," and resumed his seat. Burdette then introduced William E. Dunn, Huntington's lawyer, for the formal response. Huntington enjoyed the tributes and the manly camaraderie, but with his intense distaste for speaking in public was happy to turn the podium over to Dunn. This was, very simply, the preference of a reticent man. Dunn spoke of Huntington's love of America, his admiration for President Theodore Roosevelt, his belief in the importance of hard work, and above all his faith in the future of Southern California. Those in attendance greeted Dunn's remarks with hearty applause.[13]

Throughout his life Huntington maintained not only a marked personal reserve but a strong disposition toward independence. He seldom joined syndicates or affiliated with others in his business negotiations. He had entered the Los Angeles interurban rail venture with a number of partners but, almost immediately after moving to the city, bought them out and by 1904 became the sole owner. In a rare moment of self-revelation, Huntington expressed his reservations about partnership, suggesting why he liked to work alone:

> I am more than ever impressed with the fact that when you have on hand a big proposition that is going to require strong and continuous walking, you don't want to handicap yourself with companions who get cold feet, however excellent may be the gentlemen themselves.[14]

Huntington found that this principle, which he developed in the railroad business, worked with equal success in the competitive world of rare book collecting. If one planned carefully, identified the main objectives, trusted a few close associates—but kept control—consolidated the work of others, and

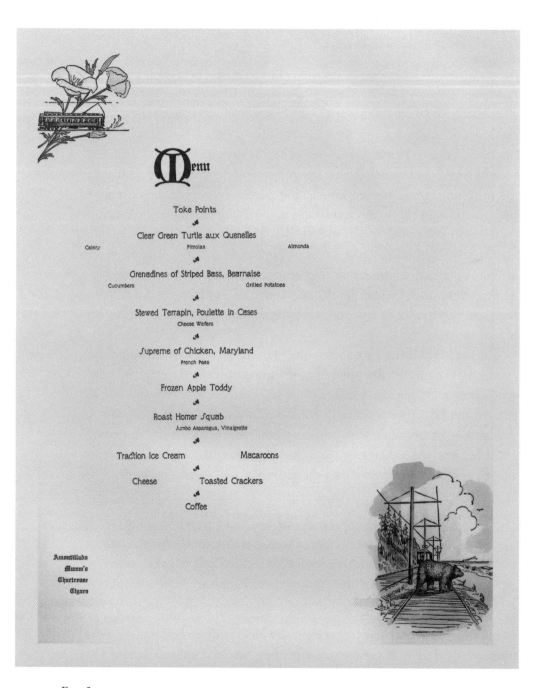

Menu

Toke Points

❧

Clear Green Turtle aux Quenelles

Celery   Pimolas   Almonds

❧

Grenadines of Striped Bass, Bearnaise

Cucumbers   Grilled Potatoes

❧

Stewed Terrapin, Poulette in Cases

Cheese Wafers

❧

Supreme of Chicken, Maryland

French Peas

❧

Frozen Apple Toddy

❧

Roast Homer Squab

Jumbo Asparagus, Vinaigrette

❧

Traction Ice Cream   Macaroons

❧

Cheese   Toasted Crackers

❧

Coffee

Amontillado
Mumm's
Chartreuse
Cigars

Fig. 5
The menu for the dinner given in Huntington's honor at the Hotel Maryland, Pasadena, 3 October 1906.

made decisions quickly, success would follow, whether the objective was the acquisition of a rail line or the first edition of Jonathan Swift's *Gulliver's Travels*. Beginning with the purchase of the Schneider library in 1907 and the Henry Poor collection the following year, Huntington's business approach began to show positive results. Applied on a continuing basis, it set the pattern for the development of one of the world's great rare book collections.

The Schneider collection, with its early printed books and fine bindings, offered Huntington a ready-made scholarly library. With fifteen ecclesiastical manuscripts, some dating from the tenth century, sixteen incunabula, and a variety of examples of sixteenth-century printing, the collection displayed a wide historical perspective. It was this very quality that had initially attracted the faculty and library staff at Columbia University. Columbia's chief librarian, James H. Canfield, had examined the books and hoped to raise the money to add them to his institution's collection. In a letter to Professor W. H. Carpenter, the head of the Germanic language faculty, he described what he had seen:

> The possession of the library would undoubtedly add largely to the reputation of Columbia. The collection contains a large number of manuscripts, perhaps four of which are very remarkable and all of which are rare. The collection about printing and illustrating early printing is more than usually complete and valuable, containing a large number of early printed books, all of them in good condition and some of the utmost rarity. I think we shall have good reason to congratulate ourselves if we are the fortunate recipients of such a gift.[15]

When Canfield was unable to find a donor, Juliet Brown, the owner, was forced to place the books on the open market. Huntington found the collection to his liking and bought it in the fall of 1907.[16] With this collection of slightly under five hundred items, Huntington acquired a number of remarkable items—a late-thirteenth-century Anglo-Norman biblical text on vellum with eighty-three historiated initials, and sixteen incunabula including a French Renaissance *Heures de Notre Dame* (c. 1495) with forty miniatures, two Bibles printed in Nuremberg in the 1470s by Anton Koberger, a woodcut Plenarium done in Augsburg in 1474, a Eusebius *Historia*

Ecclesiastica printed in Strasbourg about 1475, a stunning group of eighteenth- and nineteenth-century costume books, and four hundred fifty Hogarth prints in the first state of issue, with impressions representing the second, third, and fourth states. In addition to these high points, the collection contained some fifty works in the Swabian dialect, a collection of watercolor drawings by Charles Hamilton Smith, and a variety of German titles on geography, natural history, art, and the occult. The library offered a veritable history of the development of the book and book illustration from the manuscript period through the end of the seventeenth century. Further, the acquisition of the Schneider library marked the first time Huntington had invested in early manuscripts or incunabula, specialties that were to prove a strong and continuing enthusiasm.

By 1907 many New York book dealers were aware of Huntington's growing reputation as a wealthy collector—a man to be watched and courted. N. P. Chapin, one such entrepreneur, carried on a lively correspondence with Huntington over a period of three years. Chapin's position in the New York book world is somewhat difficult to trace because of his lack of a permanent address. In one letter written on Astor House stationery, he was able to offer Huntington a variety of sets at low prices since, as he boasted, "I have no rent to pay for stores." Apparently Chapin operated as a middleman for other dealers, since in one case he sold Huntington sets of Charles Darwin, Christian Bunsen, and George Grote from the stock of S. B. Luyster of 66 Nassau Street. Of this arrangement, Chapin reported to Huntington:

> You have bought of me lately a number of rare works without some inquiry regarding which it would be hard to decide whether you got them at a fair market price or no, but I wish to offer you *proof* of my bargains in this last sale of the three sets you ordered from me, Grote, Darwin and Bunsen, which I can *positively* assure you will hold good, in anything you have bought of me before. Mr. Luyster who shipped the sets to you from his stock of rare collections, assures me that I could not have bought them of *him* for the price at which you bought them of me. . . . he defies anyone to duplicate these sets in N Y C or elsewhere at the price at which you bought them of me.

Two weeks later, Chapin, ever resourceful and again defending his bargain prices, wrote:

> If you looked at the works I brought, you would agree I sacrificed myself to get free of bringing back all the works I sent you for inspection. You should not let the Kelmscott Completion [*sic*] pass, they will add much to your set. They are worth $150 but yours for $100 and unpurchasable.[17]

While Chapin sold Huntington a few selected bargains from his Astor House address, George D. Smith, operating from a small shop on Wall Street, offered him entire libraries. The story of Smith's rise through the ranks to the highest level of the New York book world has the quality of a Horatio Alger adventure. In 1884, at the age of fourteen, he started his career as a stock boy for Dodd, Mead and Company. Two years later he moved on to assist Walter E. Benjamin in his rare book shop at 744 Broadway, and by the time he was twenty-one he had established a store of his own on Fourth Avenue. Smith shrewdly took advantage of every opportunity that came his way. Through his work with Benjamin he met some of the most important collectors of the day—Beverly Chew, E. D. Church, Charles Foote, John Augustin Daly, and Robert Hoe. He won their respect with his hard-driving business acumen, his no-nonsense demeanor, and his phenomenal memory for prices and provenance. Smith was clever, determined, and tireless—some said ruthless—in his ability to find books for his favorite customers. It was only a matter of time before Huntington, the avid collector, and Smith, the aggressive dealer, would team up to challenge the New York book world.

The true test of the determination and nerve of collectors and dealers, from as early as the seventeenth century, had been the competitive setting of commercial book auctions. Traditionally, a collector or a collector's estate would deliver the books to an auction firm where they would be systematically examined, priced, and listed in a printed catalog. At the sale itself dealers and collectors would compete for the items listed, under the watchful eye of the chief auctioneer and his staff. This proceeding could be exciting or dull depending on the versatility of the auctioneer, the quality of the books displayed, and the disposition of the bidders. Usually, collectors would buy through an experienced dealer. The auction itself, with bids exchanged rapidly by the flick of the wrist or a raised eyebrow, could be a bewildering and an embarrassingly costly procedure for amateurs. In the early 1900s the two major book auction houses in New York were the American Art Association, an establishment that could trace its history back to 1886, and the newer Anderson Auction Company, founded in 1903. Since Smith was able to get extended terms of credit at the Anderson Auction Company he preferred to do business with them whenever possible. It seems clear that he introduced Huntington to the Anderson auctions and that Huntington took to them with enthusiasm. He was a trader and as a trader enjoyed the excitement and competitive atmosphere that permeated the auction rooms.

The most important event scheduled for the fall 1908 auction season was the sale of the Henry W. Poor library. Poor had inherited a fortune from the family publishing and banking business but lost it all in the panic of 1907. Creditors first seized his mansion at number 1 Lexington Avenue, then his wife's home in Tuxedo Park, and finally the paintings, jade, silver, and statuary, much of it obtained for him in Europe by the noted architect Stanford White. One of the first public indications of Poor's difficulties came with the announcement that his rare book library would be put on the block by the Anderson Auction Company in a series of five sales beginning in November 1908. Over the years Poor had accumulated an extravagant array of illuminated manuscripts, sumptuous bindings, incunabula, limited editions, association copies, and private press books. The *New York Times* characterized the library as "one of the most notable in America," and grandly prophesied that the sale would be "without parallel in the history of such affairs in this country."[18] Considering the makeup of the Poor library it is not surprising that its sale brought Huntington and Smith together in their first book buying venture.[19]

The Anderson Auction Company's lavishly illustrated catalog for the sale was a showpiece in its own right. The careful and evocative notes prepared by Anderson's chief cataloger, Arthur Swann, were calculated to draw high bids from the most sophisticated bibliophiles. Total receipts for the first three days were $47,000, more than even the most optimistic had hoped for. According to the *New York Times*, "hundred dollar bids were so common as to pass unnoticed! Nothing less than a five hundred dollar bid could give a person any celebrity as a book collector."[20] Among those most active in the early sessions were the dealers James F. Drake, George D. Smith, and Robert Dodd; and bidding for themselves a trio of active private collectors, Walter T. Wallace, William Randolph Hearst, and Mrs. Joseph Pulitzer. In the first session Smith bought 120 lots for Huntington for a total of $5,820. Among the items secured were a large paper edition of Dibdin's *Typographical Antiquities* ($176); *The Grettir Saga* (1858), bound in crushed morocco at the Club Bindery and printed on Whatman handmade paper ($295); Gower's *De Confessione Amantis* (1554) bound by Bedford ($710); the first edition (1819) of Shelley's *The Cenci* ($160); and a fifteenth-century illuminated missal ($700). As the sales progressed through December and into February of 1909, Huntington and Smith stepped up their pace. With Huntington's commissions in hand Smith dominated the final four sessions of the sale, spending $18,566 and securing over one-fourth of all the items offered. The final list of Huntington acquisitions is impressive: it consisted of fine printing from the Aldine, Daniel, Elzevir, Vale, and Ashendene presses, luxurious bookbinding by Bedford, Sangorski and Sutcliffe, Rivière and Matthews, illustrations by Cruikshank and Blake, and limited editions of the works of such well-known literary figures as Andrew Lang, Oscar Wilde, Robert Burns, Nathaniel Hawthorne, and John Greenleaf Whittier. The books Huntington bought at the Poor sale took him several steps further on the path he had been following since his acquisition of the Morrogh library in 1904. At this point he was more than ever committed to fine printing, limited editions, and handsome bindings—the traditional trappings of a rich man's library.

Although Smith rapidly took over Huntington's book commissions at auctions, other dealers continued to sell him items from stock. Prominent among those was Charles Sessler, an amiable Philadelphian who in his own way was every bit as persuasive as Smith. Sessler, known in the trade as "The Great Romantic" for his love of the old and rare, came to the United States from his native Austria in 1880 at the age of twenty-six and within two years established a modest bookshop in Philadelphia on Chestnut Street. Later, at 1314 Walnut, he expanded his stock and began to specialize, as his letterhead stated, in "The Rare, The Curious, The Beautiful." Although Sessler sold Huntington a few books before 1909, it was in that year that their business relationship blossomed.[21] In only three months, from 1 March to 1 June,

Huntington spent a total of $15,432 with the Philadelphia bookseller, obtaining illustrated works by Cruikshank, Gillray, and Rowlandson, as well as elaborate sets of Dickens, Audubon, Hood, Thackeray, and Lord Brougham. In the case of a Cruikshank collection, Sessler offered what he hoped would be irresistible bait. In a letter of February 1909, Sessler wrote,

> I must say that in my experience, since 1882, I have never seen a collection of Cruikshank which is in such magnificent, clean and perfect condition as this one. The gentleman who wants to sell it in block, asks $6000.00 spot cash. I have seen the original bills and it figures out that he paid over $12000.00 for this collection years ago. . . . Kindly let me know your decision at once, as I am afraid if we delay we may loose [sic] the opportunity.

Exercising patience, Huntington had the Cruikshank catalog checked against his already well-developed collection and bought only the items he lacked. In March Sessler wrote that he had shipped a fifty-two-volume set of Dickens to the Metropolitan Club address and had done so "immediately on my arrival here [Philadelphia], . . . knowing that you love promptness." In the same letter he adopted a teasing tone with Huntington, an approach that suggests the two were on unusually cordial terms. Sessler warned Huntington to be careful in unpacking the Dickens set, "as some of them are quite small, and may escape your vigilance, although this is hardly possible."[22] When the collector and the dealer met in New York they often became so engrossed examining books and manuscripts that they would work through the noon hour until finally Sessler would look at his watch and send a clerk out to the newsstand to buy chocolate bars for lunch. The talk and pricing then continued well into the afternoon.[23] Huntington was pleased with Sessler's advice and enjoyed his company. In answer to a request for a general letter of recommendation he wrote:

> I am glad to say that my dealings with you in books during the last few months have been very satisfactory to me, and I imagine equally so to yourself. The books I purchased from you were what I wanted for my particular purposes, and while, of course, I paid you too much for some, I got a good many at figures quite acceptable

to me and I had not the time to go shopping about for better bargains. When I paid you the tall prices, I felt at the time that I owed it to you as a tribute to your linguistic ability and your transcendent qualities as a salesman of literary commodities, both of which used to excite my sincere admiration. If I never run across a worse man than yourself to deal with, I certainly deserve congratulations, and if you always find as good a customer as myself, you will never want for the necessaries of life.

With kind regards, . . .[24]

Huntington extended this kind of warmth to very few. Smith also enjoyed membership in the inner circle, as did Rosenbach in later years. Others had to look in from outside.

Huntington's purchases at the Poor sale and those made from Sessler came at about the same time he decided to withdraw from some of his business responsibilities. With the rapid development of his interurban rail lines in and around Los Angeles between 1904 and 1910, along with the demands placed on him by the expansion of the Newport News Shipyards, Huntington had found little time for anything but work. Although work had always been his chief satisfaction, at sixty he was ready to direct his energy toward activities that would give him more personal pleasure. Huntington remembered Collis's last years, when his uncle pursued too late the pleasures that he had denied himself for most of his life. He had watched his hard-driving uncle manage the vast railroad and shipping business from an austere New York office and was determined not to follow that example. "Now, I want to have some fun," one newspaper reported Huntington as saying in anticipation of his retirement.[25] Huntington looked forward to having more time—to work on the finishing touches for his new home, now nearing completion in San Marino; and to build his book and art collections. When he returned to California in April 1910 after four months in the east, Huntington made his plans known to a newspaper reporter: "I have been trying to get out of business during the past few years and when my home is done, I am going to retire."[26] The break with the past was not as complete as Huntington made it sound. Although he did sell his Pacific Electric interur-

ban lines to Southern Pacific in November 1910, he never retired completely from the railroad business. Throughout his life he retained controlling
interests in the Los Angeles Railway Company and several subsidiary land
and utility companies. Still, after 1910 he was able to give more time to the
house and to his book and art collections.

When Huntington first came to California in 1892 he had visited the
J. De Barth Shorb ranch just ten miles northeast of downtown Los Angeles,
and its six hundred rolling acres at the foot of the San Gabriel mountains
made a strong impression. The panoramic views, the citrus groves, and the
majestic live oaks remained vivid in his mind. In 1903 he bought the property, tore down the vacant and deteriorating Shorb house, and, with plans
drawn up by his architects Myron Hunt and Elmer Grey, began to develop
the site for a residence. Early sketches called for a Georgian mansion surrounded by elaborate plantings, lily ponds, an aviary, and a Japanese garden.
The scale of the rooms and hallways suggests that from the first Huntington
wanted a house that would not only be a comfortable residence during his
lifetime but eventually serve a public purpose. Additionally, he wanted it to
be worthy of Arabella Huntington, Collis's widow, who he hoped would
share it with him. In 1907 Myron Hunt traveled to New York to show
Huntington the first set of working sketches. According to Hunt's records,
Arabella took a deep interest in the project, particularly the interior designs
and decorations. Most of the early planning was done in the living room of
her Fifth Avenue mansion. One of the chief features of the house was to be a
large library, an "L"- shaped room on the main floor, sixty-five feet long and
forty-two feet wide at the base of the "L"—dimensions that would have given
Huntington over a thousand feet of shelving space for his books. All this
changed in early 1910 when Huntington, influenced by Arabella, bought a
set of the Beauvais tapestries for $350,000 from the eminent English art deal-
er Joseph Duveen. The walls that Hunt and Huntington had intended for
shelving soon glowed with the hues of the great French tapestries. Adequate
space for books would only become available ten years later, in 1920, with the
completion of a separate library building.

Chapter 3

FROM CHURCH TO HOE TO HUTH
1911–1912

W. N. C. Carlton, director of the Newberry Library in Chicago, referred to 1911, the year of the Robert Hoe auction, in rather grandiose terms as the "Annus Mirabilis in American bibliographical annals."[1] He could easily have called it the annus mirabilis for Henry E. Huntington as a book collector. It was the year Huntington bought the Elihu Dwight Church library en bloc and went on to dominate both the Robert Hoe and Henry Huth auctions. It was the year he identified himself clearly as one of the world's most determined book collectors.

The decision to buy the Church library was one of the most important Huntington ever made. It was an extraordinary collection with respect to both its content and the superior physical condition of the books themselves. Church, a Brooklyn businessman, was known in the book trade as a careful buyer, one who understood quality and seldom added the extravagant or merely ostentatious. Working through Bernard Quaritch in London and Dodd and Livingston in New York, he purchased important literary and historical titles in the 1880s and 1890s from the Henry Stevens estate and from the auctions of the libraries of Brayton Ives, C. S. Bement, Marshall Lefferts, and Samuel L. M. Barlow. In 1905 he bought the so-called Rowfant library, a gem-like collection of English literature assembled by the poet Frederick Locker-Lampson. Although Church's library numbered only slightly over two thousand titles, each was distinctive. An editorial in the *New York Times* characterized it as "the most aristocratic collection of books on this side of the Atlantic."[2] A writer in the *Nation* referred to Church's library as "the finest, with the possible exception of the Duke of Devonshire's, in private hands."[3] Among Church's many treasures were Simon Marmion's magnificently illuminated fifteenth-century Book of Hours; the first Latin edition of the so-called "Columbus Letter," *Epistola de Insulis nuper inventis* (1493), reporting the explorer's discoveries in the New World; a unique copy of *The Book of the General Lawes and Libertyes of Massachusetts* (1648); the Bay Psalm Book (1640); *The Holy Bible*, translated by John Eliot into the Algonquin Indian language (1663); early editions of John Smith's *Generall*

FIG. 6
St. Luke painting
the Virgin Mary, one
of 124 decorated
leaves in a Book of
Hours illuminated
by Simon Marmion
(ca. 1460).
Books of Hours
were devotional texts
calligraphed on the
finest vellum and
decorated with gold
and lapis lazuli.

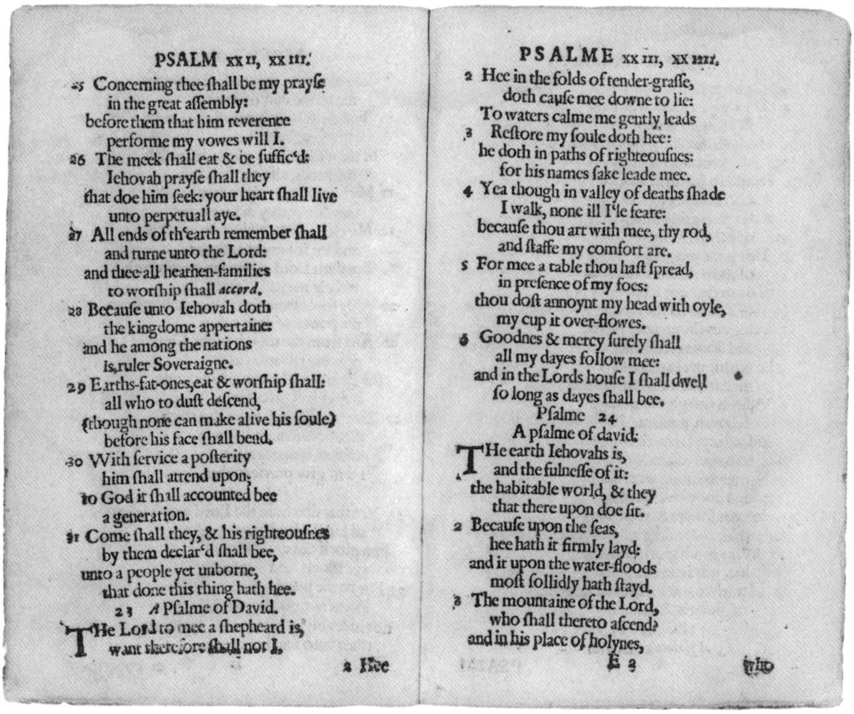

PSALM XXII, XXIII.

25 Concerning thee ſhall be my prayſe
in the great aſſembly:
before them that him reverence
performe my vowes will I.
26 The meek ſhall eat & be ſuffic'd:
Iehovah prayſe ſhall they
that doe him ſeek: your heart ſhall live
unto perpetuall aye.
27 All ends of th'earth remember ſhall
and turne unto the Lord:
and thee all heathen-families
to worſhip ſhall *accord*.
28 Becauſe unto Iehovah doth
the kingdome appertaine:
and he among the nations
is ruler Soveraigne.
29 Earths-fat-ones eat & worſhip ſhall:
all who to duſt deſcend,
(though none can make alive his ſoule)
before his face ſhall bend.
30 With ſervice a poſterity
him ſhall attend upon;
to God it ſhall accounted bee
a generation.
31 Come ſhall they, & his righteouſnes
by them declar'd ſhall bee,
unto a people yet unborne,
that done this thing hath hee.
23 *A* Pſalme of David.
THe Lord to mee a ſhepheard is,
want therefore ſhall not I.
2 Hee

PSALME XXIII, XXIIII.

2 Hee in the folds of tender-graſſe,
doth cauſe mee downe to lie:
To waters calme me gently leads
3 Reſtore my ſoule doth hee:
he doth in paths of righteouſnes:
for his names ſake leade mee.
4 Yea though in valley of deaths ſhade
I walk, none ill I'le feare:
becauſe thou art with mee, thy rod,
and ſtaffe my comfort are.
5 For mee a table thou haſt ſpread,
in preſence of my foes:
thou doſt annoynt my head with oyle,
my cup it over-flowes.
6 Goodnes & mercy ſurely ſhall
all my dayes follow mee:
and in the Lords houſe I ſhall dwell
ſo long as dayes ſhall bee.
Pſalme 24
A pſalme of david.
THe earth Iehovahs is,
and the fulneſſe of it:
the habitable world, & they
that there upon doe ſit.
2 Becauſe upon the ſeas,
hee hath it firmly layd:
and it upon the water-floods
moſt ſollidly hath ſtayd.
3 The mountaine of the Lord,
who ſhall thereto aſcend?
and in his place of holynes,
E 3 who

FIG. 7
From *The Whole Book of Psalms* (Cambridge, Mass., 1640), the first book printed in English-speaking North America. Of the eleven copies known to survive, six are imperfect; the Huntington copy has seven leaves in facsimile.

Historie of Virginia; and the manuscript of Benjamin Franklin's *Autobiography*, a record of the statesman's life from 1771 to 1790. Church had acquired the finest editions of the writings of those associated with American discovery and exploration: Vespucci, Cortes, Las Casas, Frobisher, Hulsius Levinus, and De Bry. On the literary side Church owned first editions of Spenser's *Faerie Queen* (1590), Milton's *Comus* (1637), and Goldsmith's *Vicar of Wakefield* (1766), as well as twelve Shakespeare folios and thirty-seven quartos.

Because of Church's reticence, the riches of his collection were known to very few. He had consistently refused to let his name be mentioned in connection with the books he owned and never allowed them to be shown in exhibitions. The situation changed a few months before his death, when a seven-volume catalog of his library appeared, meticulously prepared by the librarian and bibliographer George Watson Cole. In the five volumes on Americana and two on English literature, Cole provided full collations, detailed paginations, facsimile reproduction of title pages, and comparative notes on variant printings held in other libraries. The catalog set a new stan-for conducting that Examination.

I made a little Book in which I allotted a Page for each of the Virtues. I rul'd each Page with red Ink so as to have seven Columns, one for each Day of the Week, marking each Column with a Letter for the Day. I cros'd these Columns with thirteen red Lines, marking the Beginning of each Line with the first Letter of one of the Virtues, ~~~~~~ & in its proper Column ~~~~ on which Line, I might mark by a little black Spot every Fault I ~~~~~ found upon Examination to have committed respecting that Virtue, ~~~~ the ~~~~~ upon that Day.

Form of the Pages

Temperance.

Eat not to Dulness.
Drink not to Elevation.

	S	M	T	W	T	F	S
T							
S	•	•		•		•	
O	•	•	•		•	•	•
R							
F		•			•		
I			•				
S							
J							
M	•						
Cl.							
T							
Ch.							
H							

dard for bibliographic excellence.[4] A reviewer in *The American Historical Review* commented, "The catalogue, for its part, is the best-made catalogue of Americana of any such magnitude that has ever been published."[5] The result was a tribute not only to Cole but to the care and discrimination Church had exercised in forming his library.

Shortly after Church's death in August 1908, book dealers and collectors began to speculate about the disposition of the library. The most persistent rumor was that a group of New York book dealers planned to form a syndicate and divide the books among their wealthy customers.[6] When George D. Smith brought this scheme to Huntington's attention, the collector decided, characteristically, to act on his own. "I won't join your syndicate," he is reported to have told Smith, "but if the collection can be had reasonably, I will buy it myself."[7] In late March 1911, Huntington signed an agreement with the executors of the Church estate to purchase the library, along with all available copies of the printed catalog, for $750,000. The arrangements for payment bore the unmistakable mark of Huntington's business experience. He agreed to pay the Church estate $50,000 in cash, $100,000 in refunding five percent Los Angeles Railway Corporation mortgage bonds, and $600,000 in thirty notes of $20,000 each, bearing interest at five percent per annum, to be payable on a regular monthly schedule. Huntington used this system of installment payments repeatedly over the next fifteen years. It served the interests of both parties. From Huntington's point of view, there was no reason to pay large amounts of cash immediately if the seller could be talked into a more protracted arrangement. From the seller's point of view, the final result was guaranteed. Huntington exercised the right to act as his own banker, a position he was well qualified to assume.

For a few days Huntington's role in the Church sale was kept secret. In the meantime Smith, with typical bombast, reported the purchase to the newspapers as a personal coup, inflated the price by $500,000 to an entirely fictitious total of $1,250,000, and outlined a plan by which he might sell the books to the United States government or, failing that, market them in London.[8] Huntington put a stop to these extravagant claims by announcing to the press that he was the buyer. Notes of congratulation began to arrive immediately from bibliographers and collectors who understood the importance of the purchase. Luther Livingston, a dealer who had sold many of the books to Church, wrote, "For number of volumes the library is the choicest and most valuable collection ever brought together."[9]

The purchase of the Church library was crucial in Huntington's development as a collector. Up to that time he had gathered books somewhat haphazardly, indulging his interests in literary sets, first editions, fine printing, elegant bindings, and richly illustrated works. Now, with the Church library as a base, he began to focus on British and American history and literature, an emphasis that would occupy him for the remainder of his collecting career. The Church volumes never lost their luster. In December 1919, when Huntington arranged a private exhibition of thirty-five of his favorite books and manuscripts for the members of the Authors Club of New York, eleven of the total carried the Church bookplate.

The week after he secured the Church library Huntington bought a small but significant collection of Americana from Russell Benedict, a judge of the New York Supreme Court. The Benedict library, consisting of some eight hundred pamphlets, broadsides, session laws, and reports relating to the period of the American Revolution, provided a complement to the more majestic Church collection.

With the Church and Benedict purchases behind him Huntington now contemplated an even more exciting event, the sale of the Robert Hoe III library. In mid-April 1909, Huntington received a letter from Emory S. Turner, president of the Anderson Auction Company, congratulating him on the purchase of the Church library and expressing the hope that "this will not prevent your being a buyer at the sale of the Hoe Library. Now that you have taken such a great place among the world's collectors you should not miss certain items in this sale."[10] The invitation was unnecessary. Huntington was already planning to play a dominant role in the sale of one of the world's finest rare book collections. Unfortunately, there is no surviving record of the strategy sessions that doubtless took place between Smith and Huntington as they prepared for the sale. Both men lived in New York and could talk over their plans on a daily basis in Huntington's rooms at the Metropolitan Club or in Smith's shop on Wall Street. There was no need to resort to letters or notes. It is safe to assume however that the collector and his agent spent many hours working together as the date of the sale approached.

Robert Hoe III, heir to a successful printing-press manufacturing company, began to collect books as a young man. As the profits from the business

THE BLOODLESS BATTLES

ARTHUR HOE DR.S.W.A.ROSENBACH A. EISEMANN MAJOR E.S.TURNER

THE SHADES OF GROLIER, GUTENBERG, AND ALDUS THE PRICES PAID FOR SOME OF THEIR BOOKS

FIG. 9
These caricatures accompanied an article on the Hoe sale published in the *New York Herald Tribune* on 14 January 1912. The first book sale of international rank to be held in the United States, it began in 1911 and continued throughout the next year.

grew so did Hoe's bibliomania. In the 1880s and 1890s he took advantage of the dispersal of the libraries of such notable American collectors as Brayton Ives, Abbie Pope, Charles Kalbfleisch, and Almon Griswold. He bought heavily from the Beckford (1882–83) and Ashburnham sales (1897–98). The result was a library rich in manuscripts, fine bindings, incunabula, English literature, French illustrated books, and Americana. Hoe died suddenly in 1909, and the sale of his library began some two years later. In the graceful foreword to the sale catalog, the noted collector Beverly Chew spoke warmly of Hoe's informed appreciation of books and the quality of the library.

> Not only was Robert Hoe the greatest collector the country has produced, but he was a great student as well. . . . The old reproach, so often undeservedly said of a collector, that he was one who never read his books, could not be applied to him. Possessed of ample means, with knowledge and the true booklover's taste, this library he has brought together is, beyond all question, the finest this country has ever contained, and its final dispersion by auction the greatest of book sales. Happy will be the booklover to include among his treasures gems from the library of Robert Hoe, the possession of which will give his library distinction.[11]

The officers of the Anderson Auction Company did everything they could to fulfill Chew's prediction. In order to create the proper atmosphere they rented the elegant Clarence Hyde mansion at Madison Avenue and Fortieth Street, assigned reserved seats to the four hundred invited participants, and

FOR BOOKS OF THE BIBLIOPHILES

ARTHUR SWAN   GEORGE D. SMITH   DR. GIUSEPPE MARTINI   ROBERT ROSE

imported the debonair English auctioneer Sidney Hodgson to lend the correct tone to the sale. The *New York Times* heralded the event over a period of weeks with long articles about the treasures to be sold and the prices that might be reached. The editors commented at length on the great Shakespeare folios, illuminated manuscripts, fifteenth-century printings by Caxton and Mentelin, fine bindings by Nicolas Eve and Roger Payne, first editions of Burns, Keats, Goldsmith, and Shelley, travel accounts by Vespucci, De Bry, Champlain, and Hakluyt, autographs, and French illustrated books—a rich feast. The most avid speculation, however, was reserved for the Gutenberg Bible, thought to be the first book printed from movable type in the western hemisphere. Hoe had obtained this rarity of rarities from Bernard Quaritch in 1897 for $25,000. A pre-sale account suggested that one of the noted English or European dealers attending the sale would try to make sure the Bible returned to the Old World.[12] Among this group the paper mentioned Bernard Quaritch and Ernest Maggs from London, Theophile Belin from Paris, and Ludwig Baer from Frankfurt. The question in many minds was not only what prices the rarities would command but whether the Americans could compete against their more experienced European colleagues.

The sale opened Monday afternoon, 24 April 1911, with the dispersal of 196 lots for the modest return of $23,000. This was merely the warm-up for the evening session when, as the collectors and dealers all knew, the most important rarities would be offered. The first item to attract high bidding was lot 252, a perfect copy of the 1486 edition of Dame Juliana Berners's *Book of Hawking, Hunting and Heraldry*, better known as "The Book of St. Albans," the first English book to employ color printing. Smith persisted, despite a determined Bernard Quaritch, and finally secured the volume for Huntington at the unexpectedly high price of $12,000. Then it was time to display lot 269, the Gutenberg Bible, a book from the cradle days of printing, a distinguished copy printed on vellum and encased in a partly contemporary leather binding over oak boards. Smith, sitting in the front row next to Huntington, started the bidding at $10,000 and was challenged by substantial raises from A. S. W. Rosenbach, Bernard Quaritch, Robert Dodd, and Joseph Widener. After a bid of $30,000 Quaritch dropped out and left the contest to Smith and Widener. The *New York Times* provided a lively account of the events that followed.

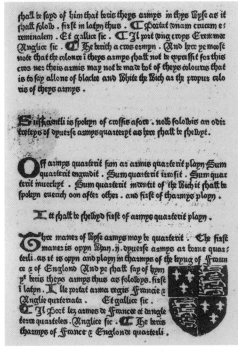

Fig 10
From Dame Juliana
Berners's *Book of Hawking,
Hunting and Heraldry*
(St. Albans, 1486), the
first English book to employ
color printing (p. 64).
Huntington acquired this
copy in 1911 in the
Hoe sale.

The price quickly went up to $35,000, then to $40,000, without a sign of quitting on the part of either. When Mr. Smith bid $48,000 Mr. Widener said $49,000 promptly and Mr. Smith made it $50,000, and amid a burst of general applause the treasure was knocked down to him.[13]

The majority of those in attendance knew that Smith was not buying for himself but acting for a wealthy client. In response to agitated inquiries from all sides and at a word from Smith the auctioneer announced Henry E. Huntington as the Bible's new owner. It was a satisfying victory with more to come. As Smith and Huntington continued to push the bidding beyond the reach of competitors they secured a 1720 Dutch printing of Pierre Bayle's *Dictionnaire* along with an assortment of fine bindings by Nicolas Eve, John Reynes, Francis Bedford, and Nicolas Derome. The second day of the sale gave Huntington the opportunity to lay the foundation for his William Blake collection. He tested the water with *The Songs of Innocence* (1789) and *The Songs of Experience* (1794) for $700 each and then plunged in, obtaining one of three known copies of *Milton: A Poem in 2 Books* (1804) for $9,000.

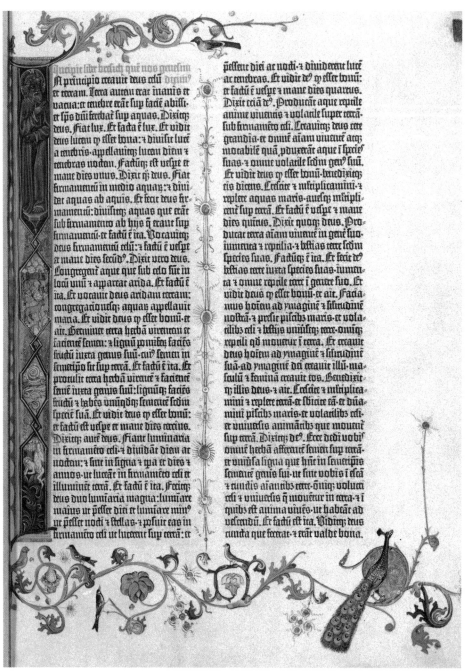

From the Gutenberg Bible (Mainz, ca. 1455), the beginning of Genesis. The Huntington copy, acquired in the Hoe sale, is unusually tall and contained in a partly original binding. It is one of only twelve extant copies printed on vellum.

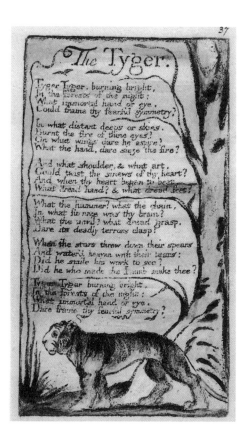

FIG. 12
From Blake's *Songs of Experience*
(1794). At the time that
Huntington bought this small
volume of hand-colored picture
poems in the Hoe sale (along
with *Songs of Innocence* [1789]),
few modern collectors had
discovered the appeal of
Blake's work.

Blake's "illuminated books," as the author himself designated these sets of
hand-colored plates, are considered by many to be among his finest productions.[14] In addition Huntington bought the first printing of *Poetical Sketche*s
(1783) and John Lavater's *Aphorisms* (1788), both with Blake's handwritten
corrections and annotations.

As the sale progressed Smith's high bids for Huntington became the topic
of heated debate. The Chicago book dealer Walter Hill was particularly vehe-
ment.

> I think many of the books have brought absurdly high prices. Take
> for instance the item "Adam Bede" sold last Monday. It is not worth
> more than $25, yet George Smith paid $250. . . . The price paid for
> the Gutenberg Bible was not perhaps excessive but the common

run of books are going at ridiculously high prices. I had [bids for] no less than 300 items which are for the Newberry Library of Chicago but not one could I obtain. It is true the books are in elegant bindings, and this explains in part the high prices, but they are also in large measure due to Mr. Huntington and to ignorance of their real market value. In bidding against Mr. Smith the rest of us are practically attacking a brick wall.[15]

An even more forthright statement of discontent came from Belle da Costa Greene, J. P. Morgan's dramatic young librarian. In Greene's judgment the prices paid at the Hoe sale were

perfectly ridiculous. They are more than ridiculous they are most harmful and establish a dangerous precedent. My point is that there are certain books which have a standard value and which are necessities to the student for reference. They are not in the class of unique volumes. Now, when the price of these volumes is raised, you injure the general public. . . . the Hoe collection is being sold practically en bloc. . . . it has hardly been an auction at all. Buyers have come from all over Europe and are getting nothing. Things have been raised to a fictitious value. It isn't even a case of paying two or three times the value of a book. Sometimes ten or twenty times the true value has been paid.[16]

The *New York Times* writer concluded:

The appearance of a new collector has been the surprise of the sale. Perhaps the old fashioned lover of books might object to the use of the term collector in this connection, for the newcomer has none of the instinct of prowling around in shops and browsing among catalogues. This has always seemed to the book-loving outsider the essence of collecting but the new man comes in with a shovel.[17]

In the first two parts of the Hoe sale, running from April to May 1911, the man with a shovel spent $320,000, nearly a quarter of the total proceeds.[18] As the sale moved along from January to November 1912 Huntington was less conspicuous but through Smith still managed to acquire important rarities. Among the high points were the Statutes of Edward III

FIG. 13
George D. Smith, holding the rare 1599 *Venus and Adonis,* which he acquired for Huntington in 1919.

and Edward IV (1482), the first printed collection of English statutes; Chaucer's *Canterbury Tales* (1477); Shakespeare's *Venus and Adonis* (Edinburgh, 1627); John Winthrop's *Declaration of Former Passages and Proceedings betwixt the English and the Narrowgansets* (1645); the Colard Mansion printing of the French translation of Boccaccio's *De casibus virorum illustrium* (1476)—a mid-fifteenth-century manuscript containing among other texts "Meditations on the Passion"—John Gower's *Confessio Amantis* (1483); Shakespeare's *Troilus and Cressida* (1609); as well as first editions of the works of Defoe, Spenser, Steele, Suckling, and Longfellow. In a few cases Huntington's bids fell short. On Friday, 28 April, Walter Hill of Chicago and Smith found themselves locked in a heated exchange over the only known copy of Wynkyn de Worde's 1512 printing of *Helas, Knight of the Swanne.* When Hill raised the bidding to $21,000, Smith dropped out and the prize went to the Chicago dealer for his customer Mrs. Edith McCormick. According to officers of the Anderson Company, the final price had more than doubled their advance sale estimate.[19] In an even greater coup Miss Greene, acting for Morgan, outbid Smith to secure the splendid Caxton printing of Malory's *Morte d'Arthur* (1485) for $42,800. Presumably, both the Wynkyn de Worde and the Caxton printings would have gone to Huntington had Smith been the successful bidder, but even Smith had his limits and was willing, when that point was reached, to say "no more." When the sale concluded in November 1912, the Hoe estate had realized $1,932,056, with Smith contributing $1,000,000 to the total. Huntington's purchases alone came to approximately $560,000.

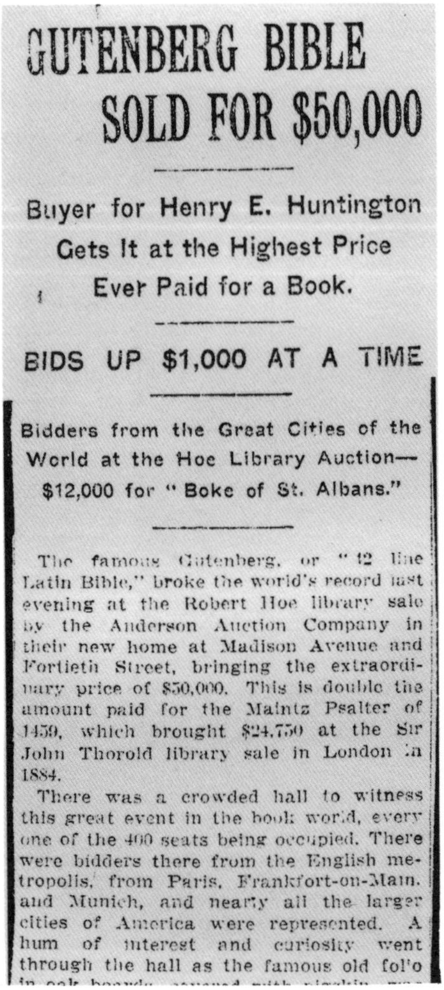

GUTENBERG BIBLE SOLD FOR $50,000

Buyer for Henry E. Huntington Gets It at the Highest Price Ever Paid for a Book.

BIDS UP $1,000 AT A TIME

Bidders from the Great Cities of the World at the Hoe Library Auction—$12,000 for "Boke of St. Albans."

The famous Gutenberg, or "42 line Latin Bible," broke the world's record last evening at the Robert Hoe library sale by the Anderson Auction Company in their new home at Madison Avenue and Fortieth Street, bringing the extraordinary price of $50,000. This is double the amount paid for the Maintz Psalter of 1459, which brought $24,750 at the Sir John Thorold library sale in London in 1884.

There was a crowded hall to witness this great event in the book world, every one of the 400 seats being occupied. There were bidders there from the English metropolis, from Paris, Frankfort-on-Main, and Munich, and nearly all the larger cities of America were represented. A hum of interest and curiosity went through the hall as the famous old folio

FIG. 14
The man who paid $50,000 for the Gutenberg Bible made the front pages of newspapers across the country, including the *New York Times* of 25 April 1911.

As a by-product of the Hoe sale Huntington found he had gained a considerable measure of public attention. Newspapers all over the country supplied their readers with a full account of the man who had paid $50,000 for the Gutenberg Bible. Most of the reports were simply factual but a few editorialized, criticizing Huntington for wasting his money on frivolities in the face of the country's serious economic problems.[20] Many people saw Huntington as a dupe waiting to be fleeced. Surely, they reasoned, a man deranged enough to spend $50,000 for one old book could easily be persuaded to buy others. Letters poured in, with descriptions of "valuable" books, usually old Bibles, that the owner, with great regret, would part with for the right price. One eager correspondent from Fort Smith, Arkansas, wrote:

I saw in the paper where you bought a Bible at auction in N.Y. printed in the 14th century. I have got one printed in Cohn [*sic*] in the 16th or 17th century. I'll let you have it for less than what you paid for the one you bought in New York.[21]

A Mr. Courtney from Somersetshire, England, was optimistic enough to send a book directly, saying he would sell it for a few shillings. This brought an immediate and angry reply from C. E. Graham, Huntington's secretary.

The Cowper book has come, the post office demanding 32c postage. Mr. Huntington does not want this book at all, having all of Cowper's works. He is much annoyed by people's sending him things he does not want and has not asked for and will not buy and as he did not ask for this book nor want it he is ready to return it when you send the unpaid postage plus enough to pay postage on its return.[22]

Even Huntington's friends had something to say about his latest purchase. Epes Randolph, who had worked with him on the Kentucky Central Railroad in the 1880s, wrote from Tucson, Arizona:

I have known for many years that you were sadly in need of the influence imparted by a constant use of Holy Writ, but I did not suppose that on short notice you would feel the need of $50,000 worth of it "in a bunch." What have you been "doing" and how does the other fellow feel at having been "done." Notwithstanding the necessity for this sudden awakening, your old friends think just as much of you as ever and are anxious to see you.

Huntington replied,

Your letter of the 2nd inst is received and I note what you say about Holy Writ. I certainly should not have paid $50,000 for that Bible if I had not needed it very much, although, as a matter of fact, I found out after I had purchased it that I could buy one for 10c, the contents of which would probably have done me as much good as the one I have, so you can imagine how chagrined I felt that I had paid $50,000 for one.[23]

The Hoe sale was a personal success for Huntington. Although he had not obtained all the items he wanted, he secured a great many and in doing so developed a measure of confidence in his ability to compete with the most powerful figures in the rare book world. This sense of assurance would work to his advantage in sales to come.

By the end of 1911 Huntington was ready to try his hand in the sophisticated London book market. This time the sale involved the books and manuscripts of both Henry Huth (1815–78) and his son Alfred H. Huth (1850–1910), long known as owners of one of the finest private libraries in England. Although he had been a collector from youth, the elder Huth's serious buying did not begin until the 1860s, when the George Daniel and the Thomas Corser libraries came on the market. Working with book dealers such as Bernard Quaritch, Joseph Lilly, W. C. Hazlitt, and Henry Stevens, Huth developed an extensive library encompassing illuminated manuscripts, early printing, English, French, Spanish, and Italian literature, autographs, engravings, and Americana. Huth's success was demonstrated in 1880 with the printing of a five-volume catalog of his library.[24] The news that the first part of the library, letters A – B, would be auctioned by Sotheby, Wilkinson, and Hodge of London, beginning 15 November, was one of the most important announcements of the 1911 season.

In mid-August Huntington received a letter from Bernard Quaritch inquiring about commissions the collector might wish to place for the upcoming Huth auction. With a history that went back to 1847, the Bernard Quaritch firm, "Dealer in Ancient Manuscripts, Rare, Artistic and Scientific Books," was one of the most distinguished antiquarian book dealers in the world. In addition to serving such notable personal customers as Lord Amherst of Hackney, J. P. Morgan, Robert Hoe, William Morris, and the Earl of Rosebery, the Quaritch firm was the official agent of the British Museum, the government of India, and the Hakluyt Society. In a handwritten note, Huntington gave Quaritch specific bids on five Shakespeare folios and quartos and asked about one hundred nineteen other lots, with the comment, "I am interested in the following numbers and if you should bid any of them in I should like to know the prices as I have not had an opportunity to ascertain their value."[25] In a surprise move Alexander Smith Cochrane, a New York industrialist, eliminated all competition for the Shakespeare section by purchasing it en bloc the day before the sale began. Of the one hundred nineteen titles Huntington had listed as being of interest, Quaritch was able to secure only thirty-two—an assortment of works by such authors as Roger Bacon, Francis Beaumont, and Richard Bentley. Including the usual ten percent commission, the transaction amounted to $2,824.88—not a large bookkeeping matter for either Huntington or Quaritch. In view of Huntington's tentative initial inquiry, the London dealer had done as well as he could. With eight sessions of the sale remaining, opportunities for more successful negotiations would not be lacking.

Although Huntington's major acquisitions in 1911 came as a result of his purchase of the Church library and his successful bids at the Hoe sale, he continued to buy from trusted independent dealers such as Isaac Mendoza, Robert Dodd, and Charles Sessler. In December he paid Sessler $11,250 for the 1460 Mainz printing of the *Catholicon,* a Latin dictionary and grammar edited by Johannes Balbus. He also began to place orders with two dealers whom he had not used before, Gabriel Wells and A. S. W. Rosenbach. These

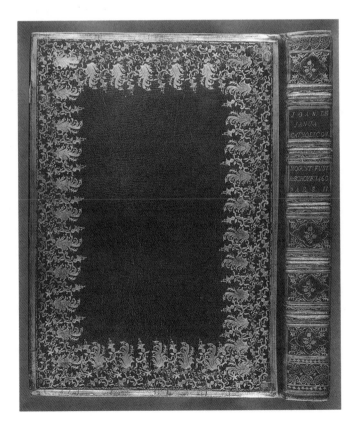

Fig. 15
The *Catholicon* of Johannes Balbus (Mainz, after 1460), a medieval encyclopedia printed by Gutenberg. The red straight-grain goatskin binding in this copy was made by Richard Wier for Count Mac-Carthy Reagh (ca. 1770–74).

men not only shared George D. Smith's shrewd understanding of the book
market but each had a profound knowledge of book history and bibliography. Wells, an active bidder on the New York and London markets, was a cultivated essayist, the master of several languages, and a thorough bibliophile.
During 1911 he sold Huntington books totaling some $7,000, including a
Doves Bible and deluxe editions of Pope, Carlyle, Meredith, and Stevenson.
Rosenbach, then only thirty-six years old, had entered the book business in
Philadelphia under the guidance of his uncle Moses Polock and was just getting started on what would be one of the most remarkable bookselling careers
of the twentieth century. Huntington, with his appreciation of expertise,
found both Wells and Rosenbach to be shrewd and energetic agents. Huntington made his first purchase from Rosenbach in June 1911—a lovely copy
of William Blake's *The Book of Thel* (1789), bound by Bedford and formerly
part of the Locker-Lampson collection. The $1,000 Huntington gave for the
book represented a profitable two hundred percent mark up for Rosenbach
over the amount he had paid Dodd and Livingston only a month earlier.[26] In
July 1911 Rosenbach sold Huntington a half-dozen English literary titles
including More's *Utopia* (1551), a first edition of Sheridan's *The Rivals*
(1775), and an album of proofs of Blake's woodcuts for Robert Thornton's
1821 edition of Virgil's *Pastorals*. In early October he attracted Huntington's
attention with more Blake material. For $17,000, the collector took a set of
Blake's pen and watercolor designs for Milton's *Paradise Lost*. Rosenbach's
price was steep but Huntington paid it without demur.

Huntington's enthusiasm for Blake's imaginative drawings is somewhat
difficult to understand when considered in relation to his earlier interest in
the playfully lighthearted illustrations and caricatures of Rowlandson,
Cruikshank, and Leech. Perhaps the principal attraction was bibliographic
rarity. Adding the Blake items gave Huntington what he often sought to
achieve, both in auction sales and private purchases: a significant degree of
control over a limited market. This was simply good business, and
Huntington was from first to last a good businessman. Also he took personal pride in knowing that his holdings were unique, that they surpassed those
of other libraries both in number and quality.

For Rosenbach, building Huntington's literary collections was a profitable
project but one he pursued judiciously. Despite his early successes with Hun-

tington, and in the book world at large, even Rosenbach was not brash enough to try to take over territory controlled by Smith. During the ten years following the Hoe sale Rosenbach kept in touch with Huntington on an informal basis, sending him complimentary pamphlets and broadsides and occasionally selling him a literary rarity. It was only after Smith's death in 1920 that Rosenbach claimed Huntington as his own.

The Hoe sale brought Huntington considerable stature in New York book circles. On 6 June 1911, August Jaccaci, the art editor for *Scribner's Magazine,* along with Beverly Chew, one of New York's most sophisticated bibliophiles, proposed Huntington for membership in the Grolier Club. He was elected in November and participated in club activities whenever he was in the city. The Grolier Club, established in 1884 by a community of wealthy book collectors, was the most prestigious organization of its kind in the country. In addition to providing a place for social interchange at the East Thirty-second Street meeting house, the club sponsored exhibitions and published a series of well-edited bibliographies. At the meetings Huntington was able to mingle and exchange views with such knowledgeable collectors as William Loring Andrews, Theodore Low De Vinne, Brayton Ives, William Bixby, and William A. White. Some of these men would be his rivals in the auction rooms, but all provided Huntington with an opportunity to increase his knowledge of books and collecting.

A month after he became a member of the Grolier Club, Huntington and a group of twenty friends and acquaintances, among them Henry Folger, John Quinn, Theodore Vail, and George Plimpton, launched the Hobby Club of New York, an organization with a somewhat less serious intent. The stated purpose of the club was to encourage collectors of literary, artistic, and scientific works and to aid the development of all three fields. The informal objective of the members was simply to get together for lavish dinners once every few months and to talk about their collections—stamps, ancient armor, coins, books, Civil War mementos, antique silver, or mezzotints. Following dinner the host would have an opportunity to speak about his hobby for the entertainment of the group. On such occasions, lulled by the terrapin soup, chicken mousse, saddle of lamb, and macaroon ice cream, some members would become inattentive or fall asleep, but Huntington always remained alert, apparently fascinated even by the most rambling and long-winded talks.[27] When the Club met at Huntington's home at number 2, East Fifty-seventh Street, on 16 December 1915, self-effacing as ever he gave over his right to speak to another member.

As early as 1911, Huntington discovered that being a book collector meant never having enough space. His two rooms at the Metropolitan Club,

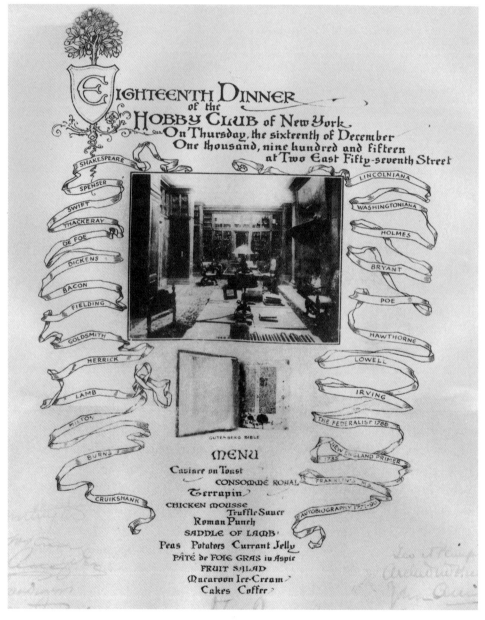

FIG. 16
Huntington's New York library is depicted on this Hobby Club menu. The decorative banner incorporates the names of major historical and literary figures represented in the collection as early as December 1915, the date of the club's meeting at Huntington's home.

once open and comfortable, were now filled with books and manuscripts. According to a fellow member:

> The room was full to overflowing with books. There were piles of books at the foot of the bed, including such valuable items as illuminated manuscripts. All the chairs were often full of books and Baron Natali, who was Mr. Huntington's private secretary, sometimes had to clear a chair for a visitor. The room was usually untidy and dusty because Mr. Huntington did not allow routine cleaning because of concern for his books.[28]

Since space was limited in New York, Huntington sent many books to California, first to the Jonathan Club in Los Angeles and later to San Marino where the new house was nearing completion. Although the tide of books was rising no one, not even Huntington, could have predicted the level it would eventually attain.

Early in 1911 Sessler sent Huntington a note hinting at the future stature of the library. "It seems to me," he wrote, "that if you make up your mind to get anything at a certain price, you get it, even to my overshoes which I left in your room."[29] In that lighthearted comment Sessler nonetheless identified a significant aspect of Huntington's makeup—a relentless determination to be first and best. It was a characteristic that had seen him through innumerable railway transactions and would serve him well in the development of his great library.

By the time the second round of Hoe sales started in early January 1912, public interest had cooled. With no Gutenberg Bible or Caxton printings to offer, the representatives of the Anderson Auction Company had to be satisfied with a total revenue that came to less than half of the $997,363 achieved in the first sales. Huntington, the *New York Times* noted, was conspicuous by his absence. With the San Marino house nearly ready and many of his East Coast responsibilities taken care of, Huntington was at last able to spend more time in California. As a celebrity of sorts, now that his book collecting habits were front-page news, he found himself immediately involved in local cultural activities. The astronomer George Ellery Hale invited him to several meetings of the newly formed Pasadena Music and Art Association and saw to it that he was elected to the board of directors. This was a step in Hale's ambitious plan to involve Huntington in a West Coast cultural renaissance. He was pleased to have secured the collector's interest and felt sure there were possibilities for more support in the future.

Although the results of the second Hoe sale had not lived up to expectations, American and British collectors looked forward to the second series of Huth sales with excitement. Now going on to the letters "C" and "D," Sotheby auctioneers would be selling Caxtons, a set of De Bry voyages, a Defoe collection, first editions of Cervantes and Dante, and two Columbus letters. After his somewhat cautious negotiations with Quaritch at the first Huth sale, Huntington was now ready to buy in earnest. In a letter of 17 May he commissioned the dealer to use his best judgment in bidding for some 175 lots. Convinced that Quaritch would represent him fairly, Huntington wrote:

> I regret that I have been so extraordinarily busy of late that I have not had time to go as carefully as I ought to over the catalogue, so as to give you an idea of the prices I am willing to pay, but I am quite willing to leave that in your hands and trust to your known judgment in such matters.

As a cautionary reminder, he added:

> Of course, I do not want to pay unduly extravagant prices, but such I know you would not pay anyway.

Quaritch was quick to assure Huntington that he understood. He answered immediately:

> I note what you state about not paying extravagant prices, it often happens in these much advertised sales that comparatively common books fetch prices beyond their value. These I usually let my opponents buy as one can generally succeed in finding other copies.[30]

By the middle of June 1912, Quaritch had fulfilled most of Huntington's commissions. The dealer reported however that he had let six items go to Mrs. George D. Widener because they were books wanted by her son, Harry, who had drowned when the *Titanic* sank just two months earlier. Quaritch explained to Huntington,

I felt sure that you would not wish to oppose her in this matter, as she was most anxious to carry out his wishes upon which he set so much store. I think the wish to see the Huth books was the great inducement that brought him to Europe on his last unfortunate journey.[31]

Huntington had no quarrel with Quaritch's approach. Neither had he any reason to complain when the London dealer wrote about a substantial reduction in prices secured from the auctioneers.

Some of the books bought at the sale I have returned, others [on the basis of defects] I have made claims for, with the result I have obtained a reduction of £518.6.0 upon books purchased by you. The most noteworthy reduction is upon Dante [*Divine Comedy*, 1481, large folio bound by Bedford with engravings by Baccio Baldino after Sandro Botticelli] lot 1987, I obtained a reduction of £400. Entre nous, the defect was of very little consequence but I was in a position to demand a big reduction and did so.

My cataloguers are very careful in collating books, and you will find their remarks noted at the end of each volume in pencil. I shall be glad to receive any criticism upon the manner your commissions have been executed, so that it may be a guide upon future occasions.[32]

Clearly, Quaritch was looking to the future, when he again might assist in the development of the Huntington library.

While Quaritch was buying books for Huntington on the London market, Smith engaged himself with a number of private collectors at home. After the conclusion of the first session of the Hoe sale Smith talked with Beverly Chew about selling a portion of his library. Smith emphasized the high prices realized by the Hoe estate and argued that the time to sell would never be better. After a continued barrage from Smith and Huntington, Chew offered his sixteenth- and seventeenth-century English poetry, a meticulously selected gathering, for $230,000, a price he felt sure would be rejected.[33] Huntington recognized the quality of the library and was happy to meet Chew's figure. When it came time to complete the transaction, however, Chew had a change of heart. According to Huntington's librarian George Watson Cole,

> [Huntington] was met at the door by Chew who said, "I have not slept a wink all night for thinking about parting with my books." Mr. Huntington with his characteristic magnanimity said to him "If that is the way you feel about parting with them Mr. Chew, I will not take them, but if you decide to dispose of them I wish the first opportunity of acquiring them."[34]

In less than a year Huntington had added Chew's splendid twenty-two-hundred-volume library of English poetry to his ever-growing collections.

Chapter 4

FOLLOWING THE AUCTION MARKET
1913–1914

In the years following the Hoe sale Smith and Huntington continued to do a major portion of their book buying in New York at the Anderson Auction Company. Established in February 1900 by John Anderson, Jr., and located in modest quarters on West Thirtieth Street, the firm at first received little attention from collectors and agents. In April 1903 Anderson bought out Bangs and Company, one of the city's oldest and best-known auction houses, and began to attract more customers. Even so, Anderson found it difficult to compete with the American Art Association (AAA), a prestigious firm that had dominated the New York auction scene since its founding in 1886. After struggling for survival for seven years Anderson sold the auction house to Major Emory S. Turner, a Civil War veteran and a shrewd businessman. Turner's greatest coup came in 1911 when he convinced the trustees of the Hoe estate to designate the Anderson as the location for the sale of Robert Hoe's library.[1] The effect of that decision and the publicity surrounding the sale gave the Anderson a new position of strength in the book auction world. Collectors and their agents began to realize that the staff at the Anderson understood how to evaluate and sell rare books.

The Anderson's chief cataloger, Arthur Swann, helped attract buyers with a series of meticulously edited and artfully designed catalogs. Turner had discovered Swann working in William Jaggard's bookshop in Liverpool in 1901 and immediately offered the bright and enthusiastic young man a position as a cataloger on the Anderson staff. It was a fortunate move and one that enhanced the Anderson's standing with bibliophiles and their agents. Swann knew book values, appreciated bibliographic niceties, and understood how to flatter collectors. Huntington, for example, found Turner and Swann appreciative of his collecting interests and easier to work with than Thomas Kirby, the somewhat taciturn president of the AAA. That was not to say, however, that Huntington would not buy from the AAA if the books were important and the prices right.

Early in 1913, Smith urged Huntington to become active in the season's upcoming sales. Their system for settling bids was simplicity itself. If Huntington was in New York, he and Smith got together at the Metropolitan Club and worked out bids for desirable items. If Huntington was in California, Smith passed along his personal recommendations after checking the New York holdings. With this advice in hand Huntington made the final decisions on bid limits. On 3 February, for example, Smith wrote to Huntington suggesting he purchase several items from the libraries of Mathew C. D. Borden and Mrs. L. D. Alexander:

> I had forwarded to you by Wells Fargo Express the marked copy of the Borden Catalogue, which I trust reached you in good shape. The books are all in very fine condition and in exceptionally choice bindings. I have placed fair values on them, and the rarer items, as in the previous Daly sale, I think will sell far below their value.

In the same letter Smith urged Huntington to authorize a bid in the upcoming Alexander sale for the famous seventeenth-century tract by Richard Mather known as the Cambridge Platform. Huntington already owned a printing of this document, secured in the Church purchase, but Smith claimed the Alexander copy was an earlier version. He wrote:

> Number 195. This is the famous Cambridge Platform for which they asked $8000 privately sometime ago. It differs very much

from the copy in the Church Library, and I think is the earlier of the two. As it is one of the most important of the early books of Americana, I think you should get it to go with the other copy, but I do not think under the circumstances, I would care to give more than between $4000.00 and $5000.00 for the book if I were in your place. Kindly let me have your views in the matter.

A week later Smith triumphantly wired Huntington:

PAID THIRTY FOUR HUNDRED AND TWENTY FIVE DOLLARS FOR CAMBRIDGE PLATFORM NUMBER 195 ALEXANDER SALE TODAY MOST IMPORTANT BOOK YOU NEED SAME TO GO WITH CHURCH I THINK VERY CHEAP DO YOU WANT SAME ANSWER YOUR LETTER BORDEN BIDS RECEIVED WILL ANSWER TOMOR-ROW NIGHT LETTER

Huntington's laconic penciled note at the bottom of the wire, "Not at that price," settled the matter.

Later that month Smith reported that he had secured most of the books Huntington wanted from the Borden sale at reasonable prices, including an inscribed copy of Shelley's *Adonais* (1821) for $1,200 and Wordsworth's *Descriptive Sketches* (1793) for $600. Not all of Smith's purchases were bargains, as he admitted when he wrote Huntington that he had to go "a little above your bid" and pay $821 for *The Right Pleasant and Goodly Historie of Four Sonnes of Alma* printed by Wynkyn de Worde (1554) because it was "an extremely rare book and is said to have cost [Borden] over $1000." Although Huntington had not bid on item 775a, a limited edition of Thackeray's *Unpublished Verses* (1899) with manuscript pages and two original Thackeray drawings, Smith dangled it invitingly.

I bought the rare Thackeray item 775a at $1650.00. It is worth $2500.00. If you want it at 10% you may have it. It is not includ-ed in your set of Thackerays.

Huntington added the slim volume to his already overflowing shelves at the Metropolitan Club.

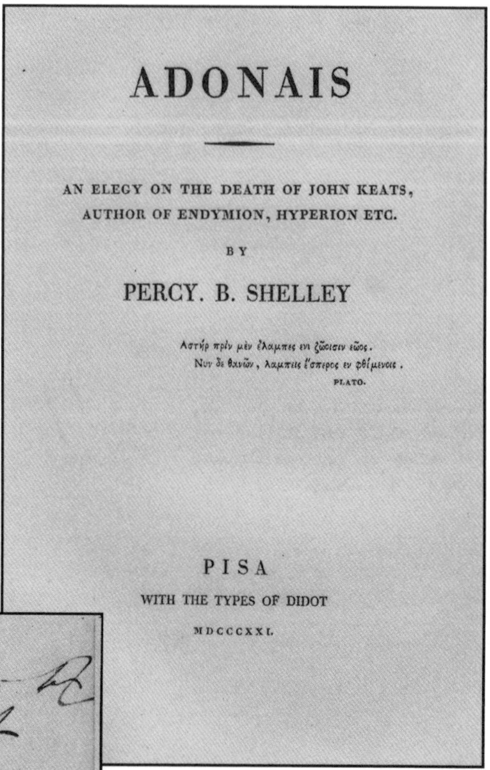

ADONAIS

AN ELEGY ON THE DEATH OF JOHN KEATS,
AUTHOR OF ENDYMION, HYPERION ETC.

BY

PERCY. B. SHELLEY

Αστὴρ πρὶν μὲν ἔλαμπες ενι ζῶοισιν εῷος.
Νυν δε θανὼν, λαμπεις ἕσπερος εν φθίμενοις.

PLATO.

PISA

WITH THE TYPES OF DIDOT

MDCCCXXI.

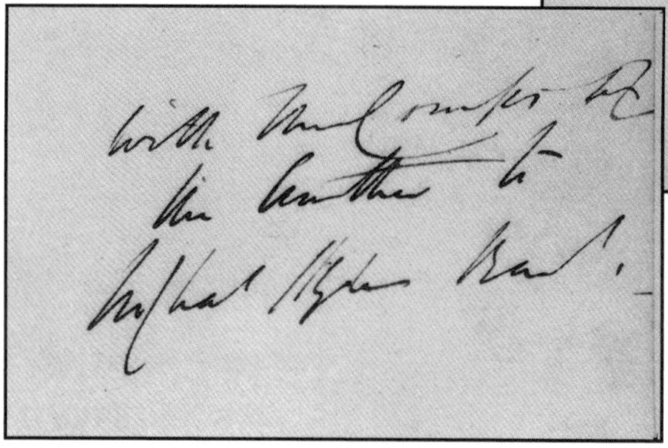

FIG. 17
Huntington bought two copies of this famous elegy by Percy Bysshe Shelley on John Keats: the one pictured here, inscribed by Shelley; and the Halsey copy, uncut and in the original paper covers.

An even more tempting array, according to Smith, would become available in March when the Richmond Auction Company was to place the Edward N. Crane library of Americana up for sale. Some of the Crane books, Smith wrote, were too good to pass up regardless of price.

> I send herewith by letter post a marked copy of the Crane Catalogue. It contains some of the most important items of Americana offered in years. There are a few exceptional items that we must have to go with the Church books. Number 69 Berkeley's Virginia, only two copies known, and this is the only one in

America. It is fully as rare as the Winthrop we got in the Hoe sale. You should get this at almost any price in reason. Also many of the important Jersey items we should get to complete our series. Number 710a and B [Original manuscript of the boundary line between New York and New Jersey 1719, with the original manuscript map to accompany the survey] are of course the most valuable, and absolutely unique. I am told they cost Crane $3500.00 many years ago. There are also a very fine series of Ptolemy that would add greatly to the Church collection. Number 683 [Original agreement as to the boundary between east and west New Jersey, 1688] is also very important as is number 690 [A letter from a gentleman of New Brunswick to his friend in Elizabethtown, 1752] which Church was never able to obtain and fills in the Church gap. Wilberforce Eames told me he knows of no other copy.

If you want me to go ahead and buy all items marked that you do not have, at or below quoted figures, you can wire me which will save you a lot of trouble and will save time.[2]

With an investment of $20,666 Huntington bought most of the items Smith had recommended. Among the rarities purchased were William Berkeley's *Virginia* (1633) for $5,100, the 1719 New Jersey survey at $2,600, and the 1688 New Jersey boundary agreement for $1,220. In addition, he secured ten sixteenth-century Ptolemy geographies, ten Thoreau first editions, and an assortment of early Georgia and Virginia imprints.

Although Smith did most of his buying for Huntington at auctions he made a few purchases directly from individual collectors. Smith stayed in close touch with the New York book world and knew when collectors wanted to sell a few items or to dispose of an entire library. Occasionally, as in the Chew purchase, Smith was able to pry books loose when the owner wasn't even sure he wanted to sell. In April 1913, Smith was able to acquire a collection of George Washington letters and manuscripts from the New York banker and yachtsman Grenville Kane. The 170 items that eventually went to Huntington in this transaction included inscribed maps, mortgage deeds, and land surveys, as well as letters exchanged between Washington and his friends and family. This manuscript purchase greatly enhanced the

Americana section of the library, already rich in printed rarities acquired from the E. D. Church estate.[3]

Another collector who found himself unable to resist the overtures of Smith and Huntington was the New York tax lawyer and literary entrepreneur John Quinn. On the basis of his friendships with George Moore, Lady Gregory, George Russell, Algernon Charles Swinburne, Joseph Conrad, the Yeats family, and others, Quinn had brought together a distinguished collection of modern books and manuscripts. By the summer of 1912, after months of worry, Quinn came to the difficult decision that he must part with some of his treasures. The previous spring he had, by chance, removed his manuscripts from the Equitable building in New York just before it had been razed in a disastrous fire. The experience had shaken him badly, making him aware of the great responsibility of owning such rarities and the difficulty of protecting them from damage. In addition, he had become actively interested in paintings and drawings and wanted to make space for an art collection in his crowded New York apartment. In a letter to May Morris, the daughter of the poet William Morris, Quinn asked for the return of several of her father's manuscripts loaned her on a temporary basis. He felt it necessary to explain his arrangements with Huntington. He was not going to part with any manuscripts given to him, he assured Miss Morris, but only those he had purchased. As to the price, he would charge Huntington only what he had paid in the first place, plus interest. "My regret at selling the manuscripts," he concluded, "is tempered a little by the fact that they will not be locked up or be the property of one individual."[4] As a result, Huntington obtained 121 manuscripts, including ninety-three handwritten pages of George Meredith's *Diana of the Crossways,* twelve poems by George Gissing, four essays by George Bernard Shaw, and the final draft of William Morris's *The Glittering Plain*—a solid foundation for the library's literary archive.

While Smith watched over the New York market, Quaritch alerted Huntington to the importance of submitting bids early for the third session of the Huth sale, scheduled to begin in London in early June. In a full-page commentary the *New York Times* referred to the event as "the greatest library sale ever conducted in Great Britain" and went on to describe some of the items that would be offered—notable works in English history and literature, and a wide selection of Americana.[5] There would be illuminated manuscripts, Books of Hours, and books from the earliest years of printing. Now thoroughly convinced of Quaritch's ability, Huntington prepared a list of some one thousand lots and asked the dealer to submit price estimates. As the sale progressed Quaritch reported to Huntington on a daily basis, with comments on items gained and lost—the latter usually explained on the basis of exorbitant prices or poor condition. Huntington had every reason to be pleased with Quaritch's work, as the dealer consistently secured items at prices far below the bid limits. On the seventh day of the sale, for example, Quaritch obtained all of Huntington's requests for a total of £1,394 under the limits agreed upon. By the end of the sale Huntington had spent $45,500, approximately one quarter of the total receipts. In this effort he secured a number of literary rarities, works by John Evelyn, Henry Fielding, Robert Greene, and John and Thomas Heywood, as well as a pristine copy of Wynkyn de Worde's 1495 printing of Higden's *Polychronicon*.

The Huth sale, important as it was, engaged only part of Huntington's attention that summer. On 17 July 1913, under the headline "Two Colossal Fortunes United by Wedding," the *Los Angeles Times* announced his second marriage. He had traveled to France to marry Arabella Yarrington Huntington, the widow of his uncle Collis. Because the couple had been closely allied in business and social affairs since Collis's death in 1900 the possibility of their marriage had been a topic of speculation among friends and family members. The long delay can probably best be understood as a result of Arabella's deep devotion to the memory of Collis, a devotion she continued to cherish throughout her life.

As early as 1908 Arabella had taken an active role in planning the construction of the house in San Marino. She worked with the architects at the outset, and many of the final decisions on furnishings and interior decoration were entirely hers. In her travels abroad Arabella had learned to appreciate high style from the English art dealer Joseph Duveen. When he agreed to help plan the interior of the San Marino house, Huntington was assured of furnishings and paintings worthy of the grand halls and high-ceilinged living areas. First came rich wooden paneling and column sheathing from England, a set of the Beauvais tapestries from France, and finally the masterpieces in oil by Gainsborough, Reynolds, Lawrence, and Romney.

Before the wedding and throughout the following weeks Huntington kept his sister Caroline Holladay informed about his plans. On 13 July he wrote, "Before you receive this I expect I shall be married, the ceremony to be at the American church Wednesday, noon." Then, in an uncharacteristic moment of self-revelation he continued, "I cannot tell you how happy I am my dear sister and I hope to make up for all I have lost and again have a home and a home such as I never had. Bell is so good and kind to me and I know she will make my life a very happy one."[6] Seven days later, from Fontainebleau, Huntington wrote, "Bell is so sweet, good and kind, wishing me to have the best of everything, which is something so entirely new to me. I am very sure my dear sister I am going to be very very happy in my new life in fact I feel that I am just beginning to live."[7] Early in September Huntington wrote his sister that he had taken a long-term lease on the Chateau Beauregard, a "most beautiful place" of four hundred acres, on the outskirts of Paris. For the next few years the chateau was a part of the Huntingtons' itinerary—two or three months in France, three or four in New York, and the winter season, from late December to March or April, in California.

With his personal life now so happily arranged, Huntington was ready to make a major purchase for his library. On 19 January 1914, he signed a contract with C. A. Montague Barlow, acting on behalf of the Duke of Devonshire, in the amount of $750,000 for the purchase of the Chatsworth library, consisting of the Kemble-Devonshire plays and the Devonshire Caxtons.[8] The 7,500 plays and 111 volumes of playbills secured in this purchase constituted a nearly complete record of the performances on the London stage from 1660 through 1830—a veritable archive of British theatrical history. Among the rarities in this collection were four Shakespeare folios, fifty-seven quartos, a sixteenth-century manuscript of the Chester mysteries, and the original manuscript of John Bale's *Kynge Johan*. John Philip Kemble, the noted actor, had formed the library in the early part of the nineteenth century and on his retirement from the stage in 1820 sold it to William Spencer Cavendish, the sixth Duke of Devonshire. The second part of the library, the Devonshire Caxtons, consisted of twenty-five examples of the work of England's first printer—among them Raoul Lefèvre's *The Recuyell of the Historyes of Troye* (1473 or '74), the first book printed in the English language; and a paraphrase of the *Disticha de moribus*, translated by

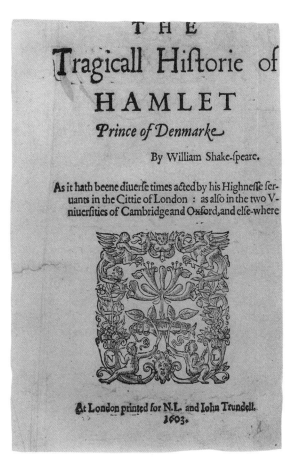

Caxton and believed then to be a unique copy. Although some outcry was raised concerning the loss in the British press, the London *Times* treated the sale with stoic resignation. According to an editorial, the sale was consummated for the Duke "in order to meet the heavy burden of death duties." As far as the Caxtons were concerned, it was a matter for some remorse since, as the editorial continued, "their sale removes from Great Britain almost the only remaining series in private hands of the monuments of the first English printer." The next day in a fuller text, the *Times* claimed that it was possible to view the entire transaction with a certain equanimity since the books would be as well cared for in America as in England, and furthermore did not in themselves represent the kind of "spiritual" value that might be found, for example, in a great Rembrandt.[9] An editorial in the *New York Times* commented that the London paper's "philosophic coolness recalls that of the Esopian fox in regard to the high-hanging grapes."[10]

FIG. 19
William Caxton may be
depicted in this frontis-
piece from a book that he
printed, Raoul Lefèvre's
*Recuyell of the Historyes of
Troye* (Bruges, 1475)—the
first book printed in the
English language.
Receiving the volume in
the illustration is Margaret,
Duchess of Burgundy,
Caxton's patron.

Huntington was well satisfied with his purchase and with the contractual agreement that specified an initial cash payment of $150,000, followed by three $200,000 installments spread over a twelve-month period. This kind of settlement was effective, Huntington found once more, whether you were buying books or suburban rail lines. On 16 March, C. E. Graham, one of Huntington's New York assistants, wrote that the first consignment of books had arrived and "although the news of your purchase is fairly common property here in NY it has not yet got in the papers."[11] One of the provisos of the Devonshire contract read, "No disclosure to be made of the sale and all parties to use their best endeavors to see that it is kept private."[12] This was a typical Huntington condition, one that allowed him to disclose the facts of a sale when he wished. It was a secret, however, that was too good to keep. On 19 March, G. E. Miles, Huntington's private secretary, wrote, "The news of your purchase seems to have gotten into the papers. Smith is wondering how it became known, but a report that I have seen this morning appears to me to bear the birthmark of our bookselling friend."[13] If Smith did leak the story, as Miles hinted, he did it with gusto, adding $250,000 to the price to create a more impressive, but entirely fabricated, total of $1,000,000.[14]

While the negotiations for the Devonshire books were still underway Huntington and Smith started to work out bids for the autographs, photographs, books, and letters that made up William H. Lambert's Lincoln collection, called by the *New York Times* the finest of its kind in existence.[15] The Lincoln items were to be sold in January 1914 at the Anderson Auction Company, and the second part of Lambert's library, an important gathering of Thackeray books and manuscripts, would be offered in early March. Over the three-day January sale, Huntington spent $27,313 and obtained a variety of rarities, including a scrapbook of newspaper accounts of Lincoln's speeches with annotations in the president's own hand, books from Lincoln's library, and playbills from the Ford Theater, where Lincoln was shot. He also bought a number of letters, perhaps the most interesting of which was one written by Lincoln to a friend, explaining how Mary Owens had rejected his proposal of marriage. The Lambert purchases supplied an important supplement to the Ward Hill Lamon collection of Lincoln documents that Huntington had purchased two months earlier. Lamon had been Lincoln's law partner in Illinois and had formed a large collection of letters, speeches, legal briefs, and memoranda. The collection also included the extensive manuscript files of William Herndon, another Lincoln partner. All together the Lamon collection included three hundred letters in Lincoln's hand, over two thousand from contemporaries, and a miscellany of autographed documents, law briefs, notes, and lectures. Huntington bought the Lamon collection for $12,500, a price Smith immediately inflated to $50,000 for publicity purposes.[16] Smith enjoyed seeing his name in the newspapers, particularly when large amounts of money were involved. Huntington never openly endorsed these fanciful press releases, but neither did he do anything to stop them. In any case the purchase of the Lambert and the Lamon collections, completed over a four-month period, provided Huntington with one of the largest Lincoln archives in the country.

Although the Lincoln portion of Lambert's library was highly regarded in the United States, his Thackeray holdings were said to be world renowned.

F𝗂𝗀. 20
Letter in Lincoln's hand to Captain James N. Brown (18 October 1858), acquired from the collection of William H. Lambert. Huntington purchased the Lambert Lincoln collection, one of the finest of its kind, through Smith in 1914.

Lambert had spent almost twenty years gathering manuscripts, books, and letters, in many cases buying directly from Thackeray's family. Early in February, Smith sent Huntington a copy of the "Thackerayana" catalog, and a letter with price estimates and suggestions on potential purchases. "As you know," he wrote, "this is the finest collection on Thackery [*sic*] extant." After considering the twenty suggested lots, Huntington wrote "yes" in the margin of the letter by only three: 781, "The Mahogany Tree," 806, "The Whitey-Brown Papers," and 1087, "Thackeray at Clevedon Court." Of "The Whitey-Brown Papers," a small quarto of ten lithographed leaves containing text and illustrations for a planned periodical, Smith said, "You should get this by all means. I think it will bring from thirty five to forty five hundred dollars, but it may go higher as it is unique." Aside from the printed books, Smith hoped that Huntington would bid on two manuscripts, "The Rose and the Ring" and "The Adventures of Philip." According to Smith "The Rose and the Ring" was the "finest item in the sale and without doubt, the choicest Thackery manuscript that will ever be offered." As to price, "It has been appraised at between forty and fifty thousand dollars, but I think it can be bought for less. You should get this by all means. I think from twenty to thirty thousand dollars would but [*sic*] it, although it may go higher." The "Adventures of Philip," according to Smith, was hardly less interesting, as it was

> the largest and most important Thackery manuscript in private hands, and the best of his manuscripts ever likely to be offered. It contains 519 pages all in his writing. This is one of his really great books and most important manuscripts. I think it will probably bring from twelve to fifteen thousand dollars.[17]

Although Huntington had indicated no interest in the manuscripts, Smith was not one to give up easily. On 12 March he wrote again.

> I purchased the two great Thackeray Manuscripts of the Collection, No 1016. "The Rose and the Ring" at $23,000.00; this Manuscript is worth over $30,000.00 and is the finest extant. Magnificent Drawings are in Thackeray's best style and more finished than any I ever saw; many are beautifully colored by Thackeray himself.
>
> No 1104 "The Adventures of Philip" is one of his famous novels and is the largest of Thackeray's Manuscripts ever offered for sale or in private hands. It only brought $12,100.00. You should have both for your library, as the opportunity will never present itself again.

On 2 April, Smith tried once more:

> I still have the two important Manuscripts from the Lambert sale and would very much like you to see them, as they are both really wonderful. When do you expect to return to New York?[18]

Four years later Huntington succumbed to the ever-insistent Smith and bought "The Adventures of Philip" but held his ground on "The Rose and the Ring."

By the middle of 1914 Huntington's attention was focused on London. Experienced book buyers knew that even though late spring signaled the end of the auction season in New York, it promised the beginning of the London sales. In March, Edmund H. Dring, representing Quaritch, wrote Huntington a long letter stressing his firm's continuing eagerness to handle his bids in the forthcoming Huth sale. After congratulating Huntington on the Devonshire purchases he proceeded to outline some of the changes that had taken place recently at the Quaritch firm:

> I hope that you will not think that Mr. Quaritch's death will affect the business in any other way but that of shifting its responsibilities on to the shoulders of his confidential colleagues. At the last Huth sale, with the results of which you were so much gratified, the entire work connected with it devolved upon myself and Mr. Ferguson. Mr. Quaritch was even then hors de combat and was unable to visit the sale room on a single occasion. . . . The knowledge of the staff are at my disposal as they were at Mr. Alfred's, while I hope that not only the traditions but also the prestige of the house will be as strongly followed and upheld under my management as they were under Mr. Alfred Quaritch."[19]

The Huth books would not come on the market until July and in the meantime, Huntington already had an agent at work in England. On his first trip abroad, but hardly as a naive tourist, George D. Smith arrived in London in June with his pockets full of Huntington commissions. Smith introduced himself to the British book dealers and collectors at Sotheby's on 25 June at the sale of the Earl of Pembroke's library. This collection, which had been in the hands of the family for generations, boasted unique copies of the monuments of early Continental and English printing. The Earl of Pembroke, plagued by financial woes similar to those faced by the Duke of Devonshire earlier that year, was forced to put his books on the market in order to meet inheritance taxes. Before the sale opened Smith had tried to obtain the whole library en bloc but was turned down because, as he reported, "The English are not accustomed to close big deals as quickly as we do on the other side. They seemed nervous and afraid to make a mistake." This only made the contest more exciting for, as Smith boasted after adding up his purchases at the end of the first day of the sale,

> I obtained practically the cream of the collection so far. I got many bargains. A lot of them I bought at far below what I had expected to pay. I believe I lost nothing by failing to buy the library en bloc, as I am getting the best part of it cheaper.[20]

Among his purchases were the third edition of Caxton's *Dictes and Sayings of the Philosophers* (1489) for $5,250, Caxton's *Godfrey of Boloyne* (1481) for $1,255, the first xylographic edition of the *Ars Moriendi* for $2,500, the Venice edition of St Augustine's *De Civitate Dei* (1470) for $500, and a volume of Cicero's letters printed in 1469 in Venice by Johannes de Spira for $1,225. The second day of the sale brought Smith even greater pleasure and more rarities. Again, as reported in the *Times*, he bought everything he wanted—a total of 99 out of 211 lots—many of them destined for Huntington's shelves. At the end of the sale, Smith gloated:

> Eighty percent of the Pembroke collection is lost to England. . . . I'm rather sorry I didn't get the whole shooting match. It would have caused such a howl to go up here. I get a lot of fun out of my business. The squeal of the English is highly amusing as when I acquired the Devonshire library.

And as if that jibe wasn't enough, he continued,

> Incidentally, I discovered that tea drinking may be a pretty expensive hobby. I went into a bookstore this afternoon fully prepared to spend $500 to $1000, and was told that the proprietor and his right hand man were both out to tea, so I walked out and bought nothing.

Mr. Smith added that he was considering opening a branch in London.[21]

With his successes at the Pembroke sale two weeks behind him, Smith proceeded to take the field at the fourth Huth auction. Although the number of lots to be offered was considerably smaller than in the previous three sales, treasures were to be had. This time Huntington decided to assign bids to both of his agents. In late June, writing from the Chateau Beauregard, he asked Dring to prepare the usual estimates. Working with that list he authorized a modest number of bids. At the same time he sent Smith an equal number of bids, although, of course, for different items. On the opening day, 7 July, Smith managed to equal his achievements at the previous sale, happily seizing both the choicest books and the boldest headlines. He took 66 of the total of 168 lots. In one spectacular burst of bidding he took almost every item in a long run of works by Ben Jonson. The *New York Times* reported this event with an impish bit of American chauvinism:

> The Englishmen fought hard to retain these examples of "Rare Ben" in their country, but Mr. Smith, despite the fact that he was suffering from illness, was not to be denied.[22]

The Quaritch firm also managed to do well for Huntington, obtaining runs of seventeenth- and eighteenth-century editions of such notable figures as Edward Jenner, John Lydgate, and Christopher Levett. Of the $93,055 total revenue in the fourth sale, Huntington spent $14,000 through Quaritch and only slightly less through Smith. Smith's bids, however, attracted the bulk of the comment from the London press, where he was dubbed "The Quaritch of America" and his purchases "American loot."[23]

With the fourth portion of the Huth sale nearing an end, Huntington devised a plan, hoping to skim the cream off the remaining lots. He asked Dring if Sotheby's and the Huth family would let him pick what he wanted from the rest of the library. Dring raised the question but found, as he told Huntington, "none of [the Sotheby partners] were prepossessed with the idea of selling a selection of the Huth books separately, as they think such a procedure would materially affect the sale of the remainder."[24] Dring proposed that Huntington make an offer for the entire remaining stock—a suggestion that Huntington told Dring to pursue. As months went by the chances of such a purchase seemed less likely. By early February 1915 Dring was only able to report small progress.

> I have today received a letter from Messrs. Sotheby in which they say "we have just received a letter from Mr. Huth in which he commits himself to nothing beyond a willingness to sell privately if an

adequate offer be made. Therefore we cannot say at what sum he would sell, but speaking privately, we have no doubt that an offer of £80,000 or more would be accepted. At least we would try to get him to do so, though we do not think he would even consider less."

Dring commented that £80,000 "seems reasonable," and concluded his letter with a crucial question, "Will you authorize me to make an offer of £80,000 for the lot?"[25]

Huntington was not willing to make a commitment of that size. He continued to place bids with Smith and Quaritch on individual items as the Huth sales continued over the next five years.

Although the big sales of the London season were over, Smith still held a number of Huntington commissions. Over the three days of the T. G. Arthur sale in July 1914 Smith spent $19,380, securing more than half of the items offered. He obtained a signed presentation copy of *Two Poems* (1854) by Elizabeth Barrett and Robert Browning for $205, *A Descriptive Catalogue of Pictures Painted by W. Blake* (1809) at $122, a large-paper copy of *Gulliver's Travels* (1726) at $1,250, and William Blake's copiously annotated copy of R. Watson's *An Apology for the Bible in a Series of Letters Addressed to Thomas Paine* at $235.

At the close of the Arthur sale Smith dropped a publicity bombshell. In a special cable dispatch to the *New York Sun* he announced that he had smashed what he called the London book ring, a claim that made all of his previous bombast and hyperbole seem tame indeed. In speaking to the *Sun* correspondent, Smith explained that a number of London dealers often joined together to control auction sales by agreeing to keep bids under a specified limit.

> They invited me to become a member of their association, but I refused and I have succeeded in breaking up the ring. The only independent buyer in London is Mr. Quaritch, who purchases on commission for the British Museum and similar organizations. My high prices caused the rest of the dealers to lose heart and they do not know what I am capable of.[26]

The event was important enough to elicit an editorial in the *New York Times* praising Smith for his "faith in the continuance of American prosperity" and for beating the ring "in the familiar American way, by high bidding."[27]

Two days after his conquests at the Arthur sale, Smith achieved another American victory, as the New York newspapers were calling it, by purchasing W. C. Prescott's Shakespeare collection. For the bargain price of $6,000, Smith obtained an extra-illustrated set of Knight's pictorial edition of Shakespeare's works, expanded from eight to ninety-five volumes with the insertion of thirteen thousand drawings, prints, portraits, and playbills. The set was shelved in a bookcase ten feet tall and elaborately carved, made from timbers of forty different buildings associated with Shakespeare's life or mentioned in the plays. After Smith purchased this curiosity for Huntington, he found out that Henry C. Folger, the noted Shakespeare collector, was also interested. Smith wrote Huntington,

> I enclose herewith a letter from Mr. Folger who is very anxious to get the Shakespeare Bookcase, I sold you. The case and set of books have been delivered to your 57th Street house. Do you care to sell the bookcase and if so, at what price? I told Mr. Folger I doubted very much that you would part with it.[28]

Although Huntington considered the possibility of an exchange, nothing came of this or of later approaches by Folger after Smith's death. The much-discussed bookcase (with its contents) remains a showpiece at the Huntington Library, now displayed in the Ahmanson Reading Room.

Smith completed his domination of the London summer sales by buying a collection of Robert Louis Stevenson autographs and manuscripts; first editions of the works of Spenser, Ben Jonson, and Keats; some fifteenth-century illuminated manuscripts; and the clock that had inspired Dickens's story "Master Humphrey's Clock." Smith had every reason to be pleased with his accomplishments. In a note to the *New York Times* he reported, "Have had a very successful trip. It was a long hard battle but I have won out O. K. "[29]

Backed by substantial Huntington commissions he had acquired some extraordinary books and had at the same time managed, as he might have put it, to show the English a thing or two. Certainly he had made substantial additions to Huntington's library. The movement of books from England to America in general was important enough to warrant coverage in a long

FIG. 21
Huntington and
Henry C. Folger
often competed
over the same rare
editions. Huntington
acquired this book-
case, made of timbers
from buildings
associated with
Shakespeare, through
Smith, but learned
soon after that Folger
wished to purchase it.
The bookcase is
still in use in the
Ahmanson Reading
Room of the
Huntington Library.

article in the *New York Times*. Referring to Huntington as a "lover of books" with catholic tastes, the writer claimed, "No other book collector in America . . . has ever purchased in so wholesale a manner."[30]

In July 1914, with the beginning of war imminent, Smith was concluding his negotiations in London. The Huntingtons, who were enjoying their annual stay at the Chateau Beauregard, found themselves dangerously situated between the battle lines as the German forces occupied Amiens and Compiègne in the north. At first Mrs. Huntington refused to leave but finally, on the advice of Myron T. Herrick, the American ambassador to France, agreed to go. The *New York Times* featured an account of the Huntingtons' last-minute escape to the coast of France that read like an adventure novel.[31] The Huntingtons arrived in London in the middle of August, spent some time with Arabella's son Archer, and were finally able to secure passage home in early September. Book buying necessarily took second place behind world events. For Huntington, it seemed a good time to take stock.

Chapter 5

THE PASSION BECOMES A PLAN
1915–1916

Huntington had been extremely active in the book auction market beginning with his purchases at the Poor sale of 1908–9. His collection had grown to such a size that a more efficient system of control was essential. As books arrived at Fifty-seventh Street, the house staff checked them against invoices and made brief entries on five-by-eight cards. Since shelf space in the handsome third-floor book room was limited, most new acquisitions had to be crated up and stored or sent to California. Considering the sheer number of books acquired and the informality of the system, it is not surprising that Smith and Huntington had only a vague idea of what the collection held.

In November 1914, while Huntington was visiting in the offices of the publishing firm of Dodd, Mead and Company, Robert H. Dodd introduced him to George Watson Cole. The sixty-four-year-old Cole was well known both as a library administrator and as a bibliographer. His most important piece of work, produced between 1902 and 1909, was the meticulously edited catalog of the E. D. Church library. Huntington was of course familiar with Cole's bibliographic skill since in 1911 he had purchased the Church books, along with all the remaining copies of the printed catalog. The two men had much in common: they were the same age, had grown up in small towns in the east, and believed in the importance of the work ethic as the means to success. After their conversation, Huntington is said to have remarked to Dodd, "That is the very man I have been looking for."[1] Although it is unrecorded, Cole might well have expressed the same enthusiasm. Nothing came of the meeting immediately, but over the next ten years Cole was to play an important part in the development of the library.

In early February 1915 the Huntingtons arrived in San Marino in their private rail car for the winter season. One newspaper account mentioned a stop in New York, where Huntington purchased a rare edition of *Pilgrim's Progress*. "I thought I had lost it," Huntington is reported to have said, "but my agent got it at last." Then, in a rare moment of public disclosure, Huntington commented gleefully, "You know this book fad is the only hobby that grows on you and keeps you agitated all the time." In that brief statement Huntington revealed not only his pleasure in getting a book that appeared to be out of reach but his enthusiasm for collecting in general. The newspaper article concluded by stating that Huntington's English literature holdings were "without parallel" and that he was a "bibliomaniac of parts."[2]

Although Huntington's bibliomania may have been intense and his resources extensive, he still needed the assistance of those in the trade. That help was never lacking. During the war years Smith was Huntington's chief agent while Rosenbach, Sessler, and others worked around the edges, selling him a few titles whenever they could. Many dealers wanted Huntington as a customer but they knew better than to antagonize Smith, who was capable of crushing any opposition. Late in 1914 Rosenbach sent Huntington two impressive catalogs, one offering titles from Harry B. Smith's "Sentimental Library" and the other describing the holdings of the Robert Louis Stevenson collection presented to Harvard by Mrs. Eleanor Widener.[3] Rosenbach was a master of bibliographic flattery. Those receiving his catalogs understood that they were among the chosen few, possessed of both the taste to appreciate the finer things and the money to afford them. Huntington was not entirely immune to this kind of flattery, and early in 1915, through Rosenbach, bought three Shakespeare quartos—*Julius Caesar* (1684), *Othello* (1687), and *Hamlet* (1676)—for a total of $750. At the same time he took a number of Rosenbach offerings from stock, including a Pynson printing of Sallust's *The*

Famous Chronycle of the Warre (1525?) for $600, the proofs of Blake's *Illustrations to Shakespeare* at $410, and Robson's *A new yeeres gift. The Courte of Civill Courtesie* (1582) for $700. These were isolated items, however, and in total fell far short of Huntington's purchases from Smith over the same period of time. In January 1915 Huntington asked Smith to bid on a collection of George Washington letters and some assorted literary titles to be offered at the Adrian Joline sale. Smith got all the items Huntington wanted for just under three thousand dollars.

Although the war in Europe did not affect the number of book auctions held in New York, it did discourage buying.[4] Perhaps the biggest sale of the 1915 spring season, and the most disappointing from the point of view of the consignors, was that of the literary and art treasures of General Brayton Ives. At one time president of the New York Stock Exchange, Ives had built two impressive libraries. After selling his Americana in 1891 he proceeded almost immediately to build a second collection around the chief literary figures of the nineteenth century. On Ives's death in October 1914 the representatives of his estate turned over the books and art objects to Thomas Kirby and the American Art Association. The gallery issued a deluxe large-paper catalog with elaborate descriptions of faience snuff boxes, ivory netsuke, Italian majolica vases, Persian prayer rugs, and 1,121 lots of "literary treasures." The treasures attracted some of the chief American book trade luminaries—Gabriel Wells, A. S. W. Rosenbach, Joseph Sabin, George D. Smith, Charles Sessler, Walter Hill, and Lathrop Harper—all looking for bargains. Since Ives had purchased many of the books at the 1911 Hoe sale it was easy for observers to draw comparisons. For those managing the Ives estate these comparisons were decidedly grim. Smith, bidding for Huntington, secured a late-fifteenth-century French Book of Hours printed on vellum for $510 (Hoe price $800), a tall copy of the 1482 first edition of Euclid's *Elementa Geometriae* for $310 (Hoe price $450), and one of the fifty-two copies of the 1906 "Mirages" by Sliman ben Ibrahim, printed on Japanese paper with etchings in two states and bound in full dark brown levant morocco for $230 (Hoe price $810). The Ives books brought a disappointing total of only $87,441. For those with money to spend, it was a buyer's market.

For Huntington the temptation to buy was tempered by his knowledge that a number of his major collections were already crated and in storage in

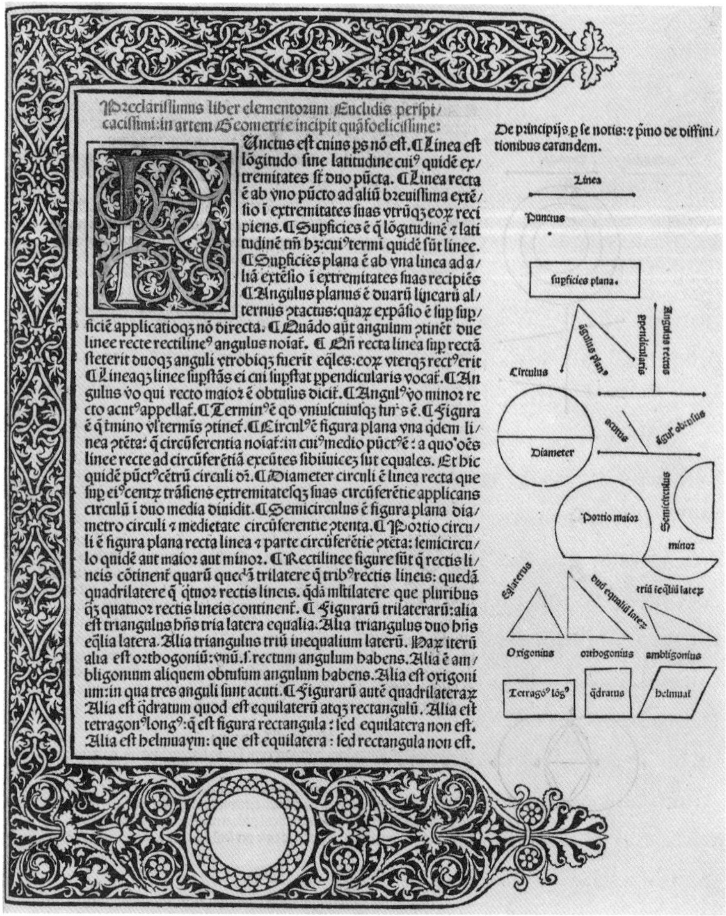

FIG. 22
First leaf from
Euclid's *Elementa
Geometriae* (Venice,
1482), a handsome
first edition of this
classic of ancient
mathematics.
Huntington
acquired the Hoe
copy at the Ives
sale in 1915.

New York and California waiting for proper bibliographic verification and
cataloging. It was time to recruit a professional staff.

In the late spring Huntington called on George Watson Cole at his home
in Hollywood and asked him if he would be willing to move to New York and
catalog the library. Cole accepted happily. In July he wrote Huntington setting out his ideas for managing the job.

> My dear Mr. Huntington:
>
> You doubtless remember that during your call I told you it would
> give me pleasure to undertake the cataloguing of your library for
> $6000 a year. I should require the assistance of one competent
> stenographer and typewriter [typist] and in order to do effective work
> and push it along as rapidly as possible two or three young women

assistants. These latter would have to be trained to their duties, and later their number might well be doubled. The catalogue should be typewritten and these assistants would each require the use of a machine. I have no doubt that bright young women can be found who have had the advantage of some library training, in which case they will soon adapt themselves to the work required of them.

As to space, I should judge a room about 16 x 24 feet, or rooms approximating that size, would be ample for all purposes. Should the above terms and plan meet your approval I will make arrangements to be in New York after the middle of September so as to be ready to begin cataloguing about October first.

Huntington's reply of 27 July, sent from his summer residence at Throgg's Neck, contained a surprising condition.

My dear Mr. Cole:

Your letter of the 19th received. I would be very glad to have you undertake the cataloguing of my library.

The only obstacle is the employment of women which for reasons of my own, I object to. I know that in employing men the cost will be more and I presume this is your principle [*sic*] reason for employing women. I hope you will not object to this or think I am set in my idea. I do not think aside from this idiosyncracy [*sic*] of mine you will regret taking up this work. I certainly intend to give you a free hand and I shall be most happy to know that you accept.[5]

Cole accepted Huntington's terms, saying that although he was accustomed to working with young women he felt could find men who were equally "bright, alert and intelligent." In late September he arrived in New York to take up his new duties. He found Huntington seriously ill with doctors and nurses in constant attendance. It was several days before Cole was even allowed to talk with Huntington, and then only long enough to get the keys to the library. Cole had seen and worked with important rare book libraries in the past, but Huntington's collection was beyond anything he had experienced. Years later he reminisced about his first impression:

I have had two great thrills in my lifetime—the first was on the 24th of June, 1913 when I visited Abbotsford and stood in the very rooms where Sir Walter Scott, the hero of my boyhood days, had written some of the works that made his name a lasting one in English literature. The second thrill came when on this occasion I opened the door to Mr. Huntington's library, walked in, and saw the shelves filled with the nucleus of the present Huntington Library. Here were my old friends the books of the Church Library and those of several less important collections, but there were also the more important ones; the Chew Collection of English poetry, the Kemble-Devonshire Caxtons, and the Kemble English drama.[6]

The task was challenging from the first. When Cole took over the collection it numbered some forty thousand volumes. That figure had quadrupled by the time he resigned nine years later.

One of the new librarian's first duties was to hire a competent staff. Cole approached Wilberforce Eames but the noted bibliographer was unwilling to give up his work on the collections at the New York Public Library. Eames however recommended two former associates, Chester Cate and Lodewyk Bendikson. Cate came immediately and Bendikson followed early in February. Cole then asked James Ingersoll Wyer, director of the New York State Library School in Albany, for suggestions, and obtained the name of Leslie E. Bliss, a young graduate of the school then working in the legislative reference section of the New York State Library. Bliss came to work early in November 1915, the beginning of a fifty-year career with the Huntington collections. During the next three years the staff doubled, with the appointments of Herman Mead, Cecil Edmonds, Philip Goulding, Clifford Clapp, and Robert O. Schad.

Cole was fortunate in his new assistants. Already trained through previous experience, the men were eager to pursue the task at hand. It was well that this was so since only rudimentary bibliographical records existed for the huge and growing accumulation of books. Before Cole arrived, the cataloging—or rather record keeping—had been done by George E. Miles and other members of the office staff, and consisted of little more than brief notes transcribed on cards. This of course was ludicrously inadequate. Cole's scheme for cataloging was ambitious and went far beyond what was then considered standard library practice. As one aspect of the job, Cole planned to produce an elaborate multivolume bibliographic catalog with detailed notes, similar to the one he had done seven years earlier for E. D. Church. When carried to completion, Cole's catalog, tentatively titled "English Literature in the Huntington Library," would list twenty thousand items in some forty thousand

pages of text. Cole presented the construction of this massive bibliography to the staff as one of their principal tasks.[7] In addition, of course, the men had to check in and catalog the continuing flow of acquisitions.

The ability of the staff to balance these two separate lines of endeavor was tested in December 1915 when Huntington purchased the twenty-thousand-volume Frederick R. Halsey library. Halsey, a prominent New York lawyer and early member of the Grolier Club, had spent over thirty-five years forming a carefully selected collection of American, English, and French literature, and Americana. Known as a fastidious collector, Halsey allowed no book on his shelves unless its binding and general condition met his exacting standards. Among the rarities in the collection were first, third, and fourth Shakespeare folios, a long run of the quartos, and a first edition of the *Sonnets* (1609) with the scarce Aspley imprint, as well as first editions of Milton, Shelley, Dickens, Longfellow, Melville, and Poe. It was the Poe section of the library that was perhaps of greatest strength: among other titles there were two first editions of *Tamerlane and Other Poems* (1827), two volumes of the *Broadway Journal* annotated by Poe, and a first edition of *Al Aaraaf, Tamerlane and Minor Poems* (1829). Originally, when the Halsey library had been scheduled for sale on the open market, a number of collectors had been interested. William L. Clements, an avid Americana collector from Michigan, had discussed the purchase of some of the items with his agent Lathrop Harper, but before they could make an offer Smith moved in and acquired

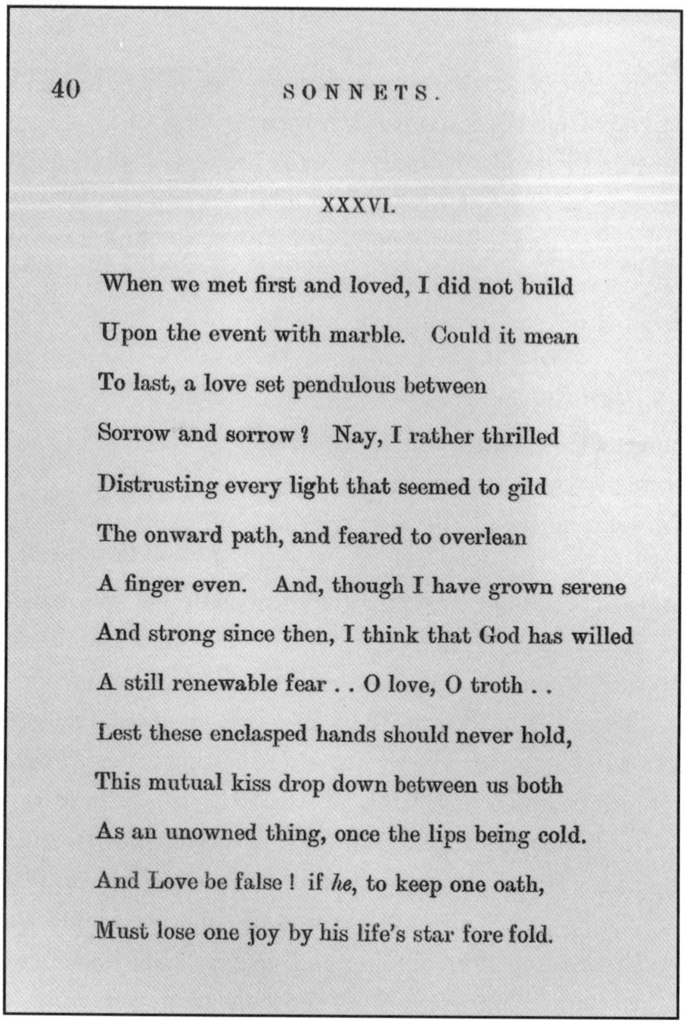
40 SONNETS.

XXXVI.

When we met first and loved, I did not build
Upon the event with marble. Could it mean
To last, a love set pendulous between
Sorrow and sorrow ? Nay, I rather thrilled
Distrusting every light that seemed to gild
The onward path, and feared to overlean
A finger even. And, though I have grown serene
And strong since then, I think that God has willed
A still renewable fear . . O love, O troth . .
Lest these enclasped hands should never hold,
This mutual kiss drop down between us both
As an unowned thing, once the lips being cold.
And Love be false ! if *he*, to keep one oath,
Must lose one joy by his life's star fore fold.

FIG. 24
The purported first, privately printed edition of Elizabeth Barrett Browning's *Sonnets* (Reading, 1847), was actually a forgery created circa 1890 by the infamous Thomas J. Wise and his associate Harry Buxton Forman. Huntington unknowingly acquired this and many other forgeries with the Halsey library.

the entire library for Huntington.[8] It was the same powerful alliance of money and decisiveness that had brought Huntington the Church books in 1911 and the Kemble-Devonshire plays three years later. As for Halsey, the sale only whetted his zeal. He immediately bought back one of the copies of Poe's *Tamerlane* at a Huntington duplicate sale and began to build another library. When the second Halsey library came on the market in 1919 shortly after the collector's death it netted the estate an impressive $158,749.

With the appointment of a professional staff, the library's selection process began to develop along more formal lines. In the past Smith and the other dealers had simply suggested titles to Huntington and he agreed or declined based on his own judgment and interests. Now, with trained bibliographers on hand, decisions could be handled more carefully. In the spring of 1916, for example, Smith wrote to Huntington saying he had passed some Dickens letters and manuscripts along to Mr. Cole for examination "as per your request." Later that same month Huntington wrote to Smith:

> It seems to me I have several of the Dickens you mention. I wish
> you would go over the matter with Mr. Cole.[9]

At first the staff was asked only to verify records in order to avoid duplicate purchases, but over time they assumed greater responsibilities, since Huntington found their knowledge and judgment helpful in the more sophisticated aspects of selection.

Huntington's en bloc purchases created special problems of verification for the cataloging staff. There were many titles in the Halsey library, for example, that apparently duplicated books already in the collection. Each suspected duplicate had to be carefully compared with the copy already in the library. It was a time-consuming but necessary task. In addition, many Halsey books represented fields in which Huntington had no interest—for example, a large number of works by nineteenth-century French essayists and novelists. Huntington decided to place the duplicates and unwanted items on the market, some to be handled directly by Smith and Rosenbach, others to be offered in a series of sales at the recently renamed Anderson Galleries.

The idea of selling duplicates appealed to Huntington on several levels. In the first place, he was a trader. He enjoyed the give-and-take of the market and the prospect of refining his holdings by replacing less desirable copies with better ones. And, of course, there would be some cash return. Even after the auction house took the usual ten percent commission he could expect to get back a considerable sum of money. The final factor was more personal and concerned Huntington's relationship to Mitchell Kennerley, the new president of the Anderson Galleries.

Kennerley's entry into the New York auction scene had been made possible by a change in the ownership of the Anderson. In October 1915 Emory Turner, tired of the responsibilities of management, sold his controlling interest to the Philadelphia bibliophile John B. Stetson, Jr. Although Stetson had the financial resources to buy the Anderson, he knew nothing about managing the firm's day-to-day operations. Clearly an experienced professional was needed, and Kennerley seemed to have excellent qualifications. A charming, audacious, and literate Englishman, he had arrived in the United States in 1899, married well, and thereafter pursued a number of careers—editor, bookseller, and publisher, sometimes combining all three at once. The titles that appeared over the Kennerley imprint from 1906 to 1914 included works by such well-known writers as Edgar Saltus, Van Wyck Brooks, William Butler Yeats, D. H. Lawrence, and Edna St. Vincent Millay. He knew many of the key figures in the New York literary world and furthermore had some influence on that world. Although he had no experience in the auction business he was confident and persuasive and counted many book dealers, collectors, bibliographers, and authors as close personal friends. Huntington liked Kennerley for his forthright, jaunty manner and was happy to trust his duplicates to the new man at the Anderson.[10]

In February 1916 Kennerley issued the first in a series of fifteen Huntington duplicate catalogs. Over a nine-year period the sales would earn the collector approximately five hundred fifty thousand dollars.[11] At the 29 March

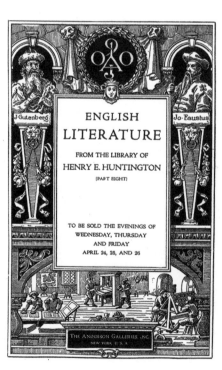

Fig. 25
Mitchell Kennerley issued catalogs over a nine-year period to accompany sales of Huntington's duplicates at the Anderson Galleries. The one shown dates from 1918.

sale, a warm-up for things to come, Huntington contributed only 230 of 1,140 lots while the remaining titles came from the estate of E. D. Church and the library of the St. Louis collector William Bixby. The New York dealers bid vigorously for the duplicates, many of them reflecting Huntington's earliest purchases—standard literary sets and English color-plate books from the Poor and Morschhauser libraries. In all, Huntington realized $8,927, with many of the higher-priced items going to Smith and Rosenbach. Although the total was small, individual items brought good prices and Huntington and Kennerley were satisfied with the results.

While preparations for the first duplicate sale were still underway Huntington entered into another important transaction with Smith. In July 1914, on his first trip to England, Smith had achieved one of his greatest triumphs, buying over half of the incunabula and other early printed works offered at the Pembroke sale. He sold some immediately to Huntington but kept others for stock. The following year he produced a handsome list of these rarities along with a few purchases from the Hoe sale under the title *Monuments of Early Printing . . . 1460–1500*. In the catalog's introduction Smith wrote:

> The collection of Early Printed Books now on Exhibition at my new store and offices at 547 Fifth Avenue has been selected principally by me from the Magnificent Library of the Earl of Pembroke, a portion of which, comprising the Illuminated Manuscripts, Block Books and Incunabula, was recently sold at Auction in London, at which Sale I was the Largest Purchaser.

Then, as an additional lure, he warned:

> Attention must be paid to the fact that the Opportunity to acquire these Noble Monuments of the Early Printers is becoming of immensely greater difficulty every day.[12]

Smith's prose implied that individuals wise enough to purchase these monuments would achieve immediate acclaim. This was not altogether misleading, as libraries and collectors had always achieved renown on the basis of their holdings of incunabula. Although the purchase of books of this kind might not place the buyer on equal footing with the British Museum or the

Bodleian Library at Oxford, it would be a start. Huntington could seldom resist the temptation to compete. He had acquired a few incunabula by chance through the Church, Hoe, and Chatsworth library purchases but had made no special effort to seek them out. Now, he had the opportunity to own a notable incunabula collection in one stroke. For the altogether reasonable figure of $90,000 he took 136 items from Smith's catalog, including a copy of the xylographic second edition of the Dutch *Speculum Humanae Salvationis*, probably printed before 1471; the editio princeps of the works of Saint Ambrose (1492); and the Hoe copy of Ratdolt's *Euclid* (1482). In addition, he acquired titles printed by William Caxton, Aldus Manutius, and Peter Schoeffer, along with examples of the work of the first presses of Strasbourg, Cologne, Nuremberg, Ulm, Basel, Florence, Venice, Milan, Lyons, Bruges, Paris, Bologna, Haarlem, Westminster, and London. Considering the quality and importance of these titles Huntington did extremely well in this, his first bulk incunabula purchase.[13]

Huntington applied his shrewd bargaining skills not only to purchases that created newspaper headlines but to smaller negotiations as well. In March 1916, Robert E. Cowan, a well-known San Francisco book dealer, offered him Augustin Macdonald's fifteen-hundred-volume California and Pacific Coast library for $25,000. Cowan claimed that the collection was the largest of its kind outside of the Bancroft Library at the University of California and that the purchaser would obtain, among many riches, a number of unique San Francisco imprints. Maneuvering for position, Huntington noted that he already owned a great many items described in the catalog and that many others he found to be of "no value." But Huntington's next paragraph held out some hope: "If I could exchange real estate here for the books, I think I might be inclined to take them. If not, I will return the catalogue." In early April Macdonald and Cowan visited Huntington in Los Angeles and the three men struck an agreement. Two weeks after the meeting Cowan put the terms in writing:

> [Macdonald] authorizes me to state as a final proposition that he will accept 10,000 in real estate and the remaining 15,000 in bonds.[14]

While this was going on, Henry R. Wagner, the noted West Coast bibliographer and collector, was watching with intense interest. He had hoped to extract a substantial number of books from the Macdonald library and was unhappy to hear that Huntington, whom he once referred to as "that shark," got there first.[15] Wagner, an avid collector-bibliographer who took keen delight in building collections piece by piece, saw Huntington as a rich man who simply gobbled up books with a stroke of the pen. In this case Huntington's pen sealed the agreement. Macdonald got both bonds and property.

The exchange of letters between Huntington and Cowan suggests something of the nature of the two men. On 28 April Cowan wrote:

> As far as the real estate is concerned, as no definite piece of property has been suggested by you, we must trust implicitly in your judgement that it will be something that represents a value of $10,000.

From Paso Robles Hot Springs, Huntington replied in the same gentlemanly manner.

> We have a list price on each separate piece and we shall charge Mr. Macdonald no more than we would if we sold for cash.[16]

The Macdonald books and manuscripts provided Huntington with his first substantial stock of western Americana.

With the Macdonald books still in packing cases, Huntington captured the headlines in August 1915 with another important Americana purchase. This time the books were offered in London from the Britwell Court library of S. R. Christie-Miller. The catalog prepared by the auction firm of Sotheby, Wilkinson, and Hodge enumerated 346 items, including an exceptional run of the De Bry *Voyages* along with an assortment of important editions of the works of such well-known chroniclers as Thomas Harriot, Peter Martyr, Sir Walter Raleigh, and Captain John Smith.[17] The library had been formed in the early part of the nineteenth century by W. H. Christie-Miller, an Edinburgh lawyer and bibliophile who bought heavily from both bookshops and auction sales. His scrupulous attention to details of binding and size, which he verified with an ever-present ruler, earned him the nickname "Measure Miller." After his death in 1848 the library passed through the hands of various family members down to S. R. Christie-Miller, who early in 1916 decided to offer the books in a series of public auctions.[18] Although

Huntington already owned a considerable number of the titles in the Britwell catalog, many obtained from the 1911 Church purchase, he was always eager to acquire finer copies. Both Smith and Quaritch were ready to act in Huntington's behalf. On 15 July Quaritch suggested that it might be advantageous to buy the collection en bloc.

> . . . [the en bloc purchase] would be more favourable than buying what you want by auction. Duplicates would sell readily. Should be glad to act for you.[19]

Smith also saw the chance to make an important sale and wrote Huntington two weeks later:

> I am negotiating for the Christie-Miller collection of Americana and hope to buy it privately before this letter reaches you. If I secure it will write you further in the matter. It is a wonderful collection and some of the very important items you do not seem to have. I was surprised to find so many not in your library.[20]

Huntington evidently saw the Britwell sale as an opportunity to play the two dealers against each other. In late July he asked George Watson Cole to write to Quaritch giving the dealer commissions for 104 items from the Britwell catalog, "if sold at reasonable prices."[21] At the same time he wrote Smith about his interest in selected items. In a preemptive sweep Smith bought the entire collection for approximately two hundred thousand dollars.[22] The other American dealers who had traveled to London to take part in the sale found that their trip had been made in vain. When asked about his colleagues' frustration, Smith with tongue-in-cheek buoyancy replied that he didn't see any reason for their complaint since "they had a nice sea voyage anyway."[23] E. H. Dring, who had taken over the direction of the Quaritch firm after the death of Bernard Alfred Quaritch in 1913, was particularly unhappy since he had been given to understand that his firm was to handle some of the buying. He wrote curtly to Huntington.

> Dear Sir:
> You will have learned from my cable that G. D. Smith has bought the collection of Britwell Americana "en bloc."

I am sorry you did not allow me to bid for the lot for you as I feel sure it would have been to your advantage to have done so.[24]

The arrangement with Huntington, however, was less comprehensive than Dring imagined since as late as 1 September, Smith was still negotiating to sell specific selected items. He wrote:

Dear Mr. Huntington

Your favor in regard to the Britwell Library received. I purchased the collection privately, but it has not yet been received. I am expecting it daily.

My intention was to sell the collection privately in block, if possible, and have not been able to price the items separately. As soon as I am able to go over the books I will be pleased to give you a list of the prices. I am sending herewith a copy of the printed catalogue.

Along the bottom of the letter Smith scrawled, "P.S. Will hold above collection waiting your return."[25]

Although Huntington's original idea had been to select certain items from the library he eventually decided to take it all. One of the most important sections consisted of a long run of the rare Latin editions of De Bry's *Voyages.* In this set, certain pages had been removed and specific passages erased in order to satisfy the "Index Expurgatorius." According to George Watson Cole, no other set in the country contained similar obliterations. The De Brys were not only historically significant but, handsomely bound in 102 red and orange morocco folio volumes, were a treat for the eye.

The en bloc sale of the Britwell books not only caused ill feelings at the Quaritch firm but angered a number of American collectors. William L. Clements, an American collector from Michigan, was unhappy since he had intended to add the De Brys to his own growing library. Like many other collectors, Clements stood in considerable awe of Huntington. When it came to the question of who would succeed in any given competition he felt, quite correctly, that he had little chance against the Huntington fortune. When he learned that Smith had purchased the Britwell books he assumed that they would go to San Marino. If that were true then perhaps a number of duplicates would come off Huntington's shelf. In some cases, he reasoned, if the original Huntington copy was a better one, a buyer might expect to be able to obtain the Britwell copy. Would it be possible, he asked Smith, to examine those duplicates? In late November of 1916 Clements made a bibliographic pilgrimage to Huntington's gray granite mansion on Fifty-seventh Street. In a letter to Clarence S. Brigham, the director of the American Antiquarian Society, Clements described his visit and his impression of the library.

> Dear Sir:
>
> I had the liberty of spending the greater part of the morning in Mr. Huntington's library, and examined the Americana. A large number of duplicates are to be sold in January and February. I brought home with me five or six rare books from the Britwell Christie-Miller lot, which of course, were duplicates in the Huntington Collection. Everything is so congested in this library that it is almost impossible to get a fair idea of it, but its scope is so extensive that it is altogether beyond an ordinary mortal to fully appreciate it.[26]

Clements was quite satisfied to take Huntington leavings.

Although Dring had been outmaneuvered in the matter of the Britwell Americana, he managed to secure all of Huntington's bids for the fifth Huth sale. The series of auctions, begun in 1911 and postponed for one year in 1914, was scheduled to resume in July 1916. In June Huntington wrote asking that bids be placed on one hundred forty items. The letter contained his familiar proviso against paying "fancy prices."

> I am in receipt of catalog of Huth Collection, Fifth Portion and I have not had time to look up the value of the books, and I shall have to trust it to your discretion as to what you shall bid on them.
> I do not care to pay fancy prices, as you of course know.

Dring was able to get most of the items wanted and following Huntington's orders, demurred only when the prices went to levels he believed excessive. In July, at the end of the sale, he wrote:

> You will I am sure be pleased to see from the daily reports which I have sent you that I have been successful in buying everything that you required, except in three instances, and in each case I thought

the prices the items fetched were altogether unreasonable. With many thanks for the confidence reposed in me.[27]

The purchases, totaling some $75,000, enhanced the solid coverage of the sixteenth- and seventeenth-century poets, playwrights, and divines with works by Christopher Marlowe, John Marston, and Cotton and Increase Mather. Huntington had every reason to be pleased with Dring's efforts.

In early April, three months before the Britwell and Huth sales, Huntington negotiated with Smith for some important books and manuscripts to be offered in New York at the Edwin W. Coggeshall sale. Coggeshall had spent years assembling what was regarded as one of the best private Dickens collections in the world. In addition, he had gathered an important Thackeray library and a rich selection of autographed literary and historical manuscripts. Smith was eager to have Huntington take advantage of this opportunity. He wrote:

> This is the finest collection of Dickens ever offered for sale. The Pickwick is the finest copy extant and the most important of all Dickens' Books. You should get this by all means.
>
> The Lincoln Collection #15 [16 Autographed letters from Lincoln, Grant, Farragut, Stanton etc.] is also extremely interesting. It cost Coggeshall $3500 many years ago and should be worth $5000 although I think we may get it for about $3000.
>
> No. 22 [an extra-illustrated set of *Battles and Leaders of the Civil War*, extended from four to twenty-five volumes with 1722 engraved portraits, views and maps and 921 letters] is the famous Daly Copy which Mr. Coggeshall broke up and added many fine and important autographs and had rebound. The letters are all of exceptional interest.

Huntington's reply was guarded:

> Yours of April 11 received. You can purchase the following at prices quoted, if you are sure I do not already have them:
>
> Nos 22 [*Battles and Leaders of the Civil War*] 154 [Dickens's reading copy of *Doctor Marigold*] 392 [Helen Hunt Jackson *Ramona* with water-color sketches by W. H. Drake] 490 [Robert

Louis Stevenson *The Edinburgh University Magazine,* 1871] 541 [Appleton's Popular Library 1852–53] I am interested in other Dickens items, but it seems to me they are high priced. I would like no. 15 [Autographed letters of Lincoln etc.] but it is more than I care to pay.

It seems to me I have several of the Dickens you mention. I wish you would go over the matter with Mr. Cole. I do not care to buy them simply because they are presentation copies.

You can buy 402 [Walter Savage Landor, *Imaginary Conversations,* 1826–28] if it goes cheap.[28]

It wasn't until May that Huntington found out what he had bought. As usual, Smith had overstepped his commissions. Of the items secured he explained:

I had to pay a little more for the Collection of Lincoln, Grant and Farragut correspondence [$3950] but if sold separately the Lincoln letters alone would have brought the money.

The Pickwick I bought for $5300 and sold it to Mr. Bunker the same day for $6000. Am sorry you did not send me a bid on it.

Number 209, the famous Walkingmatch [Dickens] I secured for you at $950. This sold very low considering the prices realized for Dickens books in this sale. . . . I got a great many of the fine Dickens letters for you. This series with the others from the next sale, if we can buy the balance at reasonable prices would make a most extraordinary Collection of Dickens Letters. They could be bound up in a number of octavo volumes and would make a great addition to your collection.

Number 392 Jackson's "Ramona," I had to pay $305 for but it is a most beautiful book. If you do not want it, I easily could sell it at a handsome profit.[29]

With the first Coggeshall auction out of the way, Smith promised the second sale would be another "exceptional opportunity."

Dear Mr. Huntington:
The Dickens letters are extremely important. No such series has

ever been or ever will be offered again. You should get all the Dickens letters possible, if they sell at reasonable prices. The long series of letters to Wilis costs [*sic*] Mr. Coggeshall $12000 and would be cheap at that figure now. Perhaps I can pick them up at about this figure and possibly for a little less.

Smith's final paragraph took a somewhat different turn:

I also wish to call your special attention to #116 [An antique Italian shell-shaped silver reliquary with interior compartments containing on one side a lock of John Milton's hair and on the other a lock of Elizabeth Barrett's hair]. This I think a most important item and may appeal to Mrs. Huntington if you are not personally interested.[30]

This "most important item" elicited no enthusiasm from either of the Huntingtons. Smith reported the results of the second Coggeshall sale with customary bravado.

The Dickens letters sold at less than half their value. They are a most important series and with what you already have will make the largest and finest collection in existence. I am sure you will be pleased with them and at the low prices which we were able to secure them for.

The sheer quantity of Smith's purchase, some four hundred Dickens letters, brought forth a mildly reproving letter from Huntington:

My dear Smith:
    I had no idea you were going to buy so many Dickens letters, and several things I did not order—they may be all right though, if you have purchased them.
    Cogswell [*sic*] sale nos. 111, 125, 132, and 149 I do not remember ordering, but I will talk with you about that when I come to New York.

Clearly no hard feelings remained on Huntington's part, as he closed on a friendly note:

. I ordered Graham to send you the twenty thousand as requested [an advance against purchases]. We are all quite well here and have had a delightful summer.[31]

As if to clear himself once and for all of extravagant spending Smith answered on 31 July:

I purchased about all of the Dickens letters as they sold at ridiculously low prices and the series with what you already have will give you the finest collection of Dickens Letters extant.[32]

While Smith was helping Huntington secure books from the New York auctions, Rosenbach kept him informed about a few choice items from stock. During the years 1916–20 Rosenbach was able to work sales against the credit he had built up from taking some of the Huntington duplicates. In this way, late in 1916, Rosenbach gave Huntington credit for $15,000 worth of Americana from the Britwell library and in turn "sold" him, for nearly the same amount, a series of Blake's watercolors for Milton's "Hymn to the Nativity," along with the Mentelin Bible of 1468. In another agreement the same year, Rosenbach supplied Huntington with a 1466 Fust and Schoeffer Cicero on vellum, a run of early Connecticut laws, James Madison's correspondence with Alexander Dallas, and Blake's watercolors for *Comus*. Smith had a similar arrangement with Huntington for the disposal of duplicates but apparently was less energetic about pursuing sales. In 1918 Huntington wrote a chiding letter:

My dear Sir:

On February 26, 1916 you received from me books to the number of 741. To January 29th, 1918, you have sold 29. At this rate it will take 49 years to sell the balance. Do you not think this is quite a long time?[33]

Although the private sale of duplicates to Smith showed minimal returns, the public auctions went forward successfully. Kennerley scheduled a second sale for late November with a stock made up almost entirely of French books secured from the Halsey library. According to the sales catalog, the items to be sold represented "the finest modern productions of the French press, illustrated by the greatest of contemporary artists with many bindings by the master craftsmen of France." In his enthusiastic letter to Huntington, Kennerley reported on the sale results.

> Lot 616 [Pastissier (1655)] cost Mr. Halsey $260 and sold for $760. Lot 438 [Le Sage *Histoire de Gil Blas* 1714–25] cost Mr. Halsey $200 and sold for $600. It is the modern books on Japanese Vellum in extravagant and ornate bindings which have suffered. . . . The first editions of Moliere had cost Mr. Halsey $40 and $60 each, and they have sold for an average of nearly $200.
>
> I hope you will feel as we do, that on the whole the sale has been satisfactory.[34]

The sale, which netted $39,900, was indeed satisfactory and suggested the possibility of even greater returns as Huntington and Kennerley planned for the 1917 Americana auction. The buying power of the European and English book dealers was of course affected by the war but at home, with the reelection of President Woodrow Wilson under the slogan "He Kept Us Out of War," prosperity still ruled. Huntington himself saw the war as an opportunity for business expansion. The European nations would need the tools of war and America would stand to profit from the trade. Commenting on the war for the *Los Angeles Times* he observed:

> It opens new fields of commerce to us with the advantages possessed by any progressive nation far removed from the scene of strife are manifest.

Asked to predict the outcome he said:

> Who will win? Well, it is a battle for life with the British and a sort of sacred conflict for the French. Personally, I believe that the war will be a long one and that it will end in the defeat of Germany.[35]

As 1916 came to a close Huntington, now sixty-six years old, regarded the future with enthusiasm. His marriage to Arabella had turned out to be everything he had hoped, he had fought off a serious illness, the Los Angeles Railway and the Pacific Light and Power Corporations were prospering, and his library, now under the guidance of a trained staff, was growing and gain-

ing recognition at a satisfying rate. It was unfortunate that many of the books
were in New York instead of California, but that too could and would be
remedied in the future. In April Huntington told a reporter that he was
"preparing to bring his world famous library of English classics and
Americana to Pasadena probably within the next two years." To facilitate this
he would "construct a special library building at his Pasadena home to house
the collection of 75,000 rare volumes."[36] Huntington looked ahead enthusiastically to a time when he could have all his books and paintings together at
the ranch.

Chapter 6

A MAGNIFICENT SCALE
1917–1918

During the war years Huntington continued to give the library and its future considerable thought. With the addition of the Halsey and Chew books, the Kemble-Devonshire collection, and now the Britwell Americana, he began to think of his books and manuscripts in terms of their usefulness to scholars, although the concept was still somewhat vague. How would the books be made available? Who would be allowed to use them? What use would be most appropriate? He had appointed a professional staff in 1915 to organize the collections and soon he would be providing ample housing in a new library building in California. The development of the collections was still his responsibility and time, he felt, was running out. At age sixty-six he could look forward to perhaps ten more years of active buying. He had started late and now needed to hurry to complete the job he had in mind. It was like the old days, when he first came to Los Angeles. He had moved in quickly, forced the competition to step aside, and in a few short years developed an impressive urban rail network. Again, he would need to move a little faster than the competition.

Since Huntington wanted results in a hurry, he had purchased the libraries already formed by such bibliographically astute collectors as Beverly Chew,

E. D. Church, and Frederick Halsey. He was always ready to buy selected items at auction but his most important acquisitions continued to come from the purchase of entire libraries. Early in 1917 the availability of the Bridgewater House library presented another irresistible opportunity.

Long known as one of the oldest and most important family libraries in England, the Bridgewater collections had been started early in the seventeenth century by Sir Thomas Egerton, Baron Ellesmere (1540?–1617), later appointed Lord Chancellor to James I. Egerton's son and grandson, the first and second earls of Bridgewater, expanded the library, and finally in the early years of the nineteenth century it came into the hands of Francis Egerton, the Earl of Ellesmere. In 1837 the Shakespeare scholar John Payne Collier—now better known as a forger—working as a librarian for the earl, produced a catalog that listed some of the rarer holdings.[1] By 1916, with taxes an ever-increasing burden, the family decided to put the collection up for sale at auction. In

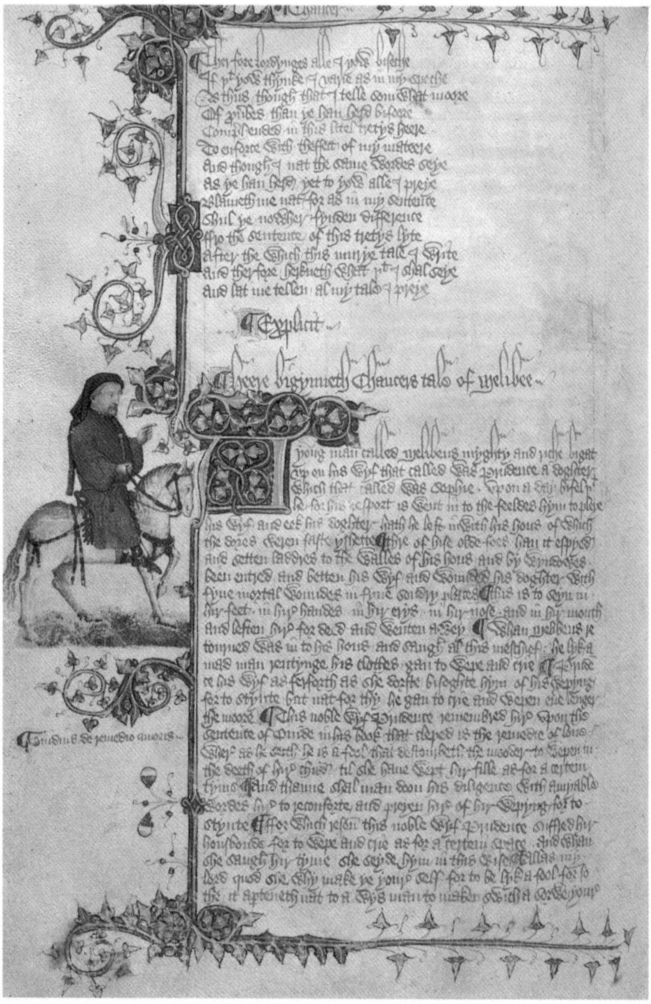

FIG. 26
The beginning of "The Tale of Melibee" from the Ellesmere manuscript of Chaucer's *Canterbury Tales,* with the portrait traditionally associated with Chaucer himself. Most readers agree that "Melibee" is the dullest of the tales. The placement of the poet's portrait thus calls attention to Chaucer's witty gesture of assigning this uninteresting tale to the narrator of *The Canterbury Tales*—in effect to himself.

all, the library included forty-four hundred printed books, exclusive of tracts, pamphlets, and newspapers, and some fourteen thousand literary manuscripts and letters. Perhaps the most distinguished item in the Bridgewater library was the famed Ellesmere Chaucer, an early-fifteenth-century illuminated manuscript of *The Canterbury Tales,* described in the Sotheby catalogue of the collection as follows:

> A superb manuscript of the highest possible importance. With the possible exception of Milton's Autograph MSS. in the Library of Trinity College, Cambridge, this manuscript is unquestionably the greatest monument of English literature in the world.[2]

W. W. Skeat had used the Ellesmere manuscript as the basis for his groundbreaking modern edition of Chaucer (1894–97), since he regarded it as "the finest and best of all the MSS. now extant."[3] The Bridgewater collection also included a number of Caxton imprints, four Shakespeare folios and numerous quartos, the most important being a *Titus Andronicus* of 1600. Additional material for literary study included works by several of Shakespeare's contemporaries. Among the writers of the Renaissance period, George Chapman, John Marston, and Ralph Crane were well represented, often by presentation copies. The Tudor and Stuart periods were more than adequately covered, with important works by Ben Jonson, John Milton, John Donne, and Inigo Jones. A notable copy of the first edition of Milton's *Comus* (1637) contained a dedication by Henry Lawes, Milton's collaborator, and corrections made in a contemporary hand—perhaps by Milton himself. The library also included a distinguished holding of Americana, with travel accounts by Captain John Smith, and a fine collection of early atlases. One of the most important segments was given over to the Larpent manuscript plays. This archive, numbering twenty-five hundred separate texts, was gathered by John Larpent while he served as Inspector of Plays from 1778 to 1824. It included scribal copies of plays submitted under the Licensing Act of 1737 and therefore represented almost all the plays performed in London during that period.[4]

Huntington knew he would never again have the opportunity to bid on this kind of library and, working with Smith, made arrangements for an outright purchase. The agreement drawn up with the auction firm of Sotheby,

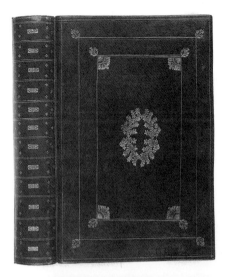

FIG. 27
When Sir Thomas Egerton (ca. 1540–1617),
later Baron Ellesmere and Viscount Brackley,
rode the law circuit in provincial England, he
took along his traveling library. The wood and
leather box contains many texts, which fold into
what resembles one large folio volume.
Egerton's Traveling Library, preserved in the
Huntington collections, is the finest example of
a few such libraries that survive from the
English Renaissance.

Wilkinson, and Hodge called for an immediate payment of $250,000 in
cash and a promissory note for $250,000, to be paid within two months of
the delivery of the first half of the library—the balance to be paid in two
more installments of $250,000 each on the delivery of the second half.[5]
Once the details of this million-dollar purchase had been settled,
Huntington, well aware of the German submarine threat, became anxious
about safe overseas transportation. In April Smith was able to assure him
that the books had left England on the *Cambria* and were well out of the

war zone.[6] Huntington and Smith kept the details of the transaction secret until 18 May, when they allowed the *New York Times* to report the delivery of 101 wooden crates of books, the largest shipment of its kind, the paper claimed, ever to cross the Atlantic. Three days later, under the banner headline "Rare Literary Gems for H. E. Huntington," the *New York Times* described the purchase in detail, concluding that the Huntington library was now "probably the finest in the world."[7]

Although Huntington had made some spectacular buys in the past, his acquisition of the Bridgewater books brought him a new level of popular attention. After almost daily exposure to headlines such as "11 Vessels Sunk by German Raider" and "France Near Exhaustion and Asks for Help," it was something of a diversion for the public to read about the sale of a million-dollar library. A month after the announcement of the Bridgewater purchase the *New York Times* ran a full-page feature story on Huntington and his library, describing him as the "prince of book collectors" and "the first bibliophile in the land." Claiming that Huntington had spent some six million dollars on books in six years and comparing his collecting prowess favorably with that of J. Pierpont Morgan, the article concluded rather fulsomely:

> Nothing on so magnificent a scale has been known before in the world's history of book collecting. Mr. Huntington has the distinction of possessing today the finest private library ever gathered together.[8]

With the Bridgewater purchase behind him Huntington was ready to participate in the sixth Huth sale, scheduled to be held in London in July 1917. Smith and Quaritch were both eager to represent Huntington's interests and in fact both carried his commissions. Quaritch had the bulk of the orders and was able to secure seventy-five lots, chiefly the writings of sixteenth-century English playwrights and essayists such as George Peele and Thomas Nash. Through Smith, Huntington bought a series of handsome navigational Portolans, illuminated manuscript charts on large sheets of vellum showing the world as it was known at the end of the sixteenth century, with detailed drawings of ports and harbors. Of the nine Portolans in the Huth library, Smith, investing $22,000, secured all but one for Huntington. Quaritch's billing was four times that amount but it was the last time he would overshadow his American rival. From then on Smith, and later Rosenbach, handled the bulk of Huntington's London commissions. Huntington had no quarrel with Quaritch's excellent service, but his friendship for Smith simply overrode all other considerations.

Although 1917 was an important year for acquisitions, with the Bridgewater and Huth purchases, it was also an extremely active one for the dispersal of Huntington's duplicates. In January Kennerley announced the sale of 308 lots of Huntington's Americana:

> This is the finest collection of Americana ever offered for sale in this country or Europe. Nearly all the books in the magnificent series of early works relating to this country are scarce and many are extremely rare.[9]

Almost ninety percent of the titles offered had come to Huntington from the Britwell Court library—and what titles they were. Wednesday evening featured a long run of the Latin and German versions of De Bry's *Voyages* while Thursday's sale included titles by such noted chroniclers as Richard Hakluyt, Bartholomé de Las Casas, Martin Frobisher, and Captain John Smith. The competition between Smith, Rosenbach, and Lathrop Harper was intense, and prices for choice items rose quickly by bids of thousands of dollars. Robert Cushman's *A Sermon Preached at Plimmoth* (1622), the earliest sermon printed in New England, brought $2,800; William Hubbard's *A Narrative of the Troubles with the Indians* . . . (1677) $2,900; and breaking all previous records, John Smith's *A True Relation* . . . (1608) went to Smith for $4,500. The sale was a resounding success for Huntington, who realized a total of $107,664, an astonishing $349 per lot. This figure was particularly impressive when compared to the $132 per lot average achieved at the Hoe sale. Smith not only controlled the bidding with total purchases of $62,148 but through a private agreement with Huntington transferred that total as a credit against the collector's future purchases.[10] What more could a book dealer ask? Smith improved his stock and assured himself sales without spending any of his own money. It was one more tie in an already strong alliance.

Encouraged by the success of the January sale Kennerley scheduled another important selection of Americana for December. On 23 May 1917 he wrote Huntington a fussy letter asking if it would be possible to prod Cole and the New York library staff into greater activity. The books for the December sale needed to be forwarded to the Anderson as soon as possible. Could Huntington order that done? Kennerley's letter concluded with a description of the Anderson's new location, a handsome four-story stone structure on the corner of Park Avenue and Fifty-ninth Street.[11] The building had formerly belonged to the Arion Club, a Germanic cultural society, which had been forced to dispose of the property when the United States entered the war. Kennerley converted the space into richly paneled galleries and sales rooms, where black-tie dinners often preceded important auctions. The new Anderson was to be a cultural mecca for the affluent. On the fourth floor Kennerley set up attractive picture galleries where he exhibited the works of Georgia O'Keeffe, John Marin, Joseph Pennell, Alfred Stieglitz, and Alexander Archipenko. Huntington's December sale was the first to be held in the new location. The sale, like most of the important auctions at the Anderson, was to be conducted by Frederick A. Chapman, the gallery's urbane chief auctioneer. Chapman, sitting on a high stool beside the podium, had a talent for entertaining the crowd with his relaxed wit, all the while extracting large sums of money from their checkbooks. With the war occupying everyone's thoughts, and with excess profit and income taxes starting to take a direct toll on the wealthy, even Chapman's graceful style sometimes fell short. It was not surprising that the 493 lots offered on the first day of the Huntington sale brought a somewhat disappointing total of only $46,212. For once Rosenbach had the distinction of stealing the headlines from Smith by paying the highest price for a single item, in this case $3,450 for a copy of Shelley's *A Refutation of Deism* (1814) in a binding stamped with the name "Mary" and with corrections that may have been in the author's hand. Smith regained his reputation the next day however by giving $4,750 for the first issue of the first edition of Dionyse Settle's *A True Report of the Laste Voyage into the West and Northwest Regions* (1577). Neither Huntington nor Kennerley was particularly pleased with the $152,238 realized for the two-day sale but buyers looking for bargains had cause to celebrate.[12]

During the war years the Huntingtons suspended their summer trips to France but continued the family routines in California and New York much as before. There were the homes to maintain, roads and gardens at San Marino to improve, books and paintings to consider, and the children and grandchildren to entertain. On the ranch there were numerous diversions—horses to ride, a bowling alley and a billiard room, croquet on the vast lawns, and often bridge in the evening. The Huntingtons seldom participated in outside social activities and were quite content with the pleasant routines that revolved around their family and a few close friends. Mr and Mrs. Huntington each had a personal secretary/companion and while in residence at San Marino kept a staff of about twenty, including gardeners, butlers, and cooks. Even when they dined alone in the evening they were attended by two butlers and two footmen. Meals were served precisely on time since Huntington believed in promptness. This was a carryover from his railroad days: if you are not on time the train goes without you. Usually the Huntingtons arrived in California in late December or early January and stayed until April or May. Mrs. Huntington preferred the East Coast, where she could be close to her son Archer and a variety of museums and galleries, while Huntington would have been content to stay year-round at his beloved ranch. Although Huntington had officially retired from business, he kept his title as president of the Los Angeles Railway Company and when he was in California worked in the downtown office on a regular basis. Huntington's son Howard had become general manager of the company in 1911 but was forced to retire in 1918 because of ill health.[13]

As for the management of the New York library, Huntington was delighted to have been able to turn that responsibility over to Cole and his staff. Cole continued to give a high priority to the production of the elaborate bibliography that was to describe in meticulous detail the twenty thousand rarities in early English literature held by the library. A bibliography of this kind went far beyond conventional cataloging practices and included detailed information on pagination, order of gatherings, binding, physical condition, and provenance. The gigantic project was well underway, as Cole reported to Huntington in January 1918, but would require two extra men to carry it out.[14] In February 1919 Cole circulated the first fascicle of his *Check-list or Brief Catalogue of the Library of Henry E. Huntington: English Literature to 1640* to various libraries and collectors around the country in order to identify additional copies and to gain further bibliographic information on the titles already included. Huntington had originally approved Cole's plan but as time went on became reluctant to commit more money to it in view of the pressing day-to-day requirements of the growing library. After the book collections and staff moved to the new library building in San Marino in the fall of 1920, work on the bibliography was essentially abandoned. According to Lodewyk Bendikson, a longtime Huntington staff member, it soon "collapsed under its own weight like a bibliographic tower of Babel." It might have been possible to complete such a bibliography, according to Bendikson, if a separate division had been organized and if Huntington had been willing to pay the enormous cost of printing and engraving.[15] Obviously, Huntington had other priorities.

For many business firms the declaration of war in 1917 raised the question of staffing. If the men volunteered or were drafted, who would do the work? Cole felt it was the responsibility of his men as professionals to stay on the job, war or no war, and was annoyed when his assistant cataloger Chester Cate volunteered for the Ambulance Corps and went to France as a supply sergeant.

A more serious annoyance, as far as the library was concerned, was the sudden disappearance in September 1917 of Cole's secretary, Herbert Holden, with a number of valuable books.[16] Huntington employed a detective agency to track Holden down, and although that effort failed, some of the books turned up in the Dodd, Mead bookstore. Robert Dodd, an old friend, was chagrined to have his firm unwittingly involved and wrote Huntington an apologetic letter. When he had tried to get an appointment, he told Huntington, and had been turned away at the door "so uniformly" he had started to think there must be something wrong and hoped it had nothing to do with the stolen copy of Copland's *Virginia's God Be Thanked*. Once the staff recognized the book as stolen property, Dodd reported, they had returned it immediately. He concluded his letter:

> I think you are too fairminded not to acquit me of anything but the most open and fair dealing in this matter.

Huntington replied,

> I regret very much that the thought has come to your mind that our relations were, in any way, strained. This, for my part, is surely not so, and I shall be glad, as I always have been to see you at any time when I am free. I sincerely hope that you will be assured that my feeling has not changed at all.[17]

Although Huntington's relations with booksellers were generally cordial there was never any doubt about who was in charge. If he thought an asking price was too high or the discount too low he was quite ready to say he was "out of the market" or that he was simply not interested. When the rare book dealer Ernest Dressel North wrote that he ran a "one price shop and . . . made it an unvarying rule not to allow a discount to anyone," Huntington answered briskly, "This is, of course, all right if that is your rule but many numbers of your catalogue which I wanted I can get at the same price or little less, with discount allowed."[18] If, however, the agent was Smith, Sessler, or in later years Rosenbach, he was more likely to accept what was offered at the quoted price.

During the early months of 1918 Smith called Huntington's attention to a number of important opportunities, among them the sale of the small but choice Ross Winans library. From it Huntington selected several manuscripts, some thirty incunabula, and an assortment of sixty other titles, many of them printed before 1640. Among the manuscripts were a 1420 Virgil, a 1400 *Piers Plowman*, and a 1320 *Jus Canonicum*. The incunabula included editions of Homer, Aristotle, Livy, Virgil, and Flavius Josephus, and represented the work of many of the most important early European presses. A number of volumes, such as Gunther Zainer's printing of the *Speculum Humanae Salvationis* (1473), were remarkable for their woodcuts. From later centuries came important editions of the work of John Dryden, Jonathan Swift, and Thomas Hood. Winans had originally asked $108,770 for the ninety-five items Huntington wanted but the wily Smith was able to get an unprecedented twenty percent discount, reducing the total to $87,016. The Winans library made an important addition to Huntington's holdings of incunabula, already well established with purchases made from Juliet Brown (1907), Church (1911), and Smith (1916).

In February Huntington received $90,000 worth of manuscripts and early printed works from Herschel V. Jones in trade for some $50,000 worth of duplicate Shakespeare quartos and folios. Jones was happy to keep the credit for future trades. It was characteristic of him to build up one collection, sell it, and start another. His constant buying and selling tempted some to say he was less a collector than an entrepreneur. In the first three decades of the twentieth century he sold more books than any of his fellow collectors. Many of his dealings with Huntington and the library staff reveal a contentious but knowledgeable bibliophile. He was ready to buy, swap, and sell only if it suited his purposes. Among the important items Huntington obtained from Jones in the 1918 trade were a thirteenth-century Latin Bible on uterine vellum with seventy-eight historiated initials, an illuminated Renaissance Book of Hours, a copy of Higden's *Polychronicon*, and thirty Bret Harte manuscripts. Similar trades with Jones continued over the next five years.

Back in the auction rooms in late February 1918 Huntington gave $9,000 for a collection of imprints of works by Cotton and Increase Mather, $19,783 for assorted Americana at the Mark Robinson sale, and $11,107 for fine bindings and extra-illustrated sets at the John D. Crimmins sale. For $6,200 he took Crimmins's prize item, a Douay Bible, originally owned by John Augustin Daly and expanded by Daly with eight thousand original prints, sketches, letters, and drawings into a sumptuous forty-two-volume set. In May, at the second Robinson sale, still eager to buy Americana, Huntington spent $29,700 for Lincoln letters and a collection of books on the American theater. In one more effort to clear duplicates from his shelves Huntington exchanged twenty Shakespeare quartos and five Caxtons originally secured in the Kemble-Devonshire purchase with the New York collector Charles Baker. In return he obtained a collection of Civil War letters, along with a selection of American and British literary and historical manuscripts valued at $80,000. The arrangement left him with an $8,000 obligation, one he would settle easily with future trades.

The general preoccupation with the war in Europe that had depressed sales in 1917 still prevailed when Huntington's next group of duplicates came up for auction in February 1918. The $88,028 realized for the 1,035 lots of English literature was hardly encouraging. Over two hundred items came from the Bridgewater library while other volumes bore the distinguished ownership marks of E. D. Church, Beverly Chew, H. W. Poor, F. R. Halsey, and Robert Hoe. Again, Smith was the heaviest buyer, picking up important editions of Thomas Heywood, Ben Jonson, Charles Lamb, John Marston, and James Shirley. For $9,200 he obtained the showpiece of the sale, the annotated copy of Milton's *Comus*. Jones, delighted with the pur-

peachments of Officers of the United States; to all cases of Admiralty and Maritime Jurisdiction; to Controversies between two or more States ~~(except such as shall regard Territory or Jurisdiction)~~ between a State and citizens of another State, between citizens of different States, and between a State or the citizens thereof and foreign States, citizens or subjects. In cases of Impeachment, cases affecting Ambassadors, other Public Ministers and Consuls, and those in which a State shall be party, ~~this jurisdiction shall be~~ original; In all the other cases beforementioned it shall be appellate, with such exceptions and under such regulations as the Legislature shall make. ~~The Legislature may assign any part of the jurisdiction abovementioned (except the trial of the President of the United States) in the manner and under the limitations which it shall think proper, to such Inferior Courts as it shall constitute from time to time.~~

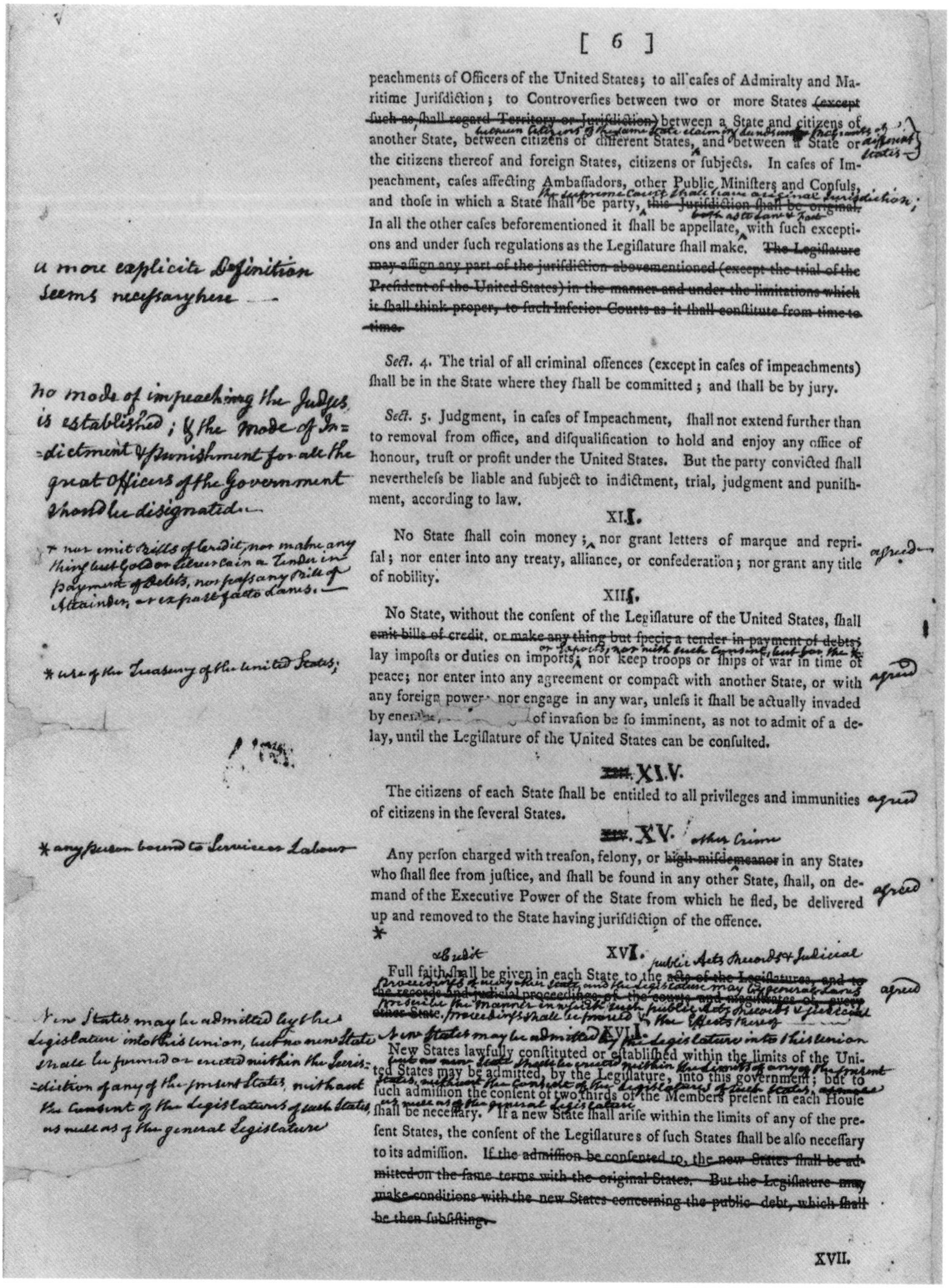

Sect. 4. The trial of all criminal offences (except in cases of impeachments) shall be in the State where they shall be committed; and shall be by jury.

Sect. 5. Judgment, in cases of Impeachment, shall not extend further than to removal from office, and disqualification to hold and enjoy any office of honour, trust or profit under the United States. But the party convicted shall nevertheless be liable and subject to indictment, trial, judgment and punishment, according to law.

XI.

No State shall coin money; nor grant letters of marque and reprisal; nor enter into any treaty, alliance, or confederation; nor grant any title of nobility.

XII.

No State, without the consent of the Legislature of the United States, shall ~~emit bills of credit, or make any thing but specie a tender in payment of debts;~~ lay imposts or duties on imports, nor keep troops or ships of war in time of peace; nor enter into any agreement or compact with another State, or with any foreign power, nor engage in any war, unless it shall be actually invaded by enemies, or of invasion be so imminent, as not to admit of a delay, until the Legislature of the United States can be consulted.

~~XIII.~~ XIV.

The citizens of each State shall be entitled to all privileges and immunities of citizens in the several States.

~~XIV.~~ XV.

Any person charged with treason, felony, or ~~high misdemeanor~~ in any State, who shall flee from justice, and shall be found in any other State, shall, on demand of the Executive Power of the State from which he fled, be delivered up and removed to the State having jurisdiction of the offence.

XVI.

Full faith shall be given in each State to the ~~acts of the Legislatures, and to the records and judicial proceedings~~ of ~~the courts and magistrates of every other State.~~

New States lawfully constituted or established within the limits of the United States may be admitted, by the Legislature, into this government; but to such admission the consent of two thirds of the Members present in each House shall be necessary. If a new State shall arise within the limits of any of the present States, the consent of the Legislatures of such States shall be also necessary to its admission. ~~If the admission be consented to, the new States shall be admitted on the same terms with the original States. But the Legislature may make conditions with the new States concerning the public debt, which shall be then subsisting.~~

XVII.

Handwritten marginal annotations:

a more explicit Definition seems necessary here —

no mode of impeaching the Judges is established; & the mode of Indictment & punishment for all the great Officers of the Government should be designated —

+ nor emit Bills of Credit, nor make any thing but Gold or Silver Coin a Tender in payment of Debts, nor pass any Bill of Attainder, or ex post facto Laws. —

* use of the Treasury of the United States;

* any person bound to Service or Labour

New States may be admitted by the Legislature into this union, but no new State shall be formed or erected within the Jurisdiction of any of the present States, without the Consent of the Legislature of such State as well as of the general Legislature

agreed

agreed

agreed

agreed

agreed

chase, gave Smith a check for the auction price plus a ten percent commission. Dealers and collectors found it curious that Huntington and Cole would release this unique treasure for public sale while keeping a run-of-the-mill copy from the Church library. The matter was never explained.

When the next group of Huntington duplicates came up for sale in April, the tide of the war had started to turn in favor of the Allies and prices reflected a new optimism. George Sargent, in his review of the sale in the *Boston Evening Transcript*, noted the upturn and commented, "In spite of the demands made upon the wealthy by war, income taxes, excess profit taxes, Liberty bonds, Red Cross subscriptions and other expensive things growing out of the present war, the American people still have money left to buy rare books."[19] Sargent was no doubt influenced in this judgment by the prices Smith gave for a fine run of Shakespeare quartos—obtained by Huntington from the Bridgewater, Church, and Devonshire libraries—starting with $1,500 for a third edition of *Hamlet* (1611) and increasing to $10,000 for a perfect copy of the first edition of *Much Ado About Nothing* (1600). Huntington and Kennerley were pleased with the average price of $157 per lot. At this point the duplicate sales had raised some $405,000. Seven more sales would follow but the returns for these would only add another $150,000 to the total. Aside from western Americana included in 1923,

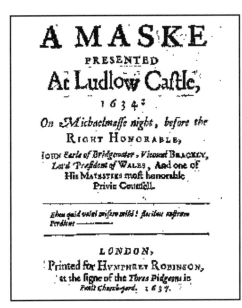

Fig. 29
The Church library copy of Milton's great masque, *Comus*. The Bridgewater copy, more valuable because of its annotations, was acquired from Huntington by Herschel V. Jones; it is now in the Carl H. Pforzheimer Library at the University of Texas.

most of the books in the later auctions were leftovers. Overall, the transactions had been a success and had worked to the advantage not only of Huntington but also of Kennerley, the Anderson Galleries, and American book collectors. After paying the Anderson's ten percent commission Huntington realized some $540,000 from the public sales. To this total he added approximately $200,000 more from private dispersal of duplicates to Smith, Rosenbach, Charles Baker, and Herschel V. Jones. As far as Huntington was concerned, the proceeds came almost as a bonus. In a hurry to build the library, he had not taken the time to indulge in comparative buying but had proceeded instead to buy entire libraries. This inevitably resulted in the acquisition of many duplicates—a situation that called for the refining process of the auction rooms.

Although the high prices realized at the April 1918 sale were encouraging, the real turning point for the auction market occurred in May, with the disposal of the Winston H. Hagen library. Hagen, a New York lawyer and a devoted bibliophile, had put together a collection of the major works in English literature modeled on the concept of the cabinet library—a small collection of highly significant titles—developed to a high degree of sophistication at the turn of the century by Frederick Locker-Lampson. Hagen had, in fact, bought many of his prize items in 1905 from the Locker-Lampson sale. In the foreword to the Hagen sale catalog, Beverly Chew commented that "a better planned collection within its well defined limits has never been dispersed by auction."[20] Apparently bidders agreed with Chew, since for selected titles they sent sale prices skyrocketing two and three times above previous records. Shakespeare's *Poems* (1640), which had gone for $2,700 in the Hoe sale of 1911, brought $5,010 to the Hagen estate. Huntington was able to buy some choice John Donne and John Dryden titles but his major purchase, identified by Chew as the "scarcest item in the sale," was a small octavo bound in purple levant morocco (ca. 1528) containing four poems by John Skelton. For this edition, unknown in either the Hoe or Huth libraries, bearing the distinguished Locker-Lampson bookplate, Huntington gave $9,700, a record figure for a single sixteenth-century literary work.

After the New York auction rooms closed in May, American buyers moved their base of operations to London, where the Huth sale was ready to resume. Smith was on hand and again he held Huntington's commissions.

Fig. 30
J. Goldsborough Bruff drawing, *View from Summit of Independence Rock,*
acquired in 1918. Bruff led a wagon train across the plains to the gold
fields in 1849.

According to the *Times,* the most important item in the sale, and one that
Huntington wanted badly, was the copy of Caxton's *Royal Book* (1487).
Smith got it for £1,800, along with one of two known copies of Nicholas
Bayard's pamphlet *Journal of the Late Actions of the French at Canada* (1693),
and a number of early editions of the poetry of Sir Philip Sidney and John
Skelton. Smith reported his successes to Huntington in a letter of 14 Sep-
tember and got back an immediate confirming order. When Huntington
next wrote he turned away from business for a moment to congratulate
Smith on a personal matter:

> I am very glad to see that you are going to sell your valuable
> string of horses, and I think that by so doing you will be able to
> keep in the book business. If you should have succeeded in the
> horse business, you would have been a wonder, for I think that
> there is hardly one in a hundred keeping at it who do not go

"dead broke" before they turn up their toes. I have lived in Kentucky too long not to have seen the fatal results.[21]

Five days later it was back to business as usual. In a crisp letter to his New York financial manager Huntington wrote:

> Dear Graham:
>
> I know that you have given Smith $20,000. Of course I should have been glad to let him have this amount if we owed it to him but we do not. And I should also have been glad to help him if we ourselves had not so many obligations.[22]

One of the obligations to which Huntington referred was $600,000 paid the month before to William K. Bixby for his prize manuscript collection. Bixby had made his fortune by starting at the bottom and climbing up through the ranks to achieve the office of president of the American Car and Foundry Company. Through a series of purchases going back to the Locker-Lampson sale of 1905 he developed a superb collection of books and literary and historical manuscripts. Bixby not only acquired these treasures but also made an effort to make manuscripts in his collection available to a wider audience, with a series of facsimiles published by the Bibliophile Society of Boston. Among these keepsakes were handsomely printed copies of Major John André's *Journal,* Shelley's *Notebooks,* and the Charles Dickens-Maria Beadness *Private Correspondence.* By 1915 Bixby found that competing for English literature in a market controlled by wealthy bidders such as Folger and Huntington was a waste of time and decided to switch to Americana, where he hoped he could achieve greater success. As a matter of practical concern he knew it would be impossible to start a new collection unless he could arrange to sell part of his existing library. The manuscript collection was sure to be marketable and Huntington seemed a likely buyer. By the time Bixby decided to sell, the two men had become social friends, first through the meetings of the Grolier Club and later at the lavish Hobby Club dinners. When Bixby spent the winter at the Hotel Raymond in Pasadena he made a point of visiting Huntington at the ranch. In 1916 and 1917 they had joined forces to sell off duplicates at the Anderson Galleries.

With Smith acting as the intermediary, Bixby agreed to sell Huntington the manuscripts for the not inconsiderable sum of $601,575. It was another coup. In one stroke he became the owner of Shelley's *Queen Mab* inscribed to Mary Godwin, the manuscript text and sixteen original drawings for John Ruskin's *The Seven Lamps of Architecture*, Hawthorne's love letters to his fiancée Sophia Peabody, the manuscripts of the journals of both John André and Aaron Burr, Jefferson's account book, and a selection of letters from George Washington, John Wesley, John Paul Jones, Benjamin Franklin, U. S. Grant, Samuel Taylor Coleridge, Charles Lamb, and Samuel Langhorne Clemens. It was the kind of purchase that appealed to Huntington's love of the unique and the personal: here were the great figures of literature and history revealed not in formal published texts but in their more intimate moments. Others may have owned first editions of *Queen Mab,* but only Huntington had the copy inscribed by the author, "You see, Mary, I have not forgotten you." For treasures like that, $601,575 seemed reasonable indeed.

As the library grew in size and importance the question of its future became even more pressing. Early in September several eastern newspapers reported that Huntington planned to turn his library over to the Board of Supervisors of the county of Los Angeles. Huntington responded by making his own announcement. As soon as the war was over, he said, he would bring all the books from New York to California and house them in a modern library building on his San Marino estate. With typical directness and brevity Huntington concluded, "I am going to give my library to the public, but not until after I am dead."[23] It was not a decision he had arrived at easily. Some had urged him to keep the library entirely under family control as a private institution while others, including George Watson Cole and Archer Huntington, believed that the move to California would be a serious mistake.[24] As far as Huntington was concerned, there was to be no debate about location. The library would be housed in San Marino, testimony to his long-held belief in the abundant promise of Southern California. From the turn of the century, when he had formed the Pacific Electric interurban rail system, the Huntington Land and Improvement Company, and the Pacific Light and Power Company, Huntington had been a California booster. It seemed clear to him that Los Angeles was not only the fastest-growing urban area in the

Fig. 31
A Samuel Clemens letter of 17 June 1868 to his mother, Mary Mason Fairbanks (first and last leaves). Signed "Your Returning Prodigal," it expresses the wish that he will see her soon. The letter was acquired in 1918 in the Bixby sale.

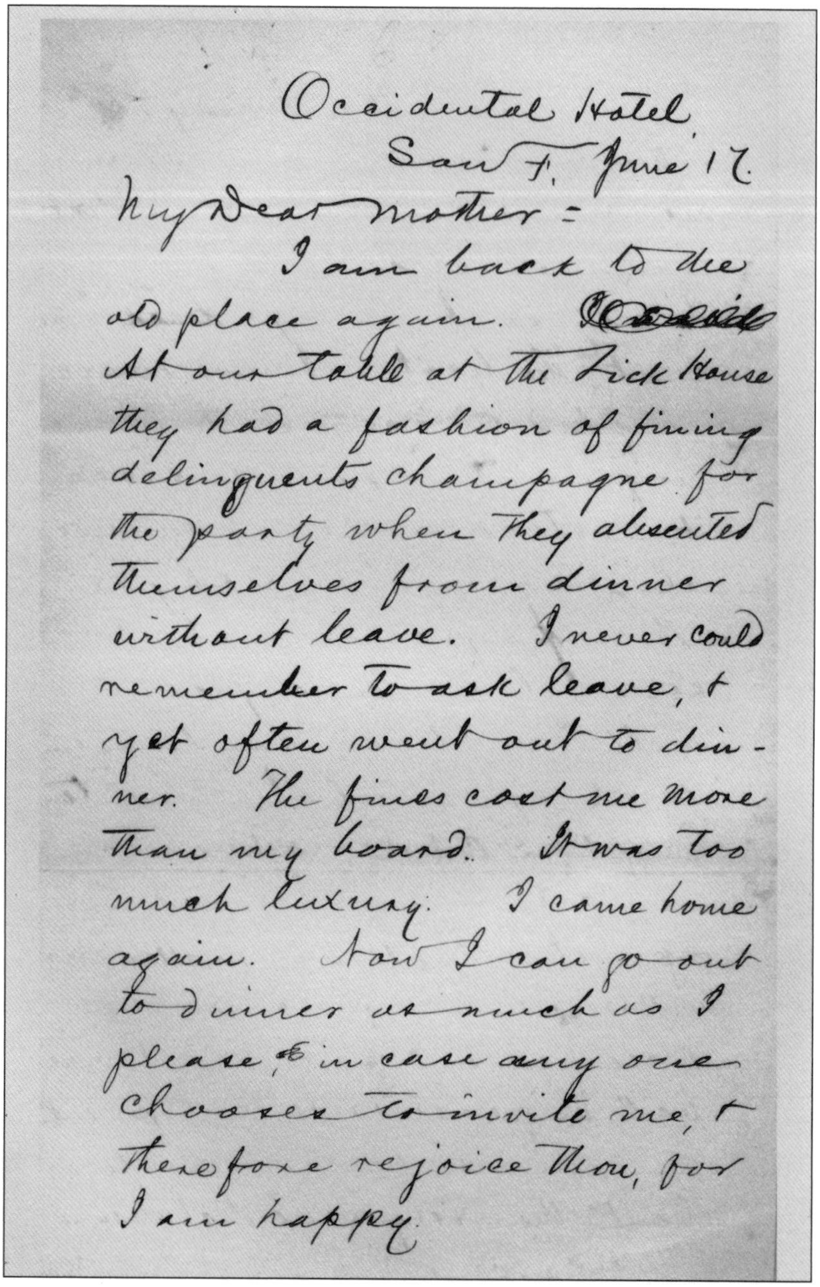
Occidental Hotel
San F. June 17.
My Dear Mother =
I am back to the old place again. At our table at the Lick House they had a fashion of fining delinquents champagne for the party when they absented themselves from dinner without leave. I never could remember to ask leave, & yet often went out to dinner. The fines cost me more than my board. It was too much luxury. I came home again. Now I can go out to dinner as much as I please, & in case any one chooses to invite me, & therefore rejoice thou, for I am happy.

country but the land of opportunity as well. In 1914, discussing the California potential with a reporter from the *Los Angeles Times*, Huntington stated, "If I were given twenty years in New York and ten years here I should choose Southern California."[25]

10

ther cub? How is the dog? If he neglects to wipe his feet on the mat before he comes in, & is in all places & at all times blundering & heedless, he will do no discredit to his name. But don't chain him. It makes me restive to think of it.

"When will I come?" Just as soon as engagements in New York & Hartford will permit. — Write me, care of Dan Slote, 121 William street, & say when any of the other pilgrims will be likely to be there. As I am "touching them on the raw" occasionally in the book — albeit very gently — I would like to shake hands with them — Church especially, who is a bully pilgrim. [There it goes again.]

My kindest regards & fervent good wishes unto yourself & all your your household.

And now I will tackle the Sphynx again.

Your Returning Prodigal
Saml. Clemens.

Although Huntington resolved the question of location quite easily, the matter of administrative control still presented a number of thorny alternatives. If he were to turn the library over to the state university, as Clements planned to do in Michigan, some independence of operation would be lost.

If he gave it to the county of Los Angeles, shifts in political power might jeopardize the collection's usefulness. That must be avoided at all costs. Over time, influenced by George Ellery Hale and others, Huntington came to believe that scholars, whom he expected to be the chief users of the collections, would best be served by an independent public institution. The specific details could be worked out later.

For most Americans the signing of the armistice on 11 November 1918 promised prosperity and a return to the good life. Those in the book business shared that dream. They looked forward to active trading, rising prices, and large profits. Book collectors, with memories of the Hoe and Huth sales still fresh in their minds, anticipated even greater buying opportunities. For Huntington, the postwar years were to be the most important in his collecting career.

FIG. 32
Plate CCI, the
Canada Goose,
from John James
Audubon, *The
Birds of America*
(1827–38). The
four-volume
double-elephant
folio was acquired
in the Bixby sale
in 1917.

Chapter 7

So Little Time
1919

During the early weeks of 1919 the New York
newspapers reviewed world and local events with
unrestrained optimism. The men who had served
on the battle lines were starting to come home,
President Wilson was in Europe trying to achieve
his vision of a peace with honor, Harry Lauder, the "Wee Scot," was entertaining enthusiastic crowds at the Lexington Theater with his rendition of a
song that began "Don't let us sing any more of war, just let us sing of love,"
and the society crowd was celebrating the New Year with gala costume balls.

The most important event scheduled to take place in the auction world
during that postwar winter was the sale of Herschel V. Jones's books. Jones,
the owner of the *Minneapolis Journal*, had already gathered and disposed of
two large collections, one of American literary first editions, the other covering the Dickens-Thackeray period. Now that he had amassed some two
thousand more titles he decided to sell again.[1] Jones, the quintessential
entrepreneur, offered his books at the Anderson Galleries in a series of sales
beginning in December 1918 and continuing to March 1919. Smith wrote
to Huntington in November with details of the sale and, as usual, suggested a number of purchases, among them a fifteenth-century manuscript on

vellum of Brut's *Chronicles of England,* an elaborately illustrated Malermi Bible (1494), a series of early Brathwaites, a set of Bulwer, and some Defoes. "You will see," Smith pointed out, "that there are many important items in the Jones catalogue that you need, particularly among the early printed books and a few of the more important Bibles."[2] After checking with Leslie Bliss, one of his trusted bibliographers, Huntington sent bids for almost all the recommended titles. Smith himself was the largest investor, spending $264,418 of the $391,854 realized in the three sales. The annotated Bridgewater *Comus* came back to Smith from Jones, but for $14,250—almost $5,000 more than the price of a year before.

Perhaps the most talked-about item in the sale was the imperfect 1609 quarto edition of Shakespeare's *Sonnets.* Jones had purchased this copy directly from Huntington for $20,000. When the staff at the Anderson Galleries examined the book before the auction they found it included two facsimile leaves inserted in place of the originals. In February Jones wrote to Huntington asking for restitution:

> Chew says the title page and dedication to the Sonnets are not genuine. This, of course, is a shock and a disappointment to me. I believed them genuine and I know you did also. I suggest it is only right for me to return the book to you and take others in its place.[3]

Once the matter was adjusted to Jones's satisfaction, the Anderson Galleries offered the *Sonnets* for sale, since even with facsimiles it was clearly a significant edition. Henry Folger, the relentless Shakespeare collector, took the flawed volume for $10,500. As the Jones sale moved into March Huntington continued to buy, but limited himself to run-of-the-mill literary items such as Robert Louis Stevenson's *In the South Seas* (1900) for $4 and John Millington Synge's *Well of the Saints* (1905) for $8. The total for his purchases at the third session, including Smith's usual ten percent commission, came to a modest $4,040.

The Huntington library staff found it was much easier to deal with Jones through the neutralizing screen of the auction house than to confront him directly. In his transactions with Huntington's staff, Jones could be capricious, acrimonious, or just plain misinformed. In January 1919, in response to a letter from Lodewyk Bendikson, Jones wrote that he wanted to buy a copy of Hugh Crompton's *Poems* (1657), offered at $1,400, adding, "I shall appreciate these little remembrances from time to time on good things, and will pay as much as you get from book sellers." By May his mood had changed: he claimed the library had overcharged him for the Crompton and that the book was not even worth $500. Bendikson replied that since there were only three known copies, one in the British Museum, one in the Huntington, and the one Jones now owned, the price was indeed valid. Jones was not appeased. That same spring, unhappy with another purchase, Jones asked to return Francis Quarles's *Shepheards Oracles* (1646) since it was, he said, a third issue, and "I buy nothing but firsts." When Bendikson replied that there was no third issue the Minneapolis collector shot back, "Your letter does not in the least change my opinion of the Quarles." In a final salvo Jones informed Bendikson, "I do not want to collect books, but want to buy a book occasionally."4 Jones went on buying books, more than occasionally, but after 1919, having worn out his welcome, did little or no business with Huntington or his staff.

While the Jones sales were still in progress Huntington forged ahead with a number of bids at the Frederick Halsey-Henry S. Van Duzer auction. Most of the lots, first editions of works by well-known American and English literary figures, came from Van Duzer's large, eclectic library. Huntington was able to secure, almost in bulk, 151 copies of works by W. H. Ainsworth, 124 of Bret Harte, and 190 of Samuel L. Clemens. He bought a copy of the second edition of John Eliot's Indian Bible (1685) and Francis Segur's "Liber Amicorum" (1599–1611), containing autographs of Sir Walter Raleigh, Inigo Jones, and Ben Jonson. In three days Huntington spent $27,542, deepening several veins in the library's literary mine.

Later in March, trying to keep abreast of the auction market, Huntington bought the entire four-hundred-item G. W. Michelmore railroading library just days before the Anderson Galleries planned to place it up for public sale. Because of its connection with Huntington's own career this was, of course, a collection he had to have. Working both sides of the Atlantic, Huntington then gave Smith commissions for a number of sixteenth-century English plays that were to be sold at the March auction of Lord Mostyn's library. The London *Times* described the collection as of "the highest literary interest," comprising works that "appear to be entirely unknown to students."[5] Huntington's bids, sent by wire from New York, overpowered the competition. For six thousand pounds he secured two of the prize items in the sale, Henry Medwall's *Goodely Interlude of Fulgens* (c. 1512), one of the earliest English comedies, of which the only other known copy existed as a fragment of two leaves in the British Museum; and an equally rare copy of W. Wager's *Inough Is as Good as a Feast* (1570?).[6] In both cases Dring of the Quaritch firm was the underbidder. Huntington's total bill at the Mostyn sale ran to a substantial £10,012.

The problem of managing the library efficiently with part of the collection in New York and part in California became more serious as time went by. In April 1919 Huntington wrote to both Smith and Bliss trying to locate a copy of the Emancipation Proclamation signed by Lincoln. A dealer had given Huntington the document to examine on approval and now it was lost. Bliss reported he had been through everything in the New York library including the safe, the "wooden cupboards under the window and even the tin boxes," but could find no trace of the missing Proclamation. He remembered an earlier bit of confusion with this same item when, the year before, Smith sold them a duplicate and then took it back when the original appeared.[7] Now the original was missing again. Such disorder could not continue. Huntington urged his architect Myron Hunt to speed up the plans for the new San Marino library building. Hunt, a gregarious workaholic, with considerable experience in producing buildings quickly for aristocratic customers, said he would try to break ground by the middle of the summer.

Huntington, who had turned sixty-nine in February, felt the tide running against him. In his remaining years, how could he achieve the greatest benefits for the library, for the art collections, for the estate in general? Dealers like Smith and Rosenbach were hard at work seeing to it that opportunities to buy books and manuscripts were never lacking, and Duveen was equally energetic in supplying important paintings. It was not uncommon for Smith, Rosenbach, and Duveen to find themselves all vying for Huntington's attention at once. Balance and careful judgment in responding to these competing demands became increasingly important. In early July, a week before the eighth Huth sale, Huntington sent an unusually cautionary night letter to Smith:

Do not buy manuscripts or pay fancy prices for books that we can pick up later. There is so little time. I shall have to rely on you. My telegraph address Pasadena. Mail me numbers of books [and] prices you buy.

Smith understood the message, both written and implied. He was to buy with care but he *was* to buy—and time, for both collector and agent, would from now on be of increasing concern. Smith's report on his activities at the Huth sale was a model of circumspection. He wrote:

In general I bid low on the items with the exception of a few of the important ones which we really want. My bids were very low on the Early Printed Books. I hope we secure the Vespucius items but I think my bids were high enough don't you? No. 7396 Tewrdannck's Chronicle printed on vellum I bid three hundred pounds on and hope we will get it. This book is really worth six or seven hundred pounds. I trust my limits will meet with your approval.

In August, after Smith furnished Huntington with a final report on the Huth sale, he returned to the theme of careful buying:

The Taylors I think sold very high with few exceptions, and a few of the earlier printed books and manuscripts we did not get, but I only bid low prices on these, as per your instructions.[8]

Despite Huntington's reputation (and Smith's) for high bidding, Huntington's buying style at this point was in fact based on a somewhat more conservative approach. It also included consideration of the best way to pay the bills. In September he wrote to Graham, his New York accountant,

I have purchased from G. D. Smith books from the Huth sale amounting to £4610. The commission of £461 brings the amount to £5071. When you think the exchange is as low as it is apt to be send him a check—or you may rather pay him in pounds.[9]

Over and above his concern for thrifty buying Huntington continued to worry about the disposition of his collections and the fate of his San Marino ranch, and during the next few years he considered a number of plans for the library's future. He first thought about the family, but none of the children seemed to share his enthusiasm for books. In September 1918 he had announced his desire to give the library and the art objects to the public but refrained from disclosing specific details. The plan that Huntington ultimately adopted combined his own views with suggestions made over a period of time by George Ellery Hale, the astronomer and director of the Mt. Wilson Observatory. When Hale first met Huntington in 1907 he had urged the collector to establish the rare book library in California. Now Huntington asked Hale what he thought about turning the collection over to the Board of Supervisors of Los Angeles County. Although this may not have been an entirely serious proposition, Hale was shocked. In April 1914 he wrote a long letter to Huntington suggesting that a board of trustees, selected on the basis of their "knowledge, taste and experience," would be far preferable to the Board of Supervisors who, he claimed, would be likely to be driven by political rather than humanitarian motives. Hale pictured the library as a "center of the humanities where scholars from home and abroad could come for study and research." Warming to the subject, he wrote a follow-up letter three weeks later full of such eloquent terms as "marble palace" and "Grecian splendor." Unmoved by this overblown rhetoric Huntington responded only, "I am not ready to reply, but it is quite possible that you have planted a seed."[10]

Hale seized upon that statement as an opening for further negotiations. Two years later he buttressed his earlier arguments with what he called a "concrete plan." He outlined an elaborate organization that would include various research departments in the arts and sciences, fellowships for nonresident scholars, and a governing board of trustees. All of this brought a casual answer from Huntington.

> The mode of organization is in line with my ideas. It will probably
> be some time (at least until times are better) before I take up this
> matter actively, as you of course can understand.[11]

Hale was willing to wait since he felt that eventually Huntington would come around to his point of view. It was Hale's main idea, often repeated, that an independent board of trustees, similar to the one that governed the Carnegie Institution in Washington, would supply the ideal organizational framework. Such a board, Hale argued, would not only be free of political taint but would give the donor a considerable amount of freedom of action during his lifetime. Some of Hale's other suggestions—creating a Parthenon-like cultural center in San Marino surrounded by teaching and research departments in such diverse disciplines as Egyptology and Greco-Roman mythology—Huntington wisely rejected. An administrative board of trustees, however, seemed a workable suggestion. In August 1919 Huntington had his lawyer William E. Dunn draw up a trust indenture placing the institution under the control of a five-man board of trustees. The stated object would be, "To promote and advance learning, the arts and sciences and to promote the public welfare by founding endowing and having maintained a library art gallery, museum and park. The institution itself would be a "free public library, art gallery, museum and park, containing objects of artistic, historic or literary interest."The original trustees, to whom Huntington turned over full authority to manage the institution, were Dunn, Hale, Huntington's son Howard, his closest friend George S. Patton, and Arabella's son Archer M. Huntington. The 1919 trust indenture transferred property and specified the duties of the trustees, chiefly to manage and control the institution.[12] In effect, it provided a firm legal basis for the development of the Henry E. Huntington Library and Art Gallery during the remainder of the founder's lifetime and provision for the continued support of that institution after his death.

As time went on other collectors saw that Huntington's approach was a wise one. After reading the indenture, Henry Folger wrote, "Thank you for the copy of your Deed of Trust for the Huntington Library and Art Gallery and thank you still more for the courage and judgement you have shown in establishing this very significant benefaction. It is at once an inspiration and a guide for others who may wish to do something of the same sort, but much more modestly."[13] Once the document was signed Huntington felt relieved, free to devote himself wholeheartedly to building the book and art collections. True to his word, and as if orchestrating his plans to match Huntington's, Myron Hunt ordered ground broken for the new library building in mid-August.

Huntington saw his affairs progressing just as he wished. Back in Philadelphia, Rosenbach, perhaps sensing the West Coast euphoria, decided to test the waters with a few costly Shakespeare quartos. Earlier that year he had made one of his most successful purchases, beating out George D. Smith for Marsden Perry's Shakespeare library. Perry, a railroad developer from Providence, Rhode Island, had started collecting in the 1890s and by 1905 had amassed an extraordinary holding of folios and quartos. As a result of the panic of 1907 he had been forced to sell part of his library to Folger and in 1914, when he failed to outbid Huntington for the Devonshire quartos, decided to get out of the market entirely. Rosenbach, ever watchful, realized that the Perry books represented the opportunity of a lifetime. The sale of this magnificent collection would not only make a sizable profit for the firm but would show the book world that he, Dr. R, was a dealer of consequence. The Perry books, he told his banker friend William Elkins, would sell themselves. And so they did. Several of the finest items went rapidly to Folger, Morgan, and Widener. Then it was time to talk with Huntington. Rosenbach baited the trap with a disingenuous wire: "WOULD LIKE TO GIVE YOU FIRST OFFER OF SHAKESPEARE QUARTOS NOT IN YOUR COLLECTION."[14] Leaving nothing to chance he followed up with a personal visit to the ranch. The books, such as Lodge's *Rosalynde* (1596), *Arden of Feversham* (1592), *King John*, parts 1 and 2 (1591), *The Rape of Lucrece* (1632), and *Hamlet* (1676), were, on the face of it, splendid copies, but once presented with Rosenbach's spellbinding eloquence they became irresistible. At the "special price" of $121,000, Huntington took the lot, paying $21,000 in cash and deferring the remaining $100,000 for eight months with a promissory note.[15] Late in August he wrote cheerfully to Cole,

"I have purchased the following:

Lodge Rosalynde	1596
Arden of Favesham	1592
King John 1st Part	1591
King John 2nd Part	1591
Mucedorus	1615
Mucedorus	1626
Gosson School of Abuse	1579
Rape of Lucrece	1632
Hamlet	1674
Julius Caesar	1684
Legge Mss of Richard III	1579

These books I will bring home with me when I return. It is necessary that nothing should be said of this transaction for some time. It makes quite a reduction in the number of plays I have to secure to be even with the British Museum."

Then, almost as an afterthought, he added:

I should like to have you send me a list of all the Shakespeare plays lacking. Place the list on my desk and send me the duplicate.

Cole's reply, attached to the requested list, mirrored Huntington's competitive glee:

I am delighted to know that you have secured so many more Shakespeare quartos. The British Museum at this rate is bound to take second place in its Shakespeare collection.[16]

The officers of the British Museum may not have known they were in a race, but Huntington and Cole took it seriously. In December Huntington wrote to Smith listing twenty-six quarto editions lacking in his collection and closed with the charming request, "If you should by any chance run across any I need, bear me in mind."[17] It was the kind of invitation that booksellers dream of. Smith had already been active that fall and had secured a number of important titles for Huntington through purchases at the November Britwell Court sale. Earlier, Dring had written to Huntington soliciting his commissions but at the same time warning him that high prices would prevail. In a curious letter, Dring expressed his surmise that Huntington had already turned the books down on the basis of their elevated prices. Cole delivered Huntington's somewhat petulant answer:

I have called Mr. Huntington's attention to what you say regarding this sale, and he says that in view of the high prices expected he has been scared out and that he does not wish to bid on books where there will be high bidding. We shall watch the results of this Sale with great interest, especially to see whether the high prices anticipated from it have been realized.

With these details out of the way, Cole offered Huntington's views on current English selling practices:

> There is certainly a limit beyond which American Collectors will not go notwithstanding the prevailing idea on your side that they stand ready to pay any price for a book of which there are only one or two copies.
>
> As such are Mr. Huntington's views concerning this Sale you can readily see why we are sending you no bids to be executed.[18]

Apparently Huntington had lost some of his confidence in the Quaritch firm. Shortly after rejecting Dring's offer he supplied Smith with a long list of commissions. Although the Britwell sale catalog was only forty pages long there were important items to consider. The cover quite accurately described the books to be sold as "exceedingly choice, rare, and valuable."[19] Among the rarities were the four Shakespeare folios, the only known copy of the fourth edition of *Venus and Adonis* (1599), imprints by Caxton and Wynkyn de Worde, the Richard Heber collection of eighty-eight Elizabethan ballads and broadsides, the first edition of Gray's *Elegy* (1751), a series of sixteenth-century plays by Robert Greene, and the 1786 Kilmarnock Burns.

The physical arrangements for the sale conformed to the usual Sotheby pattern: potential buyers sat around a large horseshoe-shaped table and the auctioneer and his clerk stood at a rostrum at the open end of the horseshoe. A porter handed the books to anyone who asked for a close examination. Millicent Sowerby, a Sotheby cataloger, wrote that on the day of the Britwell sale "every seat at the table was occupied and it would have been impossible to force a pin between the standees, so closely were they packed." The auctioneer, Sir Montague Barlow, faced with Smith on one end of the table and Dring on the other, was so tense that his face, white with excitement, "matched the white carnation in his button-hole." Smith swept the day buying eighty of the hundred and eight lots for an investment of £84,705.

After disposing of a number of books of Elizabethan verse by Nicholas Breton—all sold to Smith—Barlow turned to lot 16, "Broadsides and Ballads. The Heber Collection." The ballads, described as "among the most curious and interesting portion of early literature," had been purchased in 1830 by George Daniel from a postmaster of Ipswich and then finally sold to

S. R. Christie-Miller at the Heber sale, to become part of the Britwell library. It was a collection that Huntington was determined to own. Smith fought off a number of challenges from Dring and finally bought the lot for £6,400. Next came the four folios; those also went to Smith. Barlow then introduced the item everyone had been waiting for, lot 85, the unique copy of Shakespeare's first printed work, *Venus and Adonis* (1599), bound with *The Passionate Pilgrim* (1599) and *Epigrammes and Elegies* by Sir John Davies (1599?). The little volume, measuring 4 and $^{11}/16$ by 3 inches and covered with contemporary vellum, had been discovered in the lumber room of a Northhampton estate by a representative of the bookselling firm of Henry Sotheran in 1867 and subsequently sold to Christie-Miller. Sowerby was present at the sale and described the contest for lot 85 in vivid detail:

> When the Venus and Adonis volume was put up, there were at the beginning a few odd bidders, but these soon dropped out, leaving the field to Quaritch [represented by Dring] and G. D. Smith who fought their duel during the most intense excitement it is possible to imagine. The tense silence was broken only by the voice of Sir Montague Barlow, who declared each bid after each signal. G. D. Smith's signal was a flick of the thumb. Quaritch marked his bids by a nod. At length, bid by bid, £100 by £100 the bidding rose to the sum of £14,000, then a flick and it was £14,100, a nod and it was £14,200, a flick and £14,300. The excitement was almost unbearable, but still the bidding went on. No one took his eyes off the two bidders, all heads merely turning from one to the other as they flicked and nodded. At last there was a flick from G. D. Smith and Sir Montague announced £14,900. Quaritch quietly nodded: £15,000. Back to G. D. Smith who flicked: £15,100. At this, with the whole room staring at him, Quaritch (Mr. Dring) never moved a muscle. He had reached his limit. Sir Montague gave the necessary invitation for another bid before closing the sale. Silence prevailed and the hammer came down at last at £15,100, upon which the whole room released its excitement by giving a loud cheer.[20]

It was the largest amount to be given up to that time for a printed book. Smith claimed he was pleased to have gotten the "Venus" at what he considered a reasonable price and said, with his usual bravado, he would have gone higher.[21] Other opinions were mixed. An editorial writer in the *New York Times* not only declared $75,000 a ridiculous price to pay for a book but found fault with the collector.

> He claims, and too often the claim is admitted, to be a lover of books and to have a relation to literature. In reality it is not books that interest him, but irrelevant things like date and bindings and associations. In other words he is a curio hunter and what he calls his "library" is a museum where the reading man finds next to nothing that he wants—nothing he must have.[22]

Critical opinion in the British Isles was based on different grounds. There, American book buyers like Huntington and Morgan with their seemingly bottomless checkbooks were often looked upon as dangerous raiders hauling precious books and manuscripts across the ocean by the boatload. Alfred W. Pollard, speaking for the British Museum, noted that the exodus of English books had been going on for at least forty years and that in his opinion it was "a little late in the day to ask what should be done." It would be a mistake, he wrote, to try and place any international controls on book buying as some had suggested. It would be much better if "American buyers will play the game and publish facsimiles of the unique volumes they carry off from us." After comparing the holdings of American and British libraries in certain categories of collectable books, and finding Americans somewhat hampered historically as "late starters," Pollard concluded, "it would seem that there are some rare books still in England."[23]

None of this debate bothered Huntington. He closed out the year by buying some American literary manuscripts at the George S. Hellman sale and a mixture of Americana and English literature from the Henry F. DePuy sale. The most important item from the DePuy library was a letter written by Benedict Arnold in 1783 to Lord North in which Arnold explained his treason and asked to be placed on the British Establishment in order to increase his pension. Smith got the letter for Huntington for a resounding $2,800. In mid-December of 1919, when the members of the Author's Club met at the Fifty-seventh Street mansion, Huntington displayed the Arnold letter as one of the thirty-five most important items in his collection.

Huntington's mood was buoyant. Having appointed a board of trustees he felt secure about the future of the library. Some of this assurance was reflected in an exchange of letters with the New York collector William A. White. At the Hellman sale White had been underbidder for a notebook of Thoreau's college compositions. White wrote Huntington that he had planned to present it to the Harvard library where Thoreau wrote the essays in the first place. Would Huntington sell the volume so he could place it with Harvard? Huntington replied that after giving the matter "serious consideration" he had decided to keep the book.

> I think that I should feel different about this if it were not for the fact that this book is not going to a private library, for, as you perhaps know, my Library building will probably be ready next Fall, and my library will then be deeded to the State of California. In this way, then, the manuscripts will be as accessible to the public as if they were at Harvard. My intention is to issue much of the unpublished matter and this Thoreau among them.
>
> I trust that you will understand my position and realize how much I should have liked to accede to your request.[24]

Although White may not have been pleased with the answer he could no doubt sympathize with the argument.

Perhaps the best statement of Huntington's new view of his relationship to the library and its treasures came as a result of a newspaper interview with his favorite journalist, Otheman Stevens of the *Los Angeles Examiner*. After some preliminary discussion on business conditions in Southern California Huntington got around to the library.

> Yes, I shall build the library I have contemplated. These books of mine in value to the world of thought are a great responsibility; if seriously damaged, and of course if destroyed, they could not be replaced and the loss thereby would be irreparable. So I feel it to be my duty to give them a safe and proper home, for the owner of such things is really little more than a trustee and his responsibility is far greater than attaches to ownership of articles which there is some reason for regarding as purely personal.[25]

This was not just talk for the readers of the *Los Angeles Examiner* but a sincere expression of Huntington's views on the responsibilities that necessarily accompany the ownership of precious books and paintings, a matter that had troubled him for years. Now, with the new library building underway and the board of trustees appointed, he felt that he had started to cope with those responsibilities.

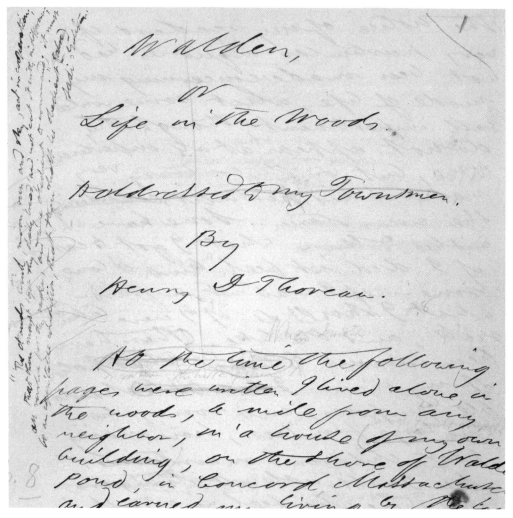

FIG. 33
From the manuscript of Thoreau's *Walden*, acquired about 1916 (p. 7).

Chapter 8

THE BOOKS MOVE WEST
1920

Among many indications of the growing strength of the library during the early postwar years, perhaps none was more telling than Huntington's response to the Arbury Hall sale. In December 1919 Sotheby's announced that 362 lots from the library of Sir Francis Newdigate-Newdegate, of Arbury Hall in Warwickshire, would be sold at auction in early January. Included in the sale were to be a number of scarce Elizabethan titles, a Shakespeare First Folio, some Americana, and a choice mixture of seventeenth- and eighteenth-century broadsides and political pamphlets. Two weeks before the auction Smith, who had stayed on in London following the sales of Christie-Miller's Britwell library, bought the collection en bloc. His jubilant cablegram to Huntington read:

JUST BOUGHT NEWDEGATE LIBRARY
YOU CAN HAVE FIRST PICK.[1]

From Huntington's point of view, however, there wasn't much to pick from. He took a scarce edition of Robert Greene's *Pandosto* (1595), the source of Shakespeare's *Winter's Tale;* Thomas Lodge's *Rosalynd* (1598), thought to be the source of *As You Like It;* added a few seventeenth-century broadsides and was content. The Newdigate books were exceptional but Huntington had four-fifths of them on his shelves already. If, as had been said, Huntington had nearly exhausted the American book market by 1912, he seemed to be approaching the same point in England eight years later.

After a rough crossing on the *Carmania* Smith arrived in New York on 24 January 1920. Securely packed in his luggage and ticketed for Huntington was the precious *Venus and Adonis* from the Christie-Miller sale, along with a few of the more spectacular items from the Britwell and the Newdigate libraries. The auction season in New York was starting to pick up again after the holiday lull and Smith, although tired from his trip, was ready to enter the fray. During the last week of January, for example, he bought $19,000 worth of Jesuit Relations for Huntington at the second Henry DePuy sale and in early February acquired some Americana at the Francis W. Fabyan sale. Although the Fabyan auction was of only marginal interest, Smith did get Huntington a copy of *The Necessity of Judgement, and Righteousness in a Land*, by Eliphalet Adams (1710), the first book printed in Connecticut. At the dispersal of duplicates from the Massachusetts Historical Society he invested $13,428 and bought Huntington a number of early colonial sermons and tracts. For Huntington and Smith the January and February auctions were only a warm-up for what they knew would be the major sale of the season— perhaps the major sale of several seasons—the auction of the Harry Buxton Forman library. From Forman's lush array of nineteenth-century English poets—Wordsworth, Coleridge, Shelley, Keats, Byron, Swinburne, and Tennyson—Smith would of course buy the best of the best for Huntington. But it was not to be. On 4 March, while talking with William Lanier Washington, a descendant of George Washington and a sometime dealer in family letters and manuscripts, Smith fell forward on his desk and died instantly of a heart attack. Many wondered if the book world would ever be the same.[2]

Starting with his buying spree at the Hoe sale in 1911 and continuing for nine golden years, Smith had all but controlled the book markets of New York and London. It was Huntington of course who had sponsored Smith's most spectacular achievements, but it was Smith himself who had remembered title pages and prices, bargained with dealers, browbeaten competitors, bid to the limit, coaxed reluctant collectors to part with their treasures—and

Fig. 34
The auction room of the Anderson Galleries in March 1920, during the Buxton Forman sale, the first major auction held after the death of Smith (photograph reproduced by permission of the Rosenbach Museum).

who was in a real sense responsible for much of the early development of Huntington's library. But now Huntington's chief agent—the most powerful figure in the New York book world—was gone. Charles F. Heartman, a fellow dealer, described Smith's role in a fanciful way that contained more than a grain of truth:

> One of my ambitions has been to go to the West Coast and see the great Huntington Library. I want to look at the bronze bust of George D. Smith in the entrance hall. Or, is there none? Well, perhaps, somewhere there is a memorial plaque, but I have my doubts. Booksellers, the makers of collectors and collections, are rarely honored.[3]

Eulogies frequently identified Smith as the greatest bookseller in the world. He had been "the Napoleon of booksellers," as poet and dramatist John Drinkwater put it.[4] Kennerley, who perhaps knew Smith better than anyone else and who set the stage for many of his triumphs at the Anderson Galleries, commented:

Since the Hoe sale nine years ago he bought and sold a greater volume of books than all the other dealers in rare books in the world put together, and he bought for Henry Huntington what is now the greatest private library in the world, ranking second only to the British museum, and in some respects surpassing it. . . . There are many collectors in America who today will look on their shelves and be grateful that they took George D. Smith's advice when he said to them about some rare volume "Buy it. You will never see another copy. Ten years from now it will be worth twice—three times—what you can buy it for today."[5]

In a lighthearted characterization of the booksellers of the 1920s, Heartman once referred to Smith as "the greatest of them all, the never-equalled 'Bulldog' George D. 'Try and take it away from me' Smith."[6] George Watson Cole, representing the sentiments of Huntington's New York library staff, wrote to his employer:

The death of George D. Smith came on us like a thunder-clap out of a clear sky. The public press has had many articles concerning him and his career. He was a most remarkable man and his place in the book world cannot well be filled. The business is to go on there as usual as they telephoned us this morning.[7]

In a rather arid note that belied his deep friendship for Smith, Huntington replied from California:

We had a good trip but marred by the sad news of Smith's death. It will be a great loss, but I am glad to hear that the business is to go on.

For those on the fringes of the book world, Smith's death was probably of only momentary interest. For the more aggressive entrepreneurs, however, it suggested that a door long shut might now be open. The day after Smith's death Thomas Kirby, representing the American Art Association, sent Huntington an outline of the services his organization was ready to supply:

Recognizing the fact that the death of Mr. George D. Smith will be a serious loss to you, I venture to write these lines with the view of aiding you to some extent at least in performing some of the duties exercised by the late Mr. Smith and I earnestly trust that you take them under serious consideration. I am prepared to execute any and all orders to purchase at sales held under our management or elsewhere in New York City and am prepared to exercise such discretionary powers as you may desire, all without charge for the service for I would deem it a compliment to be delegated to represent you.[8]

Having no great admiration for Kirby or his firm, Huntington found the offer easy to resist. Instead of making a change he decided to leave his commissions in the hands of what was now known as the George D. Smith Estate. Unfortunately, the estate was in immediate and serious financial trouble. Although the book stock was valuable, the freewheeling Smith had lived on the edge of his success and negotiated substantial loans against projected sales. To make matters worse, he had carried most of the business details around in his head and had never made a will. Since the Anderson firm was Smith's chief creditor, Kennerley found himself named as executor of the estate, encumbered with the awesome responsibility of restoring some kind of order to the business. It quickly became clear that the debts far outweighed the assets. In early April Kennerley conveyed the gravity of the situation to Huntington:

> Mr. Smith died in the midst of so many unfinished deals that we found things in great confusion; but are engaged in straightening them out. I am very hopeful that the Estate will show a very substantial equity.[9]

One of these matters affecting Huntington directly went back to an agreement he had made with Smith in 1918 involving the complicated transfer of a series of Safety Insulated Wire and Cable Company bonds. In this negotiation Huntington traded the bonds to Smith at par value of $623,000, after which Smith gave them to William Bixby as security for the purchase of Bixby's library. All of this left a $500,000 note against Smith's account in the Anderson files. Of course Kennerley wanted to clear the obligation and asked Huntington if he would buy back the bonds. The question remained unresolved until June 1923 when, after repeated appeals from Kennerley, Huntington paid the Smith estate $425,877.80. It was a generous thing to do, for as Graham, Huntington's accountant, pointed out, "you understand there is no obligation on your part at all, as the bonds were traded by you on a supposedly permanent transaction, and just because Mr. Smith squandered the fortune which he made, is no reason why you should go out of your way to help the Estate, unless you have personal reasons for doing so."[10] Huntington's esteem for Smith and his desire to help the estate apparently constituted a sufficient personal reason.

The long-anticipated Buxton Forman auction required immediate attention from Huntington's staff. Months before the sale was to begin, the circumstances surrounding the dispersal of this fine English library had generated considerable discussion. The Forman family claimed they had sold the books to John B. Stetson, Jr., a Philadelphia collector, at a reduced price— $80,000—because they understood he was planning to donate them to an institution. To the family's chagrin, it turned out that Stetson had no such philanthropic aim but was simply operating as a partner in the Anderson Galleries. In that capacity he turned the books over to Kennerley for public auction and personal profit. (The sympathy expressed at the time for the Forman heirs seems less justified today, in view of Forman's complicity in the notorious Thomas J. Wise forgeries.)

In the absence of Smith, and with the pressures of the approaching Forman sale increasing daily, a subtle shift in responsibility took place among the members of Huntington's New York library staff. Leslie Bliss had been one of Cole's first appointments in the fall of 1915 and had won a place of trust through his careful work with auction catalogs and sales lists. Among his other duties were excursions to the third-floor library, where Huntington spent much of his time. In that way he came to know the collector on a more intimate basis than the rest of the staff. He also became friendly with Smith and over time came to understand something of the dealer's buying techniques.[11] Also from Smith he heard the latest gossip of the auction world and absorbed much about the ways of the other dealers—Ernest Dressel North, Walter M. Hill, A. S. W. Rosenbach, Gabriel Wells, Lathrop Harper, James F. Drake, and Robert H. Dodd. He put all this knowledge to good use at the Forman sale. On Monday afternoon, 15 March, Bliss took up his position in the handsome Anderson auction rooms, along with Dr. W. N. C. Carlton and Maurice Wolff representing the Smith estate. The dealers were there in

force. Off to the side sat Rosenbach with one of his favorite customers, the bibliophile and writer A. Edward Newton. Across the aisle the veteran New York collectors Beverly Chew, W. H. Arnold, and W. A. White thumbed through the elaborate two-hundred-page catalog. The most exciting portion of the library, the Shelley letters and manuscripts, came up for sale on Tuesday night. Bliss was on hand and faithfully recounted the events to Huntington:

> Now as to the Forman sale. The last session comes this afternoon, so I cannot report on the whole as yet. Prices ran very high on the modern items as a rule, while some good old things slipped through cheaply. I attended each sale except the one Monday night, staying in last night as the Mary W. Shelley letters [ninety autographed letters to her step-sister "Claire" Clairmont] in which you were espe-

cially interested came up then. We bid them in at seven hundred fifty dollars, which is almost the same price per letter as you paid in the Brooks Sale, where they went very cheap, according to G. D. S. I bid in two Percy Bysshe Shelley letters [to William Godwin], which I considered reasonable, considering the matters upon which he was writing. We paid a good sized price for No. 632 ["Lines Addressed to His Royal Highness the Prince of Wales" 1811] two thousand three hundred fifty dollars, but there was nothing to go by, and we needed it to make our Shelley Collection complete. When you get the marked catalog I think you will see that the price was fair considering the other prices. Please don't think that I bid in person, for I did not. Messrs. Wolff or Carlton of the Smith estate doing all that for us. I wanted to see you get some of the manuscripts if you could reasonably, and under the way things stood, I saw no other way out, so I did it on my own responsibility. We all miss G. D. S. and his wonderful memory and knowledge of prices, and lacking that, Dr. Carlton and I had to revise many of our bids after the first two sessions, so that later we did better. I was urged to go higher on some items, but did not do so, thinking it might not be our last chance, and wishing to save for bigger things.[12]

Bliss got a number of reasonably priced Shelley first editions but stayed out of competition for the costlier manuscripts and autographed rarities. Those he left for Rosenbach, who took Shelley's annotated copy of *Queen Mab* (1813) for $6,000 and *Posthumous Fragments of Margaret Nicholson* (1810) at $6,750 for Carl Pforzheimer's growing collection. Ernest Dressel North stole the newspaper publicity from Rosenbach by paying the top sale price, $16,200, for the twenty-seven-page handwritten manuscript of Shelley's poem "Julian and Maddalo. A Conversation." Never one to pay what he liked to call "fancy prices," especially for manuscripts, Huntington was pleased that Bliss had taken the conservative approach. Also he was glad to learn that he already owned two thirds of the nine hundred items offered in the first portion of the sale.[13] It was testimony, if any were needed, that his library could stand comparison with any rare book collection in the world.

Although prices achieved at the Forman sale were regarded as high, those obtained the following week for the distinguished Walter T. Wallace library fell far below expectations. During the first two decades of the twentieth century Wallace built what historian Carl Cannon characterized as "an old-fashioned library," a collection based on personal favorites drawn from English and American literature.[14] Wallace had such esteemed rarities as a Coverdale Bible, Caxton's printing of Higden's *Polychronicon*, and four Shakespeare folios, all backed by solid runs of first editions of Dickens, Hawthorne, Poe, Lamb, and Shelley. Although Wallace's collecting lines were traditional, his buying methods were unique. Most collectors employed a dealer to act for them at auctions but Wallace, querulous and independent, insisted on doing his own bidding. This angered some dealers and probably prejudiced the outcome of the sale. Furthermore, only three days before the auction the American Art Association had circulated a letter saying that instead of the usual extension of thirty days of credit, all bills from this sale would need to be settled in cash in fifteen days.[15] Eventually it turned out that Wallace knew nothing of the letter, but dealers were predisposed to be suspicious of him and they found the terms unreasonable and insulting. Unaware that a debacle was in the making, the officers of the American Art Association went ahead with plans for what they expected to be a noteworthy sale. In the end, "bloody work was done," as Newton wrote in a letter to Amy Lowell.[16] Lot after lot went for ridiculously low prices, individual items often bringing half what Wallace had paid. Rosenbach, Wells, Sessler, and Drake were among the dealers who cheerfully bought and bought and bought. Bliss, again working carefully through the Smith estate, took $6,000 worth of American literary first editions for Huntington.[17]

With Huntington absorbed in planning for his new library building, and Cole concentrating on the "Brief Catalogue of English literature prior to 1640," Bliss continued to take on more responsibility for buying. He not only began to place cautious orders on his own responsibility but moved to diversify the library's pool of agents. With Smith's monopoly broken it was possible to look around a little. In late March 1920 Bliss ordered a large collection of William Dean Howells first editions from the Dunster House Bookshop in Cambridge, Massachusetts, and in April proudly wrote that he had gone to Thomas Gannon's bookstore in New York and found some of the same Kipling first editions offered in the Forman sale at half the Forman prices.[18]

While Bliss was looking around for various ways to save money, Rosenbach continued to call attention to his wares, few of which were bargains. The flamboyant salesman and the meticulous bibliographer had little affinity for each other, and over the years they maintained a cautious relationship. Bliss kept a close watch on Rosenbach orders and frequently returned items that failed to match the doctor's sometimes overblown descriptions. Rosenbach, for his part, had little time for such trivia since he knew his books were worth anything he wanted to ask. Wasn't he, after all, the leading antiquarian book dealer in the country and, to put it bluntly, wasn't Bliss just Huntington's doorkeeper? Rosenbach had already sold Huntington a few high-priced Blakes and some Shakespeare folios, but now he saw an opportunity to move ahead on a grander scale. He knew that with a buyer like Huntington it would be important to appeal to both his pride of ownership and his taste. Perhaps a dignified New York address would help. It was all right of course to have a solid business in Philadelphia, but Rosenbach felt his growing prestige called for nothing less than a stylish Manhattan location. Late in 1919 he purchased a granite-fronted Madison Avenue townhouse, formerly owned by the Morris Loeb banking family, and with deft application of imported carpets, Barbizon landscape paintings, rich paneling, and an English butler made ready to attract wealthy New York collectors. Bliss visited the new location and, as he told Huntington, found it impressive.

In early April Rosenbach offered to bid—with no commission, just out of the goodness of his heart—on a Benjamin Franklin imprint and a John Norton pamphlet to be sold at the Stan Henkels auction rooms in Philadelphia. Rosenbach got them both for $1,500, a figure he claimed, with characteristic glee, to be the greatest bargain of the year.[19] Rosenbach then offered George Wither's *The Shepherds Hunting* (1615), obtained at the Forman sale, which still happened to be on his hands as the original buyer had backed out. Bliss, seeing a rare bargain, encouraged Huntington to take it, noting that the morocco-bound octavo could be had for $760 plus ten percent commission and that no copies had come to the market in recent years. Huntington added the volume to his shelves.[20]

Even though Huntington was glad to take his alert young assistant's advice on routine matters, he kept tight personal control of large purchases. Bliss understood this and approached the question of acquiring an important

Lincoln collection with all due deference. In April he wrote:

> A short time after you left I had another phone conversation with
> Judd Stewart, the owner of that largest Lincoln Collection, about
> which we talked several times the past winter. He has just added to
> it the only known copy of the first edition of Lincoln's First
> Inaugural Address, which Lincoln had run off for himself just
> before he left Springfield for Washington to become President. It
> alone, as you know, is a fine addition to any library, and of course
> it greatly enhances the value of that collection. I wish you would
> think it over carefully, and come back next time prepared to at least
> see it, or the rarities which he has in his office. It would be one of
> the very finest purchases you ever made for the money, and I believe
> you can buy it for ten thousand dollars less than the price he set.[21]

As far as Huntington was concerned the Stewart collection would have to
wait. The library building on his San Marino estate concerned him far more
at that moment than the books that would eventually fill it. By April the
scaffolding was cleared away and Huntington could take a close look at the
structure. Described vividly but somewhat contradictorily in the *Los Angeles
Times* as a "Bastile of Books" and a "Western Louvre,"[22] the elegant building contained both Renaissance and Mediterranean features. It was designed
in the shape of a comb, with a high-ceilinged main exhibition hall measuring one hundred by thirty-three feet as a base and three wings running off
at right angles for stockrooms, a gallery, and workrooms. The exterior of the
long south facade was dominated by two elaborately carved bronze doors
and a series of Ionic columns, the whole completed with a low-pitched red
tile roof. Located on a rise between the San Gabriel mountains on the north
and a wide valley on the south, the library had an appropriately impressive
setting.

Huntington was eager to have his books and staff brought together in
California. Originally he and Cole had planned to make the move in the winter, but now with construction ahead of schedule it seemed possible to have
some of the men come early and start the job of unpacking. Since the staff
and associated family members consisted of twenty-eight people—eight cou-
ples with nine children and three bachelors—the move would be no small

THURSDAY MORNING, MARCH 25, 1920. — PART II: 12 PAGES.

BASTILE :: OF :: BOOKS :: NOW :: NEARING :: COMPLETION

Volumes for the Western Louvre of Learning to Start Westward Journey — S...

SEEKS ANOTHER PRIZE LIBRARY.

One-Time Owner of Choice Collection Tries Again.

Sets Goal at a Hundred of World's Rarest Books.

Fellow Bibliomaniac Praises Great Huntington Gift.

Having sold in New York a year o a library of 1500 volumes of rarities that brought a price of 00,000, Herschel V. Jones of Minneapolis, publisher of the Minneapolis Journal, is now engaged in forming a collection of 100 books of formative period of the drama d poetry, before the time of akespeare. Mr. Jones, who is at Hotel Huntington, Pasadena, d yesterday of his purpose to ass another notable library.

"When I began my collection thirty years ago," he said, "I anticipated selling when 60 years old. I fell little short of that when I sold a ar ago."

This sale the London Times noted "the greatest book sale in the rld" considering the number of lumes.

Of his new collection Mr. Jones id:

"My rule in buying is to look for

Henry E. Huntington and His Library Building as It Looks Today.
Note the rails of the power magnate's specially built railroad in the foreground.

HENRY E. HUNTINGTON'S Bastile of books on his magnificent San Marino estate, with its specially built | the inside with hollow tile. The construction has been followed to insure an absolutely fireproof building of the utmost durability, and one which will entirely safeguard the priceless books | have unusually high ceilings. the building has been planned a view to its enlargement. If ne this contingency is not likely to in the near future. The capacit

Fig. 36
The *Los Angeles Times* of 25 March 1920 called the new Huntington library building both a "Bastile" and a "Louvre."

undertaking. The problems of housing and schools called for immediate solution. At the same time plans needed to be made for the shipment of books, office equipment, and card files. Huntington, engaged in a variety of activities in California, was not as sensitive to the complexities of the situation as Cole wished him to be. After learning that Huntington expected the men to be responsible for the cost of getting their household goods to the freight offices, Cole wrote a rather frantic letter of appeal.

> Perhaps I may be permitted to say that the moving from here to California is a very serious matter with all our men. Nearly, if not all of them are dependent on their monthly salaries for their current living expenses and it would be a great drain if not an impossibility for them to consider with any degree of composure the idea of bearing any of the expenses consequent upon such a move as we contemplate.
>
>   . . . I think it should be borne in mind, to begin with, that our entire staff is made up of picked men and that their value to us has been vastly increased by the experience they have had in the work they have done during the past [four] or five years. I believe, too, that better work will be done by them if all the expenses of moving are taken from their shoulders. A contented and satisfied frame of mind I am sure will turn out to be one of our best assets.
>
>   I am looking forward with pleasure to seeing you soon, as details can be so much better settled by personal interviews than by correspondence.[23]

In the end Huntington agreed with Cole's analysis and absorbed all moving costs. By the first of September the staff had settled in temporary housing in and around Pasadena, and on 10 September, with high expectations, they reported for work. The first few weeks, however, tested their enthusiasm. Since the upper floors of the building were still unfinished, everyone was jammed into the basement, an area already overcrowded with large wooden packing boxes and temporary shelving. To make matters worse, neither Cole nor Huntington was on hand to make decisions or offer encouragement. Huntington was spending the fall, as was his custom, outside Paris at the Chateau Beauregard, while Cole was in New York, forced to stay behind following emergency surgery. Slowly, under the direction of Bliss and Schad, the staff began to bring some semblance of order to the basement. In the first few weeks they set up shelving, unpacked boxes, and checked in several large collections of Americana. By the time Cole arrived in October enough progress had been made so that he could write Huntington a cheerful report saying that the second floor was almost ready and that by the end of the week the men would be occupying their own office space.[24]

For Huntington, confined in New York with a serious illness, the news heightened his sense of frustration. If he could not be on the grounds himself he intended to exert control over those who were. In a testy letter to Cole he laid down the rules.

> I have just received a letter from a young lady who has visited the Ranch and wishes to write up the gardens for an Eastern magazine. She states that you would give her permission but that she prefers to get it directly from me. I have a strict rule regarding requests of this kind. The orders are that no one is to visit the grounds except through a pass from my office in Los Angeles. Moreover I have especially forbidden any passes to be given to any one of the "movies" or the theatrical profession. Meanwhile, until my arrival, I have written my office that I do not wish any one on the grounds except those that belong there. My policy has been to keep it as private as possible, and as for writing it up, when the right time comes, I shall have the proper person do it.[25]

It was a bleak time for Huntington, relieved only by a ceremony at New York University where Chancellor Elmer Brown presented him with an honorary doctorate of laws degree for his contribution to the world of scholarship. The citation accompanying the degree as read to Huntington declared that he was a "man of affairs, a man of books, . . . who with liberal spirit and discriminating taste, has gathered from all the world a royal treasure of letters and literary memorials," in order to make, "in the fullness of time, on the far western rim of this young western continent, a treasure house of learning where scholars from all lands shall find enrichment."[26] Huntington reported the event to his sister Caroline in a brief note simply saying it had been a "pleasant gathering."[27]

Not everyone responded to the California move with the enthusiasm expressed in the New York University tribute. When Huntington first announced his plan, a number of librarians and collectors objected strenuously. It seemed obvious to them that American cultural life was centered in the major cities of the east—Boston, New York, and Washington—and that any effort to move rare books across the Mississippi would be madness. The books and manuscripts, important as they were, would languish, remote from the scholarly community.[28] With his deep belief in California's future Huntington took no notice of such arguments. The San Marino ranch was home. He once told Cole that he would be perfectly content to go inside, close the gates, and never leave again. The trips to New York and France were a diversion for Mrs. Huntington, who was almost entirely blind and needed diversions, but as far as Huntington was concerned they were a waste of time. Why would anyone voluntarily choose to leave the magnificent California climate, the sculptured gardens, and the books and paintings? In December 1920 he wrote to his sister Caroline, "Belle and I expect to start for California soon after the 1st of January—and we can't get there soon enough. New York is certainly not the winter climate for me and I fear it will sometime lay me out."[29] At seventy, Huntington was well aware of his own mortality.

During the fall and winter of 1920, Huntington decided to slow his buying. He had spent a large amount of money on the library building, and the move from New York had cost more than he planned. He told Bliss to hold off unless something of great importance came along. When Judge Russell Benedict of the New York Supreme Court, an acquaintance for many years, offered a tempting collection of early colonial laws, Huntington declined wistfully: "You may be sure I would like to possess the Laws, but of buying books, there is no end, and with all the calls made on me, I sometimes feel it will be my end."[30] In December, still watching his bank balance, Huntington sent Bliss a check for fifty dollars to cover assorted purchases. Bliss wrote back that he had been able to use the money well. "I visited Dawson's Bookshop on Hill Street . . . and bought mostly Californiana items, though I got one or two general Americana and some American authors. Among the rest of the items you will notice "The Truth-teller," an old Mormon item which I am sure would bring fifteen or twenty dollars if put up at auction, and which I purchased for fifty cents."[31]

Although the move to California occupied Huntington's thoughts during 1920, there were one or two sales he could not ignore. When the Anderson Galleries placed the rather disappointing remainder of George D. Smith's stock up for sale in a series of auctions, he bought a few items—some Jefferson Davis letters and a Bliss Carman manuscript—more as a gesture of help for the estate than as a consequence of interest in the items themselves. In the summer he asked Quaritch to handle his commissions, again few in number, at both the Christie-Miller sale and at the ninth and last session of the Huth sale. The matter of an appropriate commission on the Christie-Miller books caused a rift in his generally amiable relationship with the Quaritch staff. Huntington had placed no specific bids at the sale, but after it was over asked Francis Ferguson, handling the business negotiations for Quaritch, to supply him with several items obtained by the firm for stock. In reply to Huntington's request for billing at the usual ten percent commission Ferguson politely insisted on fifteen because, as he said, "the books were bought at risk."[32] It was not the way to deal with one of the world's most important collectors. Huntington simply turned over all future London sale commissions to Rosenbach.

Although Rosenbach had sold books to Huntington through direct negotiation for several years, he had seldom carried his commissions at auction. That had all been done by Smith and for the short time after Smith's death by the agents of the Smith estate. Now the time had come to appoint a new representative. Bliss suggested the capable New York dealer James Drake but Huntington favored the more flamboyant Rosenbach. Knowing how essential it would be to obtain Huntington's trust right from the start, Rosenbach took almost everything of importance in the Herman LeRoy Edgar sale, including Anthony Askham's *A Lytel Treatyse of Astronomy* (1552) for $3,220 and George Best's account of Martin Frobisher's expedition in search of the Northwest Passage for $4,600. In addition, he was able to buy Huntington a number of printed Indian treaties at appealingly low prices. For both men it was a promising beginning.

Earlier in the year Huntington had entered into another partnership, this time with a librarian rather than a book dealer. Clarence S. Brigham, the energetic and knowledgeable director of the American Antiquarian Society, had visited Huntington's New York library a number of times shortly after the war and in the process developed a genuine respect for the strength of the collections. In April 1920 he wrote to say he had examined the recently issued *Checklist of the Library* (1919) and was impressed with the progress Huntington had made in securing pre-1641 English printings. Brigham told Huntington he was going to England that summer and would be happy to look for the pre-1641 items to add to those already in the collection. Brigham's goal, as he explained it, would be to see that Huntington's library became "the greatest collection of English literature prior to 1640 in the world . . . with the exception of the British Museum." The effort, according to Brigham, would not be directed to high-priced rarities, most of which were already in the collection, but to less important titles that could be secured for reasonable prices. He would charge nothing for his own service since, as he wrote, "I am not in the book business, and am actuated chiefly by my love of the subject and my pride as an American in your library."[33] In order to hold prices to a reasonable level Brigham came up with a clever scheme. Huntington's name would never be mentioned in any of the transactions. Dealers would be told to ship the books to Worcester, Massachusetts, and would naturally assume that Brigham was buying for the American Antiquarian Society. He would do nothing to discourage that notion. Huntington approved and sent Brigham a list of the volumes already in the collection.

In Brigham's first week in London he managed to buy one hundred thirty titles at an average cost of fifteen dollars. No one, he wrote Cole, suspected the Huntington connection, not even the people at Sotheby's, where "I attended an auction and got several Bibles and Books of Common Prayer which I never should have been allowed to get for twice the price, if they had known."[34] Although English dealers, according to Brigham, felt no jealousy over the activity of wealthy American buyers, they expressed complete disbelief that any overseas collection could ever rival the great British holdings. By the middle of August Brigham was able to boast to Huntington that he had examined over fifty thousand books in some forty bookshops between Exeter and Edinburgh and bought over one thousand pre-1641 titles. The time was right, according to Brigham, since the English book dealers had not had much opportunity to issue catalogs since the end of the war and had large stocks on hand. By the time he was ready to come home, after visiting the

London shops of Edwards, Pickering, and Maggs, Brigham had spent fifteen thousand dollars and bought slightly under twelve hundred titles. These volumes, he told Huntington, would have brought twice that amount if sold as a collection or through a catalog.

Brigham was now completely caught up in the process of building Huntington's library as a rival to the distinguished British collections. He reported that if he made one or two more trips it would be possible to overtake and surpass the libraries of Oxford and Cambridge and perhaps even give the British Museum a stiff race. During the winter Brigham continued to buy from British dealers, securing some two hundred forty more titles. On his second trip, during the summer of 1921, Brigham found it more difficult to locate books not already in the collection. He reported that he frequently looked at one hundred pre-1641 titles to find five or six that the collection lacked. With the expenditure of twenty-three thousand dollars he bought seven hundred books, many of which, he told Huntington, were exceedingly rare.[35]

When the books began to arrive in California, however, the library staff found an alarming number of errors. Chester Cate, the acerbic assistant librarian, called this to Brigham's attention and told him bluntly: "In cataloguing the books which you purchased for us last March and subsequently, a somewhat larger number than we anticipated from your letters has been found to be imperfect. . . . Imperfect books are of small value and are of little use to us in this library."[36] Brigham admitted that in his haste to examine books, sometimes as many as five thousand a day, he might have been careless in noticing imperfections, and he offered to take such volumes back for his own library—a suggestion that was never acted upon. When Brigham traveled to England in 1922, he found that pre-1641 printings were even harder to locate than before and in four weeks managed to add only 315 new titles. "People will be impressed," Brigham told Cole, "when they see the initial 'H' following so many titles in the forthcoming bibliography of early English printing sponsored by the Bibliographical Society."[41] Cole agreed and replied that with this last batch of purchases the Huntington collection of pre-1641 titles had reached eight thousand, a figure that brought them even with Cambridge University and not far behind Oxford.[37]

Although Cole and Brigham took pride in the size of the collection, Cate continued to find fault with a number of the purchases. The dispute reached its climax in the summer of 1922 when he discovered that Brigham had loaned one of the recently purchased books to a Yale librarian without asking permission. Huntington was extremely sensitive about his ownership rights and immediately made his displeasure known to Brigham. The book in question, *Chaderton's Fruitfull Sermon*, should not have been loaned, Huntington wrote, and furthermore the price Brigham paid was considerably beyond what another copy of the book had brought at a recent sale. In view of these matters, Huntington concluded, "I think it would be well for you to discontinue your activities for this library until such time as I may authorize you to continue as our agent." For Brigham, the harsh letter was like a bombshell. In a three-page reply he told Huntington that he had put forward his best efforts for three summers, "worked day and night poring over immense book stacks to obtain some 2600 unique titles with no thought other than to improve the library. I have sometimes thought," he concluded, "that my labors in behalf of the Huntington Library have not been appreciated."[38] The only answer he got was a terse note from Bliss saying indeed, his efforts had been appreciated but that Huntington now felt all buying should be done directly from the library in San Marino.[39] It was a disappointing end to what had been, from Brigham's point of view, a happy working relationship. It did not change his view, however, that Huntington was, as he later wrote, "unquestionably the greatest of American book collectors."[40]

FIG. 37
Huntington's decision to situate his library in Southern California was generally greeted with dismay on the East Coast, but the tone of this piece from the book section of the *Boston Evening Transcript,* 16 February 1921, was celebratory.

Chapter 9

INCUNABULA AND MANUSCRIPTS
1921–1922

Huntington spent the first six weeks of 1921 in New York trying to regain his strength. It was an extremely frustrating time to be confined to the somber Fifth Avenue mansion, while his gardens bloomed in San Marino. His poor health also made it impossible for him to take part in important sales. Early in January, Brigham wired to say that for the remarkably low price of £7,000, Huntington could buy 550 early theological titles that were to be offered as part of the Christie-Miller sale later that month; but, he warned, an agreement he had made with the Sotheby firm contained the proviso that the transaction must be completed within four days. Although the offer was attractive—over half of the titles carried pre-1550 imprints—Huntington was simply too ill to consider it. The books fell immediately to the British collector Sir Leicester Harmsworth.

By 15 February Huntington's health had improved enough so that he was able to return to California. In a matter of days Rosenbach arrived with the proof sheets for the catalog of the next Britwell Court sale. He and Huntington spent hours poring over the rich array of poetry and prose, selecting widely from early printings of Homer and Ovid, essays of

Archbishop Laud, poems by Francis Quarles, and courtly plays by John Lyly. As the want list grew they decided to try a tactic that had worked well in the past—a blanket bid for the whole collection. When Rosenbach left for England he carried Huntington's note promising £50,000 if the collection could be had en bloc. The representatives of the Christie-Miller estate, with visions of an even larger total, were not swayed by this American frontal attack and politely turned the offer down. This meant that Rosenbach had to spend a little more time getting what Huntington wanted, but get it he did. With price of little consequence, lot after lot fell to Rosenbach's bids. He gave £1,450 for Samuel Nicholson's *Acolastus, His After-Witte* (1600), a poem filled with quotations from Shakespeare, and £1,080 for a unique black-letter copy of *Everyman* (1530) with a handsome woodcut title page. He not only secured almost everything Huntington wanted but also picked up the few items requested by Henry Folger and William A. White.

The English book dealers were amazed. Clearly, the days of American domination, established immediately after the war by George D. Smith, had returned with even greater intensity. This time however the buyer was no rough-hewn braggart, but a cultivated, scholarly braggart quite capable of debating the quality of binding states in Shelley's *Epipsychidion* or the frequency of cancels in early editions of *Paradise Lost*. Polished scholar or belligerent tradesman, the result was the same—the books and manuscripts wound up on Huntington's shelves. From Rosenbach's point of view, however, item-by-item bidding took much too long. Why not buy everything that remained? Rosenbach thought that purchase of the entire library—which he told Huntington was valued at £350,000—might be negotiated for a mere £22,500—perhaps a naive estimate but one Huntington was ready to try. He made the offer, and again, politely, Sotheby's turned it down.

With the Christie-Miller sale behind him Huntington had Rosenbach place bids in New York at the William Loring Andrews sale in April 1921 and at the William Brewster sale in May. For $1,200 he obtained the prize of the eclectic Brewster collection, an early draft of Edgar Allan Poe's "Annabel Lee." Rosenbach congratulated Huntington on the purchase and told him that William Randolph Hearst had been "much disappointed" not to be able to add the manuscript to his own library.[1] Aside from these purchases—and a number of small orders sent to Stevens and Brown and Francis Edwards in

London, James Drake in New York, and Arthur Clark in Cleveland—
Huntington again withdrew temporarily from the book market. Over the
course of a few weeks in the spring he turned down the offer of a blockbook
and several sixteenth-century plays from the energetic Pasadena bookseller
Alice Millard, a collection of Jack London manuscripts offered by Mrs.
London through Henry Wagner, and a request for support from the Grolier
Club of New York. To Robert Jaffray, the Grolier treasurer, he explained his
situation by saying:

> I am founding here a library and Art Museum which I intend giv-
> ing to the State of California. The Library building, although not
> completed, has now facilities for the Librarian and his staff and they
> are already here at work. You will realize, I trust, that I feel that I
> should concentrate all of my attention on this project. I should like
> to help out in the many requests that come to me, but under the
> circumstances, it is not feasible.[2]

In June, preparing for what would be his last trip to Europe, Huntington told
Cole to stop all book buying until further notice.[3] There were however a number of annuals and reference books that had to be continued. When
Huntington returned from Europe in October he let Cole know he was not
pleased to find an accumulation of bills. These expenses, although not large,
irritated Huntington since they came at a time when he had just made one of
the largest investments of his life, paying £182,000 to Duveen for *The Blue
Boy,* Thomas Gainsborough's masterpiece. When Huntington decided to buy
an expensive book or a painting from one of his favorite dealers he seldom
argued about the price, but after the purchase he often economized on other
things.[4]

Winter brought a recurrence of his illness, so for the second year in a row he
was forced to spend December in New York. But crossing the Continental
Divide had its usual therapeutic effect, and a week after he arrived at the ranch
in early January he began to feel better. As if to celebrate, Huntington broke
his usual injunction against granting interviews and indulged in a long, rambling talk with John Daggett of the *Los Angeles Times.* It was one of the few
occasions on which he spoke openly and frankly about his style of collecting:
"consolidate those private libraries which represent the life efforts of notable

connoisseurs." He also talked about how his library should be evaluated.

> " . . . Please do not mention any monetary figure in connection
> with any books or paintings which I have acquired. I say money has
> nothing to do with it. True value can only be experienced in eons
> of time, by the march of centuries to come and by the uplift of
> humanity."

It was an unusually florid comment and, according to Daggett, after making
it, Huntington turned away to gaze out over the San Gabriel Valley, as if
regretting that he had said so much. To break this introspective mood
Huntington treated his interviewer to a walking tour of the new building.
There was a stop to view the construction in the main reading rooms, a look
at the massive vault, and then a brief examination of two important new
acquisitions, the Bret Harte first editions and the Fort Sutter papers. At the
end of the interview Daggett asked Huntington if he had ever considered
writing his life story. "No, never," Huntington answered, and went on, "I
have been approached regarding a biography. I do not want that. The library
will tell the story."[5] It was the answer Daggett might have expected from this
reticent man.

While making public pronouncements on the future of the library as a
whole, Huntington still involved himself directly in negotiations for relatively minor purchases. In one such case he drove a surprisingly hard bargain,
even though he seemed to have little at stake. In early January 1922 he told
Schad to offer Emil Sauer, a veteran Los Angeles book dealer, $125 for a small
history collection priced at $167. When Schad demurred and suggested a
slightly higher figure—since the dealer had recently suffered a serious family
tragedy with the death of a daughter—Huntington sent back a crisp reply, "I
told you what to do."[6] Sauer packed up his books and left. Where business
was concerned, and in fact where most things were concerned, Huntington
had little room in his make-up for sentiment. Perhaps his firm line with Sauer
also reflected his wish to keep his book budget under control. Huntington
often followed large purchases with small economies; he would often complete the cycle by making substantial purchases again soon.

During the early months of 1922 he decided favorably on three major collections: the Charles Gunther incunabula, the Henry R. Wagner Califor-

niana, and the Britwell Court English literature. Although the items offered at the Christie-Miller sales (1916–27) varied greatly in importance, those listed in the sale catalog for February 1922 included a particularly impressive array of treasures. Again Rosenbach carried a pocketful of bids from San Marino to London. For £21,611 he managed to get all but one of the seventy-eight lots Huntington wanted, including the only known copy of Chaucer's *The Love and Complayntes bytwene Mars and Venus* (1500?) and a volume containing four extremely scarce sixteenth-century pamphlets.[7] After Rosenbach secured Huntington's specific requests, he proceeded to buy two hundred lots for stock—but with a rather clear idea of who the potential buyer might be. In a letter to Huntington he listed the purchases, noting that almost all would be unique holdings. To Rosenbach's satisfaction, if not to his surprise, Huntington wrote a check for £18,000 and took all but fifteen lots. In the midst of these substantial investments Huntington decided to bargain more carefully with Rosenbach for the manuscript copy of the fifteenth-century Towneley (Wakefield) mysteries, a series of thirty-two short miracle plays. In early January he authorized Rosenbach to bid as high as £6,000, but twelve days later cabled to change his limit to £3,500. The wisdom of that move was clear when Rosenbach bought the precious 132-leaf vellum document for £3,400.[8] As if to emphasize his prowess Rosenbach let Huntington in on some of the behind-the-scenes maneuvers at the Britwell sale. He had gone slowly the first day, he told Huntington,

> so that the dealers present could not run me, for if I began by buying everything they could certainly have played havoc with me. As I also informed you I permitted Dring of Quaritch's to purchase a few books for the British Museum and Sir Leicester Harmsworth who collects volumes of theology and religion. Consequently the prices were so extremely low some of the books selling for less than they did fifty years ago. Christie-Miller was terribly disappointed as he expected the total to have been in the neighborhood of £200,000.

Huntington congratulated his agent: "Your mission was a very satisfactory one to me and I do not see how you could have done better than you did." Then, after telling Rosenbach about the splendid spring weather (one sunny

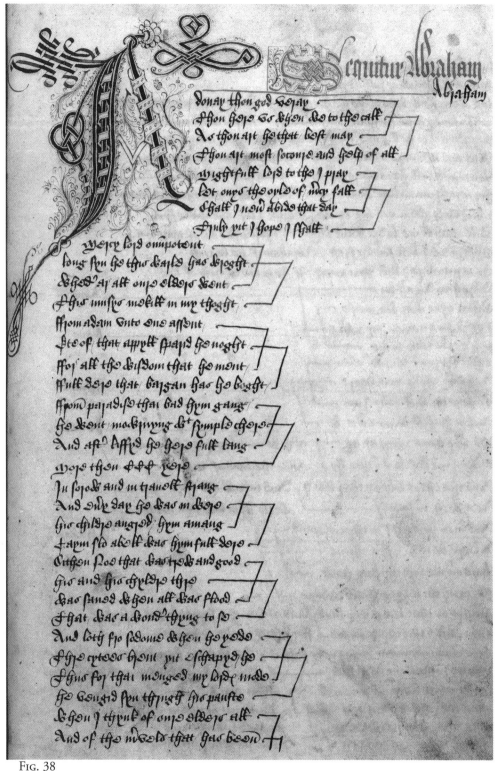

FIG. 38

The manuscript of the Towneley (Wakefield) mystery plays, the first manuscript to be formally accessioned to the collection.

day after another), and the state of his health (better than I have been in a long time), he noted seven duplicates in the latest shipment and told Rosenbach they were his to resell (you have been so kind, I think that you are entitled to the books).[9] Kindness, of course, had nothing to do with it. Rosenbach's ledgers show 1922 as the takeoff year for sales to Huntington. Earlier, Huntington's annual expenditures with the dealer had totaled anywhere from $8,000 to $250,000, but in 1922 they increased to $400,000 and from 1923 to 1925 averaged $1,000,000 annually.

Other spring purchases revived Huntington's interest in two areas of collecting that had lain dormant—early printing and western American history. After a considerable amount of negotiation Huntington offered the book dealer Walter Wyman, acting for the Chicago Historical Society, $25,000 for a collection that included seventy incunabula, four hundred Bibles, seventy-five assorted miniatures, early atlases, Shakespeareana, and a number of sixteenth-century Martin Luther tracts. These had been the property of Charles Frederick Gunther, identified by the autograph specialist Walter Benjamin as one of the greatest collectors of historical documents in America.[10] From Gunther the collection had gone to the Chicago Historical Society where, under conditions set by the heirs, parts of it had to be sold on the open market. Although it was a miscellany, it was the kind of miscellany that Huntington liked. He was particularly pleased to get the incunabula since he knew that ownership of these early European printings would bring immediate prestige to his library. As they had done while building the collection of English literature printed before 1641, Huntington and his library staff enjoyed tabulating their rapidly strengthening position in holdings of incunabula in comparison to those of the British Museum and the Bodleian Library at Oxford.

In the fall, quickly attuned to Huntington's newest enthusiasm, Rosenbach provided two assorted collections totaling 109 incunabula. With vast enthusiasm, Rosenbach described the volumes in a typically impulsive sales letter as "in the finest possible condition, . . . carefully selected, . . . beautifully illustrated," . . . and "a remarkable bargain."[11] Considering the distinguished presses represented and the variety of the titles obtained, Rosenbach's estimate was accurate—the volumes were a bargain. The $34,000 Hunting-

FIG. 39
The Vallard atlas, from the library of Sir Thomas Phillipps, was acquired through Rosenbach.
This leaf shows the landing of the colonists in Canada.

ton invested at the time seems modest enough measured against his expenditure of over $1,500,000 during the next four years for the so-called cradle books of the European presses. In the time remaining to him, it was Huntington's goal to make his collection as distinguished as possible, and buying incunabula seemed a sure route.

A month after Huntington took the Gunther books, he started negotiations with Henry R. Wagner for a sizable California collection. Wagner, the epitome of the scholar-bibliographer, who first became acquainted with Huntington at the Anderson Galleries, considered him an ambitious but unsophisticated collector. Wagner's own style of collecting, built on a lifetime of study and travel, involved the careful analysis of imprints, binding variants, collation, and provenance. In the process of building his own library he had compiled a number of landmark bibliographies, including *The Plains and the Rockies, California Imprints 1846–1851,* and *The Spanish Southwest 1542–1794.* He knew dealers and collectors world-wide, and over the years had established himself as a dominant buyer whenever western and Spanish materials came on the market. The Wagner system was to gather a substantial number of books, publish a bibliography, sell the books, and move on. In 1921, shortly after *The Plains and the Rockies* came out, he decided to clear his shelves for the next venture. At first he planned to distribute the books at auction but changed his mind midway through negotiations with the American Art Association and instead approached Huntington.

Although Wagner felt Huntington had little personal interest in Californiana, he thought he might be able to get him to buy the books out of a feeling of responsibility to the area where he had made his fortune.[12] Over a period of several months the two men exchanged offers and counteroffers. Wagner first asked $80,000 for his three thousand books, manuscripts, and assorted maps, with Huntington to pick up the collection in Berkeley and pay half of the total in cash. Huntington replied, "After a careful consideration of your library lists, I have concluded that eighty thousand dollars is a sum in excess of what I would be willing to pay for your collection. However, I will give you seventy thousand dollars for the collection *delivered here,* twenty thousand dollars payable in cash after unpacking and

Fig. 40
Zuni, New Mexico, depicted in Baduin Möllhausen's *Diary of a Journey from Mississippi to the Coasts of the Pacific* (1858), acquired from Henry R. Wagner.

checking at my library, and the balance of fifty thousand dollars in a personal note payable February 15, 1923."[13] He went on to say that although he knew the collection to be excellent, he had observed a general decline in the market values for Americana, especially in the low prices realized in the last part of the Britwell sale. It was the kind of bargaining both men understood and enjoyed. Wagner finally agreed to Huntington's terms, preferring, as always, to place the books locally rather than see them dispersed in New York. In later years Wagner claimed to have negotiated a "good price."[14]

With his salesmanship now running in high gear, Wagner sliced four hundred dollars from the four thousand he had asked originally for a miscellaneous collection of California pamphlets and newspapers. Next it was time to put his sixteenth-century Mexican imprints on the market. This was a choice assortment indeed, thirty-five titles dating from 1544 to 1600 and most of them from the estate of Count José Maria Sanchez y Agreda. Wagner told Huntington that the collection as it stood was one of the four best in the world and that with the proper development it could easily become the best of all.[15] At first Bliss wrote that the material was outside the library's range of interest, but a month later, in a surprising change of direction—and claiming he had not discussed the matter with Huntington—said he would take the purchase "on his own shoulders" and pay the $6,000 asking price.[16] Years later Wagner commented that the purchase satisfied Huntington on two levels: "He bought my collection of 16th century imprints because I suppose it represented a large section of the total output, and was cheap."[17] Wagner knew his man. Huntington couldn't resist getting a bargain and at the same time dominating a collecting field. Huntington respected Wagner's bibliographical skills and Wagner enjoyed the opportunity to introduce Huntington to new areas in book collecting.[18] Huntington, of course, always reserved the right to set his own limits or simply not to make an offer at all. In 1924, when Wagner asked $6,000 for sixty titles from his splendid collection of Spanish books, the men failed to come to terms. It pained Bliss to write,

> Mr. Huntington has decided to practically go out of the book market for some time, probably meaning till the late summer or early fall. If you are very anxious to sell them now, you had better try some other purchaser, or if not, try me again about next September,

when I might be able to go over the list again, as I know some of
the books at least should be in our collection.[19]

It was a missed opportunity—Wagner sold the books eventually to Herschel
V. Jones—and one of the last times the men did business together. In June
1925, however, Wagner offered Huntington five nineteenth-century maps for
$2,000. When Bliss countered with an offer of $1,250, Wagner replied, "In
view of many courtesies extended by Mr. Huntington and the library I am
inclined to accept any reasonable offer. On the other hand the offer you made
hardly seems adequate." On 2 July he agreed to Huntington's terms: "Your
offer seems to me very inadequate but I do not desire to negotiate with anyone else, so I accept."[20] Although it was Wagner 's opinion that Huntington
was not a "simon-pure collector," and that "there was nothing bookish about
him," he believed nonetheless that Huntington, in gathering a large library,
was making an important contribution to scholarship.[21]

While it was probably true, as Wagner claimed, that Huntington had little substantive interest in California history, his enthusiasm for collecting
American history in general was well established. Beginning with his purchase of the Church library in 1911 and continuing with the acquisition of
the Britwell Court volumes in 1916, he had added Americana regularly.
Huntington was strongly drawn to America's heroes, particularly Washington
and Lincoln. It was not surprising that he should show considerable interest
when Judd Stewart's notable Lincoln library became available. Stewart, an
assiduous Lincoln collector, had spent thirty years accumulating a vast
archive of material—some two thousand printed books along with a wide
range of pamphlets, letters, medals, sheet music, broadsides, engravings, and
newspaper clippings—perhaps the finest Lincoln holding in the country.
Negotiations for the sale stretched over several years. Huntington had no
trouble agreeing to Stewart's requirement that the materials be kept together,
but he would not waver from his top offer, $65,500, a figure the heirs found
unacceptable. The matter remained on the table for over a year, but when no
other buyers came forward the family agreed to Huntington's terms. One of
the star items in the collection was the so-called Ellsworth letter, a note of
condolence in Lincoln's handwriting sent in May 1861 to the parents of the
first Northern officer killed in the war:

"In the untimely loss of your noble son our affliction here is
scarcely less than your own."

It was a moving message and had a special significance for Huntington, who
had suffered the death of his only son, Howard, in March 1922. Howard,
who had assumed some of his father's management responsibilities as vice
president of the Los Angeles Railway Company, had never been in robust
health, but his death came suddenly and was a great shock.

In the midst of this family tragedy—and with bank balances falling around
the country—Huntington moved forward cautiously as several private collections came on the market. Although he had done most of his buying through
dealers or at auction there had always been a stream of direct offers from independent collectors. As the newspapers continued to report Huntington's five-
and six-figure purchases the flow increased. Although most could be dismissed
as worthless, occasionally a letter appeared that deserved careful attention.
During the summer and fall of 1922 three private collections of more than
average interest came to Huntington's notice. The first, a George Washington
library owned by Walter Lewisson of Boston, appeared remarkable both for its
size and quality. In a twenty-year-period Lewisson had gathered what he
proudly called the "largest collection of Washingtoniana in the world"—some
five thousand books, pamphlets, and broadsides; seven thousand periodical
excerpts; and assorted portraits, drawings, and medals.[22] He had limited editions and foreign translations of Washington's own writings, over eight hundred biographies, three hundred editions of the Farewell Address, and some
one thousand orations and eulogies. At first Huntington was skeptical, writing that "my own collection is so big there is little in the way of printed books,
pamphlets and broadsides that I do not have." After seeing the Lewisson list,
he changed his mind.[23] From that point on it was only a matter of money.
Although Lewisson characterized his price, $60,000, as "absurdly low," it was
more than Huntington wanted to pay.[24] Two months earlier he had talked
Wagner into reducing the price of the California books by $10,000—why not
try the same approach with Lewisson? Bliss conveyed Huntington's offer,
$50,000 for the entire library delivered in San Marino and accompanied by
the card catalog. Lewisson agreed but asked that the books be picked up in
Boston, a condition that Huntington accepted.

The purchase of the library was only the beginning of a useful relationship with Lewisson who, at Huntington's request, kept adding Washington items over the next several years. It was a good arrangement, since Lewisson was known in the trade as a collector of modest means and could obtain books at prices far below what Huntington would have had to pay. Huntington's name by this time had come to mean unlimited means, and regardless of economies Huntington or his staff might undertake, any number of book dealers were ready to "pay off the mortgage" with a few good sales postmarked to San Marino. In a letter of 6 January 1923 Lewisson wrote Schad that the price of the Washington books would go up twenty times if Huntington were known to be the buyer.[25]

The next two private collections to come Huntington's way had their roots in the South. In April he received a brief note from a Mrs. John Nicholson of Philadelphia, saying she had read about the library in the *New York Times* and wondered if Huntington would be interested in a collection of Civil War literature. It was a library gathered by her late husband, Lieutenant Colonel John Page Nicholson, and included books, pamphlets, government publications, diaries and journals, general orders, and periodicals, all related to the military history of the war. Many of the books were autographed presentation copies and all, according to Mrs. Nicholson, were in fine condition and beautifully bound. At first Mrs. Nicholson set the price for the collection, estimated to be about seventeen thousand volumes, at $60,000, but when Huntington demurred, dropped to $50,000. When Schad finally had a look at the books, he found that Mrs. Nicholson's count was incorrect, and in fact the library only numbered some ninety-five hundred volumes. Schad handled all the local details, including the awkward matter of the collection's misquoted size, with the utmost diplomacy. Mrs. Nicholson apparently had no idea of the exact content of the library, having made her estimate based on recollections of her husband's conversation. She was pleased to complete the transaction for $30,000 and to place the books under Huntington's care.[26]

Schad supervised the packing of both the Lewisson and Nicholson collections and then traveled south to Richmond, Virginia, to take on an even larger assignment, the examination and shipping of the library of the former secretary of the Virginia Historical Society, Robert A. Brock. Huntington first heard of the Brock collection from Earl G. Swem, the

librarian of the College of William and Mary, who had been engaged by the family to help locate a buyer. Brock had started to collect before the Civil War and added materials up to the time of his death in 1914. Schad, who had seen many fine libraries, was astounded at the size—over 130,000 books and manuscripts—and quality of the Brock collection. In an enthusiastic letter to Huntington he described how the books and manuscripts filled the three-story Brock homestead from cellar to attic. "There is not a single person alive, or for that matter, Mr. Brock himself," he concluded, "aware of just what it contains." In his first hurried examination Schad saw two Washington letters, a Jefferson notebook with 150 pages in his hand, twenty-five letters from Lord Fairfax to Washington, deeds and papers of the early governors of Virginia, orderly books from the Revolutionary and French and Indian wars, Jefferson's own copy of the Virginia laws, Confederate imprints, books from Patrick Henry's library, early Virginia newspapers, Southern almanacs, and prints and pamphlets "on every conceivable subject." Schad made the purchase for $39,000, a price he advised Huntington not to mention since the collection had been offered to several other institutions at a considerably higher figure.[27] A bitter editorial in the *Richmond News Leader* blamed the community for the loss of the books and manuscripts and reminded readers that this was a tale that had been told before, "indifference on the part of the public, inaction from the legislature, then loud indignation at the sale of the treasures."[28]

As far as Elizabeth Brock was concerned the sale had been a complete success. In early November she wrote to Huntington expressing her emotions at parting with her father's collection and her satisfaction with the final disposition.

I feel that I must tell you how grateful we are that my father's library (the result of fifty years gathering) will be kept together. While it was with grief I parted with my life-long friends, and for the past eight years my constant companions, I am glad that they are now the property of another lover of books. . . . I wish to thank you for your promptness in removing the books and the efficient manner in which the removal was effected. In Mr. Schad you have a treasure and with his intelligence, zeal and innate love of books he bids fair to become one of our great book experts. Trusting that the acquisition of our books may give you pleasure.

Huntington responded with comparable warmth,

I can imagine how you must have felt in parting from this library with its many close and loving associations going back through your whole lifetime; but I feel sure it will always be a comfort and satisfaction to you that it has fallen into good hands where it will receive the best of care and be kept intact. After it is properly placed on the shelves and the library ready for use I hope you will be able to see it in its permanent home.

I agree with you, that in Mr. Schad I have a treasure of a book-man, and one who will treat books right because he loves them.[29]

Earlier he had written Schad a more businesslike note: "I am glad the deal is consummated, and think you have done very well."[30] As a result of Schad's efforts, on 10 November Chesapeake and Ohio car 700326 moved west over Southern Pacific tracks carrying sixty thousand pounds of books and manuscripts boxed and labeled for San Marino.

With the rapid flow of books and manuscripts into the library Bliss and Cole became concerned about keeping up with accessions and cataloging. Bliss wrote to Schad, concluding with a remark on the distractions caused by Huntington himself:

When I found out that you were to pack the Brock library, I took one look at that table, completely filled with Wagner books and current acquisitions for inventorying, besides one truck of refer-

ence books, took a long breath, and started. . . . I'll pull through all
right alone if H.E.H.'s coming doesn't ball things up.

Staff responsibilities also included spending time with visiting scholars. Bliss
wrote to Schad, "I am about to propose to Dr. Cole that beginning with
January 1st, all visitors (save H.E.'s) be prohibited for one calendar year to

FIG. 42
The staff of the
library pictured in
front of the new
building in 1922.
From left to right
they are
C. Sorenson,
A. J. Gabler,
W. O. Waters,
R. O. Schad,
C. K. Edmonds,
L. Bendickson,
H. Scott,
G. W. Cole,
Huntington,
C. Cate,
L. Bliss,
P. S. Goulding,
R. Gifford,
H. R. Mead,
C. B. Clapp, and
A. Whitaker.

let us move undisturbed. They've come thick and fast this fall so far." Bliss concluded, "I suppose H.E.H. will be here the last of the week, and then the fun will begin."[31]

As the staff braced themselves for the arrival of the Nicholson, Lewisson, and Brock collections, Rosenbach continued to buy for Huntington at the New York auctions. In November Bliss forwarded firm requests for seventy-

seven lots to be sold at the Henry Cady Sturgis sale but with the warning, "when I say bid these in for us I do not mean to enter into any crazy competition with an unlimited bidder. Also please send me personally a priced copy of this sale, as I am interested to know just how much each item brings." A few months later Bliss chastised Rosenbach for neglecting to check the cataloging details on an eight-dollar western title that had turned out to be a duplicate from the Harold Holmes sale. According to Bliss, Huntington had insisted that the book be sent back for credit. "We want you to verify these books," Bliss wrote somewhat acidly, "with the same care that you would employ when you look at the Elizabethans." This was just too much. Rosenbach shot back, "Your suggestion that we send a representative to examine Western items as closely as I would look at Elizabethan ones interested me. Perhaps you do not know that Western books were my first loves and that we were the first booksellers in America to deal in them on a large scale."[32] Rosenbach deplored this watchdog review by Bliss and and whenever possible corresponded directly with Huntington—avid book dealer to avid book collector.

After the William Sheehan sale—the first to be held in the luxurious new East Fifth-seventh Street galleries of the American Art Association—Rosenbach wrote Huntington that he had passed over books in poor condition in favor of those that were cheap, like Brinton's *The Renaissance* (1908) and Combe's *Napoleon* (1815), both of which, the dealer claimed, sold for less than the cost of their elaborate bindings.[33] Another tactic Rosenbach employed to win approval from favorite customers was the shuffling of competing bids on a single item. In this sensitive balancing act, Rosenbach—and many other dealers—often decided who would have first priority and who would step aside. Although collectors sometimes failed to get items they wanted immediately, they understood the system and knew that the next time it would be their turn.

The system operated with a well-oiled efficiency—especially from the dealer's point of view—as an example involving Huntington and Folger shows. Over the years Rosenbach saw to it that in spite of their similar collecting lines the two men seldom collided. He managed both collectors so well that they remained loyal to him and cordial to each other. Rosenbach's skillful balance on this particular high wire was never better demonstrated than in the case of the 1609 *Pericles*. Folger had two copies, one fine and one imperfect. William A. White had a copy he was willing to sell and Huntington simply wanted to own a copy. Rosenbach saw a way to please everyone. He sold White's copy to Folger for $18,500 and allowed Huntington to buy the flawed Folger copy for an astounding $32,500.[34] For any other dealer it would have been the deal of a lifetime; for Rosenbach it was just business as usual. In another case Rosenbach went so far as to discard an unlimited bid because, as he told Huntington, "I know [Templeton Crocker] never desires to bid against you." Naturally such courtesies had to be returned: at Huntington's request, Rosenbach routinely refused to bid against Walter Hill, who was buying Indian-captivity titles for the noted Chicago collector Edward Ayer.[35] It was enough to confuse any but the initiated. In the end these gentleman's agreements served to bind collectors and dealers together.

In his service to Huntington and other collectors, Rosenbach could be diplomatic or domineering, depending on his particular purpose. At the Robert Emmet sale he abandoned all diplomacy. These were books that Huntington wanted. The chief item in the sale was a well-documented set of the signers of the Declaration of Independence, a collector's icon that finally went for $19,750—some $4,000 over Huntington's stated limit. Rosenbach had to do some quick explaining. For one thing, he told Huntington, competition for the signers had been fierce. The underbidder, William Ball from Muncie, Indiana, had forced the price up beyond the expected levels.

> When you think that an ordinary document of Button Gwinnett sold for $4800 in the [Elliott] Danforth sale in Philadelphia about eight years since you will see that the price paid for this set of the Signers was really a most reasonable one. But what is more important is that fact that the collection was formed by Dr. Emmet who was the greatest authority on the Signers of the Declaration that ever lived.

In a final burst of rhetoric Rosenbach added that the other lots he had purchased were bargains. The extra-illustrated fourteen-volume *Pictorial Field Book of the Revolution* by Lossing, for example, went for $1,200, and according to Rosenbach was the cheapest item ever sold at auction. The autograph material alone, he estimated, would bring a minimum of ten thousand dollars. A wire to Huntington ended with a typical flourish:

congratulations on the finest lot of
illustrated books ever offered for sale.[36]

At times it must have seemed as if Rosenbach would never run out of fine lots, each more remarkable than the last. In July 1922 the dealer sold Huntington a collection of four thousand letters written to James T. Fields, the editor of the *Atlantic Monthly,* by almost every major American literary figure of the nineteenth century. Whittier, Lowell, Emerson, and Holmes, for example, were represented by hundreds of letters on both professional and personal matters. Huntington bought this important literary archive for $12,500—undisputably a bargain. To fill out the library's growing archive of letters from nineteenth-century literary and historical figures Rosenbach next provided Huntington with the personal correspondence of Samuel A. Allibone, long-time editor of *A Critical Dictionary of English Literature and British and American Authors.* A smaller collection than the Field papers, the Allibone purchase added samples of the writing of Bulwer-Lytton, Disraeli, Macaulay, George Bancroft, and W. H. Prescott.

The next irresistible item to come from Rosenbach's bottomless reserve was the Simon Gratz library of American imprints. In a flowery three-page letter Rosenbach spelled out the significance of the books for Huntington and provided a list of the high points. It was, of course, the finest collection of such books ever assembled. Rosenbach had visited with Gratz, a Philadelphia lawyer, and after considerable negotiation obtained a price on the books, "although he did not want to sell them, stating it would be better to give the collection to the Free Library of Philadelphia."[37] The imprints were indeed choice and included Ann Bradstreet's *Poems* (1678), Bacon's *Essays* (1688), the first printed New England election sermon (1664), and best of all, twenty-four books from the Philadelphia and New York presses of William Bradford, the first printer of the middle colonies. According to Rosenbach there would be a minimum of duplication since Huntington owned only one title from the Gratz stock and that one, Keith's *Presbyterian and Independent Visible Churches in New England*, was imperfect. The asking price, $50,000, was extremely low, and Rosenbach assured Huntington that if sold at auction the books would bring at least twice that amount. Under Bliss's microscopic inspection, eighteen duplicates turned up. Back to

Philadelphia went the offer: Huntington would pay $40,000 for the books he lacked if Rosenbach would take the duplicates. Rosenbach did not appreciate having terms dictated to him and replied, "It will be difficult for me at this time of year and just prior to my departure for Europe." It was a sale, however, and he agreed, offering the usual congratulations. He told Huntington that with the Gratz purchase he now owned "the finest collection of Bradford imprints in any collection either public or private."[38]

Huntington had purchased literary manuscripts from time to time over the years but had done so cautiously and without the urge to establish primacy for any particular author or historical figure. He was proud of his Lincoln and Washington collections, but never felt as if he had to control the market for every letter and autograph that came up for sale. As his collection developed in the mid-1920s, however, manuscript acquisition took a more prominent place. Sessler, who had only made a few sales to Huntington since the end of the war, managed to collect $10,675 for a mix of manuscripts of Wilkie Collins, Charles Dickens, Joseph Conrad, Charles Lamb, Lord Byron, and others. On 15 November 1922 Kennerley, still in charge of the Anderson Galleries, sent Huntington a list of manuscripts of Arnold Bennett, Charles Reade, Conan Doyle, Joel Chandler Harris, and Bret Harte. These had been the property of the novelist George Barr McCutcheon and were offered at $3,098, a sacrifice price according to Kennerley, since McCutcheon had come upon hard times and was eager to sell. McCutcheon even agreed to pay the Anderson's ten percent commission.[39] Five days later Kennerley marked the manuscripts sold.

With his growing enthusiasm for manuscripts Huntington offered Harold Hymes $7,500 for thirty-seven items held by the George D. Smith estate. This purchase included twenty-two letters from Queen Victoria to the Duchess of Gordon, Mark Twain's "Playing Courier," and a selection of texts by William Morris, Algernon Charles Swinburne, and Robert Southey. In December, as if to close the year on a triumphal note, Huntington bought twenty-eight letters written in the late 1680s by the Jesuit priest Father Eusebio Francisco Kino. Sent to northwestern Mexico by the Holy See, Kino had been an acute observer and reporter of the customs and culture of the Native Americans of the region. When the letters, rich in local detail, came on the market for £5,500 in a Maggs Brothers catalog, Alice Millard secured them with Huntington in mind as a buyer. Eager to form a good business relationship with her San Marino neighbor she reduced the Maggs total by ten percent and when Huntington asked for a further fifteen percent discount she agreed. For both Huntington and Millard it was a highly satisfactory way to close the year. To Millard's question—"Do you have any objection to its being known that you have purchased them and that the transaction passed through my hands?—Bliss answered "no objection."[40]

During the time the library was housed in New York Huntington made little effort to secure current titles in history, literature, or the arts. His goal was to form a rare book library. This policy changed somewhat after the move to California, when Bliss and Schad took on more responsibility for ordering and collection development. They started to buy from local outlets such as Vroman's in Pasadena and Dawson's in Los Angeles, as well as from a large number of dealers across the country and in England. While shops like P. J. Dobell and Pickering and Chatto in London supplied antiquarian titles exclusively, others, such as Stevens and Brown in London and James F. Drake in New York, sent both antiquarian and modern first editions. The arrangements with Drake, a shrewd dealer and witty raconteur, were mutually beneficial. Huntington had obtained a few scattered items from Drake as early as 1918, but it was not until the summer of 1921 that their relationship blossomed. Following Huntington's directions Bliss sent Drake a letter commissioning him to bid on some two hundred fifty items to be offered at the upcoming John A. Brooke sale in London. According to the letter Drake would use his own judgment on prices; still, as Bliss cautioned, "we do not want to pay prices that are unreasonable but I feel sure you will be able to judge approximately what will be fair bids to place."[41] It was unusual for Huntington to let a dealer proceed with such a large order with no fixed bid limits but in this case he made an exception. Living up to that trust Drake sent Huntington a long report of the sale with careful comments on all items purchased and those passed up— some because of price, others on the basis of condition. By spending just over four thousand pounds Drake obtained important works of Thomas Churchyard, John Milton, Sir Philip Sidney, John Taylor, and George Wither. All of this impressed Huntington and brought Drake another assignment. Bliss asked him to organize a standing-order plan for the library so that first editions of certain living authors—Max Beerbohm, G. K. Chesterton, Joseph Conrad, John Drinkwater, John Galsworthy, Thomas Hardy, and others—would come automatically. This was a major innovation since Huntington had always worked with dealers on a specific item-by-item basis. Between 1922 and 1927, the year of Huntington's death, Drake sent the library hundreds of new books, adding another dimension to the developing collections.[42]

Drake's contribution to the development of the library went far beyond the supply of new books. In the field of modern literature he had a better stock and knew more about prices and condition than either Rosenbach or Sessler. He was also a shrewd politician and knew how to maintain friendly relations with both Mitchell Kennerley at the Anderson Galleries and Thomas Kirby at the American Art Association. With Huntington's bids in hand Drake managed to secure important Tennyson and Swinburne first editions at the Edward Butler sale of April 1922 and choice Americana at the Flora Livingston sale of March 1923. All this was excellent preparation for the major event of the 1923 season, the John Quinn sale.

Chapter 10

WORKING WITH ROSENBACH
1923

John Quinn was one of a kind, a successful and energetic New York lawyer, patron of the arts, man-about-town, aristocratic connoisseur—and monumental egotist. He had started to collect first editions and manuscripts shortly after the turn of the century as a by-product of his acquaintance with the major writers in the Irish literary movement. He bought their early works, recommended their efforts to American publishers, and in general acted as their amiable patron. As his reputation for entrepreneurship grew, he found it easy to strike up friendships with prominent poets and novelists such as Robert Bridges, Ezra Pound, James Joyce, and Joseph Conrad. In the process he gathered more manuscripts and first editions. From Conrad, for example, Quinn was able to obtain many handwritten first drafts and typescripts at extraordinarily modest prices, ranging from three to five hundred dollars. In addition to books, Quinn invested heavily in art and was one of the chief backers of the 1913 Armory Show and the 1921 Metropolitan Museum of Art exhibition of postimpressionists. From the beginning Quinn found it difficult to decide where to invest his time and money. Was he an art collector or a book collector? For a number of years he tried to be both, but early in 1922, with his apartment overflowing with books, paintings, etchings, and sculpture, he decided, with considerable regret, to sell the books. As he said in the introduction to his five-volume auction catalog:

> The agreement was all or nothing, an agreement which has been faithfully adhered to, though parting with certain personal items gave me many a pang. . . . If I attempted to tell all that the books and manuscripts have meant to me, it would require a small volume. . . . I cannot go through or attempt to write about or to tell what these books and manuscripts, which contain a world of beauty and romance or enshrine the records of friendships and of interests and enthusiasms, have meant or mean to me, for they seem to me to be a part of myself, even though I may smile a little at my own feeling.[1]

Quinn and Kennerley had been close friends for years so it was no surprise when the collector chose to sell his books at the Anderson Galleries. For this event, which was scheduled to run as a series of sales from November 1923 to March 1924, Kennerley spared no expense. The abundantly annotated catalog—a collector's item in its own right—was bibliographically precise and aesthetically pleasing. It featured a generous assortment of title-page facsimiles, portraits, and drawings as an attractive graphic supplement to the text.

The Quinn sale offered Drake another opportunity to demonstrate his expertise. He knew the collection intimately, as he wrote Huntington, since he had sold over half of the books to Quinn in the first place.[2] In response to Huntington's bids Drake obtained works of William Blake, Robert Bridges, Bliss Carman, Edmund Gosse, Lady Gregory, and Walter Savage Landor— no spectacular high spots but solid first editions in good bindings. Huntington had pointedly neglected to bid on the most talked-about items in the Quinn collection, the Conrad manuscripts. The listing of these texts in the Anderson's catalog caused great excitement in the Anglo-American book world. When they were placed up for sale on Tuesday evening, 13 November 1923, all the important New York dealers and collectors were on hand to watch the show.

Almayer's Folly, Conrad's first book, started off the run of thirty manuscripts and brought $5,300 from Rosenbach. Gabriel Wells took *Under*

Western Eyes for $6,900. After that Rosenbach had his own way with the other titles, including *Chance, Typhoon, Nostromo, Lord Jim*, and finally *Victory*, for which he gave $8,100—the highest price realized up to that time for a manuscript of a living author. When the bidding was over and the columns of figures added up, the Anderson Galleries had taken in $110,000 for the Conrad manuscripts, to which total Rosenbach had contributed an impressive $72,000.[3] In an unusual move he purchased the manuscripts without any firm bids in hand. With the right approach, he mused, Huntington might be induced to buy. For once the Doctor's superb sales-manship failed him. Huntington was not particularly interested in draft copies of novels and besides, as he wrote Rosenbach, the asking prices were simply too high.[4]

Drake continued to do a steady business with Huntington over the next few years, supplying first editions of literary works on their blanket-order agreement and buying selected items at various New York auctions. In November 1924, for example, Drake held a number of Huntington bids for books to be offered at the sale of William H. Arnold's library. Arnold, known as an author, book dealer, and bibliographer, put together not one but two impressive collections of literary rarities. After selling his first library in 1901 he started all over again, this time concentrating on autograph manuscripts and limited trial editions of literary figures, including Kipling, Keats, and Tennyson. He purchased many of these items through the British bibliographer Thomas J. Wise, who was in 1934 exposed as a consummate forger by John Carter and Graham Pollard, in their *Enquiry into the Nature of Certain Nineteenth Century Pamphlets*. Arnold had once praised Wise, whom he called his "dear old friend," in *First Report of a Book Collector* (1897)—nor were Huntington and Drake any less deceived. With no knowledge of the true nature of many of the items he was buying, Drake went forward with Huntington's bids, securing first editions of works by the Brownings, Morris, Rossetti, and Ruskin. Prices were high, as Drake reported, because "Mr. T. J. Wise of London sent over some large bids on these and Doctor Rosenbach and Mr. W. M. Hill also had some big bids. I had to take items away from them."[5] This careful handling prompted a continued flow of orders from San Marino to Drake's West Fortieth Street New York shop. Drake had won his way into that small circle of dealers whom Huntington trusted.

At about the same time that Huntington started placing orders with Drake he began to experiment with two other New York dealers, Lathrop C. Harper and Edward E. Eberstadt. Harper's stock represented a broad spectrum of Americana, while Eberstadt focused on the western states and territories. Bliss wrote to Eberstadt in the spring of 1923 asking the dealer to bid in ten items in the Charles Eliot Norton and James Terry sale and, as usual, cautioned against paying high prices. The wording of the letter made it clear that the order was given as a test. "We are inclined to let you try your hand for once bidding for us." Bliss wrote, "but you know we are not at all anxious to pay fancy prices so if you see a manuscript or printed book going too high, do not try and see how far you can go just because you are bidding for us." Eberstadt wired an ecstatic reply.

> THANK YOU FOR YOUR LETTER TWENTY SIXTH PERIOD IN APPOINTING ME YOUR LOCAL REPRESENTATIVE ON WESTERN MATERIAL I HAVE ACHIEVED THE AMBITION OF MY CAREER PERIOD UNDER SUCH CIRCUMSTANCES IT IS IMPOSSIBLE TO TELL YOU HOW MUCH I APPRECIATE THE HONOR BESTOWED AND YOUR CONFIDENCE AND KINDNESS IN THE APPOINT-MENT PERIOD SUCH KNOWLEDGE OF THE WESTERN MARKET AS IS MINE MY EFFORTS AND SERVICES MR. BLISS ARE YOURS TO COMMAND PERIOD I INTEND TO MERIT YOUR CONFI-DENCE AND CONSIDERATION.[6]

Eberstadt—characterized as "poker-faced" by book dealer Charles Heartman —did his work well and secured almost all the items Huntington wanted.[7] In a two-page letter Eberstadt explained how the sale had gone and encouraged Huntington and Bliss to continue to use his services. He reminded them that he often represented William R. Coe and Templeton Crocker, two active western collectors, and promised to make arrangements for those men to "step aside in some cases where there is a decided wish to secure a certain piece with the understanding that you too will be agreeable to let them in a similar case have other items they may desire."[8] It was the familiar quid pro quo system that Rosenbach had employed for years. Between 1922 and 1925 Huntington and Bliss used Eberstadt intermittently for small orders but never expanded the connection beyond that level.

With Lathrop Harper, a dealer of broader experience, Huntington's relationship was closer and of longer duration. Even before the library moved to California in 1920 Harper was on friendly terms with Huntington and visited frequently at the Fifty-seventh Street residence.[9] After 1920 Huntington used Harper regularly at sales where his extensive knowledge of Americana would be a factor. In March 1923, for example, Harper bought forty-two lots in the William Winters sale, including one item Huntington had identified as "very much" wanted, a unique 1848 printing of California laws. After a spirited exchange of bids with a representative of Harvard University, Harper secured the rarity for $3,150 and reported, "It seemed to me that it was an item that you simply had to have, and I was prepared to bid at least twice [what] it sold for if I had been pressed—fortunately this was not necessary."[10] The following month Harper carried forty-five Huntington bids to the Norton-Terry sale, the same event that Eberstadt, with ten bids, had jubilantly thought was his private preserve. Bliss cautioned Harper to avoid "ultra-fancy competition" but if possible to get three George Washington letters which, as he told the dealer, "would be very welcome to us if the total could be kept under $1,800." After the sale Harper reported that since prices had been "very uneven," he had experienced some success and some failure; he had been able to get the first American edition of *Hamlet* for the modest figure of $17.50, but had to pass up the Washington letters as they rose to $2,710.[11]

Harper's most important purchase for Huntington involved the sale of the colonial papers of General James Abercromby. The archive, including military memoranda, personal letters, and acts of Parliament, covered 1758–59, when Abercromby was in command of the British forces in North America. Harper assured Huntington that $13,500 was a reasonable price and that the collection would be a perfect supplement to the Loudoun papers that he had purchased the previous spring. Huntington agreed and added the Abercromby papers to his growing collection of primary materials on the American Revolutionary War. After 1924 Huntington and Harper did business regularly but on a reduced scale. Huntington directed almost all of his large orders to Rosenbach, and Harper found his time absorbed by other collectors, including William L. Clements, John B. Stetson, Jr., Henry Wagner, Alfred Chapin, and John H. Scheide.

For the purchase of the Loudoun papers in April 1923 Huntington employed the services of the renowned British art dealer and long-time family friend Joseph Duveen. In 1909 and 1910, when Huntington was putting the finishing touches on his San Marino home, Duveen supplied the art for the interior—paintings, sculpture, and a set of the famed Beauvais tapestries. He continued to sell important paintings to the Huntingtons during and after the war—Hoppners, Romneys, Raeburns, Constables, and Gainsboroughs—a galaxy of beautiful ladies and handsome gentlemen in stately poses, surrounded by idyllic children and harmonious landscapes. In 1913 he helped the Huntingtons settle into the Chateau Beauregard outside Paris and later, when staffing became too difficult, made himself available as their agent to dispose of the excess furniture and art works. In late 1921, after lengthy negotiations, Huntington paid Duveen a staggering £182,200 for what was to become one of the main attractions of his art museum, Thomas Gainsborough's *The Blue Boy*.[12] Although Duveen never handled rare books or manuscripts as part of his regular trade, he was constantly exposed to fine libraries in both England and Europe. Sometimes he would take on books along with other household goods simply to please an important client. In 1923 he agreed to act as intermediary when Lady Loudoun wanted to dispose of her family papers—an archive of some ten thousand documents relating to the Jacobite rebellions of 1715 and 1745 and to the campaigns of the American Revolution, in which her great-grandfather, John Campbell, fourth Earl of Loudoun, had served as commander-in-chief of the British forces. Duveen's wire to Huntington indicated that he felt the papers could be obtained for much less than the twenty thousand pounds Lady Loudoun had asked and that, in fact, Sothebys had suggested a value of twelve thousand. That was exactly what Huntington wanted to hear. In May he paid the Sotheby price and became the new owner of the Loudoun papers.

In December, encouraged by his success with the Loudoun archive, Duveen tried to interest Huntington in a set of 260 letters written by Lord Chesterfield to his godson. These were in the possession of Lord Carnarvon and estimated to be worth twelve thousand pounds, a price Huntington thought was much too high. Duveen, looking for directions, wired:

MAY I ASK IF YOU MEAN THAT I MUST DROP MATTER OF LET-
TERS ENTIRELY OR MUST I ENDEAVOR SECURE REDUCTION
PRICE STOP PERSONALLY I HAVE NO IDEA OF VALUE SUCH
THINGS AND WOULD APPRECIATE YOUR GUIDANCE BECAUSE
IF I TELEGRAPH FLAT REJECTION THEY WILL PROBABLY GO
ELSEWHERE AND ULTIMATE BUYER WOULD SECURE THEM
LOW PRICE THEREFORE PRAY GIVE ME SOMETHING TO WORK
UPON STOP IF YOU REALLY THINK YOU MAY ULTIMATELY
WANT THEM WHY NOT LET ME NEGOTIATE A LITTLE KIND
REGARDS.

In this case Huntington was not in a mood to bargain, and he told Duveen that because the value placed on the documents was far above his own estimate he saw no need to make an offer.[13]

By June 1923 the flow of books and manuscripts into the library had accelerated to an alarming degree. In an eighteen-month period, besides the sizable Lewisson, Nicholson, and Brock collections, Huntington had added a large number of titles from the Britwell, Quinn, Sturges, and Severance sales. During this same period he acquired the Gunther and Rosenbach incunabula, set up the standing order arrangement with Drake for current literature, and added a large number of early English titles from Brigham, Maggs Brothers, Pickering and Chatto, and Quaritch. Bliss summed up the struggle to contain the deluge somewhat wistfully in a letter to a friend: "Everything goes well but the capacity for work of our staff seems unable to keep abreast of Mr. Huntington's capacity for purchasing."[14] Huntington was not unmindful of the situation and in June 1923 decided to act. He wrote Cole in peremptory fashion from New York:

> Until my return I do not wish to order another book for the Library or the Catalogue room. In fact I do not care to have checked up the catalogues that come, as it is my plan to concentrate on two things, getting the books into the stack, and giving all possible time of the men on the Catalogue.[15]

This stern decree was in line with Cole's own priorities. Almost all the books that had been shipped from New York three years earlier were still in packing crates. It was difficult enough to work from lists to be sure of what the library owned but impossible to use them to judge such variables as binding condition or the quality of illustration. Work on the "Brief Catalogue of the Library of Henry E. Huntington: English Literature to 1640," begun so energetically by Cole in 1916, had come to a stop. Finally, there was the question of money. Huntington's resources were vast but not unlimited. What should he budget for books, paintings, sculpture, and the gardens? How much should he set aside for the estate? How much would be needed to carry on the management and development of the library and art collections after he died? For a seventy-three-year-old man in poor health these were serious questions. Having spent approximately a million dollars a year on books and manuscripts for twelve years, Huntington knew it was time to organize what he had. Letters of rejection began to outnumber letters of acceptance. In July he wrote Cole concerning a Milton manuscript: "I would say that while the item seems desirable, I am too poor to think of buying."[16] On E. D. North's letter offering the manuscript of Hawthorne's *Our Old House,* Huntington scribbled a one-word answer—"no." Even Kennerley came away empty-handed when, after offering Huntington a particularly fine portrait of Edgar Allan Poe, he heard back, "I already have a good portrait of Poe."[17]

In this mood of austerity it was easier for Huntington to turn down individual items than to resist well-organized collections, especially if Rosenbach was the agent. The Rosenbach ledger sheets tell the story. In 1922 Huntington spent $411,675 with the Philadelphia firm, a figure that he increased to an impressive $881,588 in 1923.[18] One of Rosenbach's first assignments from Huntington in 1923 was to place bids at the Herschel V. Jones sale. The mercurial Jones had established himself as one of the most active buyers and traders in the postwar American rare book market. He bought from Rosenbach and Sessler as long as he could afford it and when his funds ran low sold what he could at the Anderson Galleries. At the same time he kept a steady barrage of offers on Americana and English literature flowing to Huntington and his staff. Perhaps, Jones suggested, Huntington would like to swap a few Wagner duplicates for some "important Westerns." Huntington showed no interest. Then there was the matter of the Sir Walter Scott manuscript. According to Jones, Huntington ought to own the manuscript of a major Scott novel and by a happy coincidence he had one to sell.

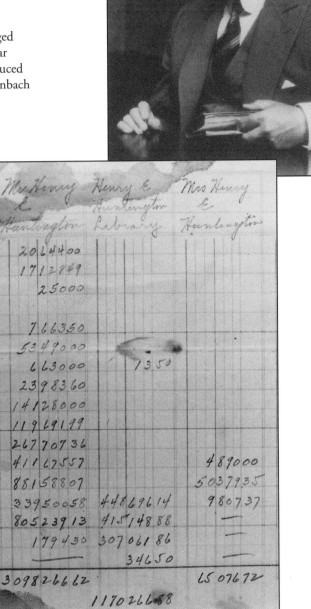

FIG. 43
Between 1923 and 1925,
Huntington's purchases
through Rosenbach averaged
one million dollars per year
(both photographs reproduced
by permission of the Rosenbach
Museum).

	Mrs Henry E. Huntington	Henry E. Huntington Library	Mrs Henry E. Huntington
1911	2024400		
1912	1712849		
1913	25000		
1914			
1915	766350		
1916	5349000		
1917	663000	1350	
1918	2398360		
1919	1428000		
1920	11969199		
1921	26770736		
1922	4162557		489000
1923	8815880 7		5037935
1924	33950058	44869614	980737
1925	80523913	41514888	—
1926	179430	30706186	—
1927	—	34650	—
	30982662		6507672
		11702668 8	

Wouldn't Huntington like to buy *The Pirate*? According to Jones, the manuscript was a bargain at $10,000. After some lighthearted haggling between Jones and Bliss, Huntington turned it down as being out of his range of interest.[19] Jones, who always had one eye on profits, argued constantly about prices asked by other collectors and assumed a prickly attitude if anyone had the audacity to question his. In the spring of 1922, when Schad made a special trip to Minnesota to look at some duplicates in the Jones library, he found bargaining impossible because "what I most wanted, he wanted to keep."[20]

When Jones placed his Elizabethans on the market in 1923, it was the third collection he had auctioned at the Anderson in as many years. The sale catalog reproduced a letter from Jones to Kennerley explaining some of the collector's motivations:

> After the disposal, four years ago, of my library of English Literature I proceeded to collect one hundred rare Elizabethan books, with accompanying minor, but important volumes, for the sole purpose of giving me comfort in the time of bereavement over the loss of my friends. Instead of proving a comfort, I find myself miserable in being compelled to face the impossibility of collecting another English Library. I shall be happier with none than with the few. Therefore, I am sending them to you for disposal.[21]

Rosenbach made a point of telling Huntington he had risen from his sickbed to attend the sale, but in fact there were only twenty items the California collector wanted. The bulk of the books went to John Clawson and Henry Folger, collectors with longer Elizabethan desiderata lists than Huntington. In reporting the disappointing monetary returns Rosenbach wrote somewhat sanctimoniously that he didn't think it was quite proper for a private collector to speculate. That being the case, he sniffed, perhaps Jones got what he deserved. [22] None of this did any permanent harm to the friendship between Jones and Rosenbach, and in fact they bought and sold happily together almost up to the time of Jones's death in 1928. With Huntington it was the same. Although the two collectors followed completely different paths they remained congenial friends, full of respect for each others' horse-trading instincts.[23]

Immediately after the Jones auction Rosenbach took on a more serious assignment for Huntington, handling his bids for the next Britwell sale in London. As usual there was plenty to choose from. In two letters, each dense with lot numbers, Bliss outlined Huntington's priorities. First there were one hundred and fifty items designated "please buy," then one hundred thirty more covered by the note "We are interested in the following if offered at what we consider reasonable figures."[24] For Rosenbach, the 1923 Britwell sale raised the old question of conflicting bids to a new level of intensity. In this case Rosenbach needed all his vaunted diplomacy to keep White, Folger, and Huntington happy with him and with each other. First it was a matter of sorting out several titles wanted by both White and Huntington. This was settled fairly easily after Rosenbach pointed out to Huntington that he already owned lots 432, *Lucanus* (1600), and 559, *King Edward* (1596). The conflict between Folger and Huntington over lot 42, Richard Barnfield's *Cynthia* (1595), described as "of the utmost rarity," was somewhat more delicate. Rosenbach, rushing to leave for England and not wanting to go through intermediaries, wrote directly to Huntington. Interest in *Cynthia*, he told his client, had been intense. White, Folger, and Clawson had all made offers and made them before Huntington had sent his bid. According to Rosenbach, Folger felt it was "only right" that the *Cynthia* should go to him, since he had been "very nice" in a number of other cases deferring to Huntington. With the gently persuasive, "I know that under the circumstances you will agree with him," the Doctor made the negotiation sound final. Rosenbach closed his letter on a positive note: "On account of this arrangement where none of the American collectors are bidding against each other, I think you will obtain [the items you want] at prices that will please you." Huntington expressed his satisfaction: "regarding the conflicting bids, I would say that it is of course right that you should consider his bid on the 'Cynthia.'" Then, in the spirit of bon voyage, he closed, "I hope your trip will be pleasant in all ways—financially and physically and I might add that I also may be benefited."[25]

Once in London the Doctor dominated the week-long sale, accumulating a billing of £53,385 against the grand total of £63,336. Huntington's share, £45,375, included hundreds of fine Elizabethans and one extraordinary American imprint. While examining the books before the sale Rosenbach had spotted an undistinguished-looking copy of Philip Pain's *Daily Meditations: or, Quotidian Preparations for and Considerations of Death and Eternity*, a small octavo with a woodcut border, printed by Marmaduke Johnson in Cambridge in 1668. After a brief exchange of bids Rosenbach bought the book for £51, a price he jubilantly reported to Huntington as "the greatest bargain I ever secured." "Cambridge" in this case was Cambridge, Massachusetts, and the book, overlooked by all the other dealers, turned out to be the first volume of verse printed in North America, worth between seven and eight thousand pounds.[26]

In addition to the Britwell books Rosenbach's chief purchases for Huntington in 1923 included the James Ellsworth incunabula, the Battle Abbey papers, the Wilberforce Eames Americana, and a number of the Sir Thomas Phillipps incunabula. Phillipps, born in 1792 and raised in privileged circumstances, spent his entire adult life acquiring books and manuscripts. His stated desire was simply to own a copy of every book printed. Shortly after his death in 1872 the library, some sixty thousand manuscripts and fifty thousand printed books, passed first into the hands of his daughter Mrs. J. E. A. Fenwick and then to her son, T. FitzRoy Fenwick, a shrewd businessman who cared little for books personally but was well aware of their value. Beginning in 1886 he placed portions of the library up for sale at Sothebys and dispersed other volumes in private arrangements with various European libraries. The break-up of the library was further assured when in April 1923 Fenwick met Rosenbach and invited him to examine the books at Thirlestaine House in Cheltenham. Rosenbach knew all about the Phillipps library with its vast ranges of Americana, English history, and incunabula. Recently Huntington had been showing more interest in obtaining examples of printing from the first European and British presses. Rosenbach was there to help. He bought 760 Phillipps incunabula, mostly religious titles, for £20,250 ($92,593) and sold them immediately to Huntington for $150,000.[27] This was only the beginning.

On his first visit to the rambling Phillipps family residence in Cheltenham, the Doctor had seen a set of early English historical documents that he felt sure would appeal to his favorite customer. These ninety-seven folio volumes, made up of court rolls, family papers, charters, and Compotus Rolls, some dating to the thirteenth century, were identified with the Abbey of St. Martin founded by William the Conqueror and thus known as the Battle Abbey papers. These precious volumes were protected by law and could not be sold without authorization from the Chancery Courts. Rosenbach set the wheels in motion and after a six-week waiting period obtained the needed confirmation. In late November, he bought the muniments from Fenwick for $18,000 and turned them over to Huntington for $50,000. This was a good piece of business but more was to come. The Phillipps shelves now provided some twenty early English manuscripts from the fourteenth and fifteenth centuries—three manuscripts of the *Canterbury Tales,* Brut's *Chronicles of England,* and various renderings of Thomas Hoccleve, John Lydgate, and Robert Langland. The manuscripts were, Rosenbach wired, THE FINEST LOT OF EARLY ENGLISH POEMS AND PROSE THAT HAS EVER BEEN OFFERED FOR SALE. Fenwick had refused to sell this part of the collection in the past, according to Rosenbach, since it was one of his favorites, but after conferring with several family members now felt ready to do so for the sake of the estate. Rosenbach bought the twenty manuscripts from Fenwick for $52,900 and sold fourteen of the choicest to Huntington for $92,000.[28]

Rosenbach's older brother Philip, who engineered the purchase for the firm, judged correctly when he predicted that the sale of the Fenwick manuscripts would bring an "extra large profit."[29] By the time Rosenbach returned to England in 1924 Fenwick had uncovered another layer of documents he wished to sell, the eleventh-century manuscript Bible of Bishop Gundulf, ten volumes of the William Blathwayt American Colonial Papers, and a dozen sixteenth-century Portolan maps. The path from Thirlestaine House to San Marino was by now so well traveled that Huntington was ready to accept the collection for $150,000 almost before Rosenbach made the offer.[30] Over a period of eighteen months Huntington had spent $442,000 on Phillipps books and manuscripts—enough to deplete anyone's bank balance. In April 1924 he wrote to the dealer Walter Wyman, "At present I am buying very little. As perhaps you have read in the papers Dr. Rosenbach is just returning from England with a fortune in books, etc. and while only a part of it is for me there are enough to make a bill of unusual size."[31]

In addition to the Phillipps items Rosenbach brought back some three hundred incunabula from the Charles Thomas-Stanford library and an

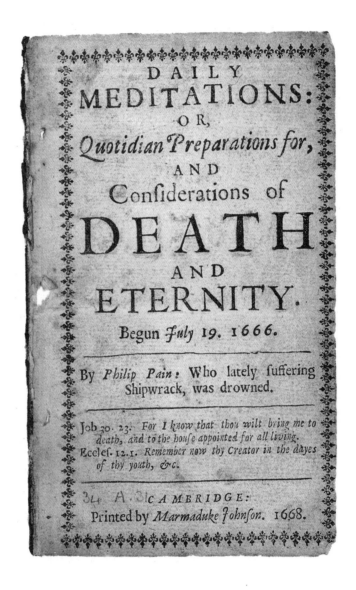

DAILY
MEDITATIONS:
OR,
Quotidian Preparations for,
AND
Confiderations of
DEATH
AND
ETERNITY.
Begun *July* 19. 1666.

By *Philip Pain:* Who lately fuffering
Shipwrack, was drowned.

Job 30. 23. *For I know that thou wilt bring me to
death, and to the houfe appointed for all living.*
Ecclef. 12.1. *Remember now thy Creator in the dayes
of thy youth, &c.*

CAMBRIDGE:
Printed by *Marmaduke Johnfon.* 1668.

Fig. 44
The only known copy of the first volume of verse printed in English in North
America. This Britwell book, misidentified in a sales catalog, was recognized as a
bargain by A. S. W. Rosenbach, and he passed the savings along to Huntington.

assortment of "fifteeners" from London's various antiquarian shops. Since Huntington was eager to build an outstanding incunabula collection Rosenbach needed to keep a stock on hand.[32] The Thomas-Stanford volumes, particularly strong in Italian printings of the Greek and Roman classics, went quickly to Huntington for $82,000, followed by a second collection of three hundred titles formerly owned by Lathrop Harper for $97,000. Then, in the next few months, Rosenbach sent two more incunabula collections west, one hundred titles from the Wilhelm Richter collection with another two hundred fifty drawn from stock. The billing that accompanied these purchases totaled $190,000.

In the course of this frenzied buying and selling Rosenbach's fine-tuned system suffered a nearly fatal breakdown. In one of the shipments to Huntington a careless packer included invoices showing the original costs to Rosenbach. Everyone knew that the dealer made a handsome profit, but to allow the exact markup to be displayed so blatantly would have been a serious mistake. Immediate action was needed. Rosenbach, using air transportation for the first time in his life, flew to California and arrived just ahead of the incriminating documents. He later told his brother Philip that the adventure had cost the firm one thousand dollars. That figure matched the amount entered in the Rosenbach ledgers as paid to George Hapgood, Huntington's personal secretary.[33] Hapgood was a useful friend. In exchange for an abundant supply of Rosenbach charm, Havana cigars, and incidental favors, he kept the Doctor apprised as to Huntington's moods, his health, and the general flow of activities at the ranch.[34]

Ordinarily the Rosenbach shop ran with a precision that brought customers back time after time. When William A. White wanted to sell some of his Elizabethan treasures secretly, Rosenbach managed the complicated arrangements with masterful style. He sold Huntington thirty-five of the White rarities in 1923 for $260,000, requesting that all details be kept quiet. "This is a confidential matter between Mr. White and myself," he wrote, "and neither of us desires that it should become public. Even Miss [Henrietta] Bartlett [White's bibliographer] does not know of these transactions and we are anxious to preserve the utmost secrecy in regard to them." Cole wrote back that although he would try to observe confidentiality, keeping such an important transaction secret would be almost

impossible, and he warned that "the suppression of the provenance will
. . . I fear cause us considerable embarrassment in explaining how these
books came to be in the Huntington Library."[35]

Another example of the Doctor's shrewd salesmanship involved the dispersal of the James Ellsworth library. Ellsworth, a midwestern collector who
had made his fortune in the coal fields of West Virginia and Ohio, had gathered an impressive library including a set of Shakespeare folios, a paper copy
of the Gutenberg Bible, a complete set of the Signers of the Declaration of
Independence, various Washington and Lincoln letters, one hundred
incunabula, and the 1502 King-Hamy Portolan map. Rosenbach bought the
library in 1923 and promptly distributed the rarities to some of his favorite
customers. Eldridge Johnson took the four folios, John H. Schiede the
Gutenberg Bible, and Huntington happily bought the incunabula and the
King-Hamy map, described by Rosenbach as the "finest piece of early Americana that has been ever [*sic*] offered for sale."[36]

At the Henkels auction rooms in January 1924 Rosenbach managed to
secure almost all of Huntington's bids in the sale of the papers of Gideon
Welles, Lincoln's secretary of the navy. The prize of the sale, lot 41, Lincoln's
23 August 1864 letter to Welles on the discouraging state of the presidential
campaign, went for $1,250—a great bargain according to Rosenbach. The
Welles papers added another strength to the already important Civil War
archive.

The year that had begun for Huntington with the purchase of the
Simon Gratz library of American imprints, and had seen him add important collections of incunabula and historical documents, now closed with
one more impressive acquisition—the early American printing gathered by
the ascetic bibliophile Wilberforce Eames. Of the several collections formed
by Eames, a distinguished staff member of the New York Public Library,
the American imprints collection was perhaps the most important. It
included some thirteen thousand pieces—books, pamphlets, and broadsides—illustrating the origin of printing in the states and territories, cities
and towns, throughout the United States. One of the major selling points
was the collector himself. With a well-founded reputation as a meticulous
bibliographer, based on his work on Joseph Sabin's *Dictionary of Books
Relating to America*, Eames had come to be recognized as an international

authority on all matters relating to American printing. Book dealers and collectors made constant use of his expertise and relied absolutely on his judgment. Rosenbach, who viewed most librarians as harmless drones, identified Eames as the greatest student of books in the whole history of scholarship.[37] He bought the Eames collection for $65,000 less fifteen percent, and in a profitable turnaround sold it to Huntington for $65,000 plus ten percent. Although Rosenbach concluded these arrangements in October 1923, the collection didn't arrive in San Marino until the end of the following year, since Eames insisted on personally labeling and packing each group of books by the name of the city in which they originated. Huntington, always impressed by careful work habits, agreed that the bibliographer should be given as much time as necessary. In early 1924 Rosenbach wrote that the "Herculean task" was going even more slowly than anticipated; Eames had wrapped the first sixty-five bundles but was only as far as "B" for Boston.[38] By the end of the year, however, the entire collection was classified, labeled, and shipped to San Marino—a jewel in the library's Americana holdings.

In view of Huntington's large investment with Rosenbach it was appropriate for the dealer to acknowledge the growing importance of the Huntington library. Toward the end of 1923, a year when the collector spent nearly one million dollars with the Rosenbach firm, the *New York Times* quoted the Doctor at length on skyrocketing book prices and determined collectors—among whom none, according to Rosenbach, was more determined than Huntington. After a passing mention of J. P. Morgan and his "wonderful library" of illuminated manuscripts, Rosenbach launched into a bravura tribute.

> Henry E. Huntington's achievement, in making his collection of English literature is unrivaled in the history of book collecting and is, in my mind, a greater achievement than the building of the pyramids or the Panama Canal. Mr. Huntington has been continually on the alert for the last fifteen years gathering, selecting, eliminating, and always improving his library. It is nothing short of a miracle that such a collection as his should have been formed in a period of only fifteen years.[39]

For the public press it may have been politic to describe Huntington's achievement as a miracle, but looked at in pure business terms the miracle was more a matter of supply and demand—and in the portions of the collection secured through Rosenbach, a matter of a shrewd dealer with an extraordinary ability to discern rarities and a collector with almost unlimited means.

Chapter 11

AN OUTSTANDING ENDOWMENT
1924–1925

As he approached his seventy-fourth birthday in February 1924, Huntington had many reasons to feel content with life. His predictions for the growth of Southern California had been borne out abundantly, his second marriage was a satisfying joy, and the San Marino ranch had fulfilled all his expectations. The estate had prospered under the direction of the board of trustees established by the indenture of 1919, and the book and art collections had grown substantially.[1] In May of the previous year he had been pleased when the state senate of California passed a resolution praising the Huntington Foundation and its goals of "educational, artistic and cultural benefit of the people of California and the United States." The resolution went on to say that the library was "acknowledged to be the most complete and valuable assembling of literature known to the world." With its art collections rivaling those of distinguished European galleries and its botanical gardens representing trees and plants from all over the world, the institution as a whole was "recognized as one of the most outstanding endowments of the century."[2]

On the negative and more personal side, both the Huntingtons had recently been plagued with serious health problems. Mrs. Huntington's eyesight had deteriorated to the point where she was almost blind and

Huntington himself had suffered a variety of serious respiratory and intestinal disorders. The winter in California however seemed to do them both good. Certainly for Huntington the mild California weather always provided a psychological as well as a physical boost. He had once written to Kennerley of a late December: "We read with interest—and with pity—of [your] weather. . . . Here we frequently sit out of doors, and are now beginning the third week of cloudless skies and bright sunshine."[3]

Huntington's relationship with Rosenbach had grown closer over the years, to the point where the Philadelphia dealer was always a welcome houseguest at the ranch. Still, this was a business partnership; they were never on a first-name basis. Huntington reserved that intimacy for his family and a few close friends. If in his dealings with book dealers Huntington kept a tight control over the social proprieties, he kept an even tighter control over the balance sheets. As a result of his early training in the railroad business, under the watchful eye of Uncle Collis, Huntington kept meticulous records of his own financial transactions. He was ever fond of repeating one of Collis's favorite homilies, "It isn't what you earn but what you save that counts."[4] He knew down to the dollar what had been spent, what was pending, where the money would come from, and under what conditions and over what time period it would be paid. Because of his precise awareness of his own financial condition, however, he sometimes would call a halt and announce himself "out of the market." It was a simple method of balancing his accounts, and one that he employed even after his estate had increased to the point where he could have gone on buying almost indefinitely. He declared such a pause in the spring of 1924, just before he turned over to his trustees a two-year accumulation of books and paintings valued at $4,100,000.[5] It was again time to take stock. When Sessler wrote that he had a collection of Americana that would be a splendid acquisition as well as a genuine bargain at $200,000, Huntington replied crisply, "I have received your letter of the 15th and all I can say is I have nothing to say."[6]

But Rosenbach was ever the exception. Even as Huntington sent out letters of rejection to most dealers Rosenbach continued to sell him a rich assortment of books and manuscripts. This arrangement suited the Doctor perfectly and supported his theory that rules made for others did not apply to him. In January 1924 Rosenbach sent Huntington the proof sheets for the next Britwell sale, pointing out that since there would again be competing bids from Henry Folger, John L. Clawson, Carl H. Pforzheimer, and William A. White, an early reply would be appreciated. Then, just to prove that he traveled in the right circles, Rosenbach described a potential acquisition from Spain, the library of the Duke of Veragua. This collection, made up of books and documents relating to Christopher Columbus, had up to that time never been examined by a dealer. "I know the Duke's cousin, the Duke of Berwick and Alba, also a descendant of Columbus," Rosenbach boasted, "who promised to give me every aid. He told me, if I could find his cousin, the Duke of Veragua, in a receptive mood, and at that particular moment short of ready money, I could probably effect a deal."[7] Huntington showed no interest in the Duke's library but did place orders for a substantial number of the Britwell books. In a letter of 18 February he asked Rosenbach to bid in some two hundred seventy lots, and two days later wrote again and added fifty more. Rosenbach acknowledged the order with a wry comment.

> Perhaps if we are lucky I can buy a few unnoticed nuggets for a song, as in previous sales, but I do not anticipate a "coup" like in the last when I purchased the only copy known of the first New England poems for the price of a second-hand book of sermons. But you can never tell.[8]

Over the eight days of the sale Rosenbach equaled his performances of the previous three years, bidding higher than anyone else and capturing the important lots. The London *Times*, after listing a few of the most expensive items, grouped everything else under the rubric, "Dr. Rosenbach also bought the following books, except where otherwise indicated." Among the items secured for Huntington were the "exceedingly rare" copy of the first edition of Edmund Allen's *A Catechisme* (1548); the Ireland-Herbert-Woodhouse-Heathcote-Dent-Heber copy of Richard Pynson's printing of Alexander Barclay's *Fourth Eclogue,* with Heber's flyleaf inscription "I know of no other copy"; and also from the Heber collection the only known copy of Henry Constable's *Diana. The Praises of His Mistres, in Certaine Sweete Sonnets* (1592)—the highest priced item of the sale, reaching £2,700.[9] Rosenbach wrote from the Carlton Hotel that "the prices were as a rule moderate, some high but many *great bargains.*" Then, almost with a wink, as if to demonstrate his loyalty to the Huntington cause, he added, "I only let Mr. Folger have three items out of nearly fifty!"[10] For the privilege of securing 249 lots of Britwell treasures Huntington paid £48,914, a high water mark for him at a single London auction.

In the midst of all this euphoria there was an occasional cry of protest. During World War I Huntington had done a considerable amount of business with the Bernard Quaritch firm, using them as his chief agent for the early Huth sales. Since 1919, however, he had sent Quaritch only occasional direct orders. In July 1924 E. H. Dring wrote to remind Huntington that his firm still stood ready to provide good service and substantial discounts.

> For some years now, you have not entrusted me with your commissions for the London sales. I have never demurred at your having discontinued doing so because I have always thought that you, being a business man, would have considered carefully whether it would be to your real advantage to put them into the hands of other agents than myself. I myself feel that you would save a very large amount by putting your commissions in my hands, but if, on the other hand, you are content with your present agents, please disregard this letter.

Huntington answered:

> I wish to assure you that I have no personal feeling against the Quaritch Corporation, although I felt a little dissatisfied at one time about orders for books purchased by you going to other patrons—just what they were I have at this time forgotten. As Dr. Rosenbach attended all important sales in London my opportunity for consultation was better with him than with others so far away. At any rate, let me assure you again that I have no feeling towards your company except the kindest.

Dring was unhappy to hear that his firm had overlooked any books Huntington wanted and explained in a four-page letter that during his eleven years in charge of the firm's book operations Huntington's bids had always been given first preference.

There are, I know, a few instances where I have deemed it advisable not to be gulled by ridiculously high reserves fixed by the auction-eers or owners and have let such lots go back to the owners. I have had forty-five years experience of English books and one lesson I have learned is that one can be too submissive in allowing one self to be dominated by the man in the rostrum.[11]

The matter was left as a standoff; Huntington continued to do most of his London business with Rosenbach and Dring continued to resent it.

After savoring his good fortune at the Britwell sale and learning of Rosenbach's sweep of incunabula from the Phillipps, Thomas-Stanford, and Richter collections, Huntington headed east. Mrs. Huntington had been in poor health for several months and, as usual, wanted to avoid the heat of the California summer. Once she arrived in New York, however, her condition worsened and on 16 September, in the gray Romanesque castle Collis had built for her on Fifty-seventh Street, she died.

Arabella Duvall (Yarrington) Worsham Huntington, born about 1850 in Virginia, left behind an unhappy early marriage and moved to New York. Later, she married two of the wealthiest and most powerful men in America, both Huntingtons, Collis and Henry. She supervised the decora-tion of their mansions, brought together several impressive art collections, and directed the affairs of their households with a haughty elegance. Unlike other women of her station and means she never figured in society. Perhaps she did not care to do so or perhaps society, not sure what to make of this strong-minded often imperious Southerner, never made the effort to meet her halfway. In any case Huntington recognized in her a strength and resourcefulness that matched his own. In addition, he shared with her a lifelong devotion to Collis—the blustering, tough campaigner who was perhaps the dominant figure in both their lives. Between Arabella and Henry, there was a mutual respect for the other's enthusiasms and a com-fortable lack of rivalry; she concentrated on art while he developed the library and the gardens. Arabella's death left Huntington with a feeling of loss and despair. He immediately turned over the house and all its fur-nishings to Arabella's son Archer and returned to San Marino in early October.

During the four months that Huntington spent in New York at the time of Arabella's death, a major change in personnel had taken place at the library. In the spring George Watson Cole had surprised him by speaking of retirement. Although Cole had originally hoped to work until 1925, rounding out ten years as Huntington's chief librarian, a number of events had intervened that made him change his mind. With twenty staff members now serving under his direction Cole found that tensions and rivalries had replaced the former easygoing mood of cooperation. This made supervision more complicated. In late 1923 it had been necessary for him to dismiss Philip Goulding, one of the catalogers, for incompetence. Goulding had been asked to check some items in a Pickering and Chatto antiquarian catalog and had cleared twelve expensive items for purchase. When the books arrived they turned out to be duplicates. Cole, who had supervised Goulding's work, took full responsibility for the error and offered to pay the cost of the duplicates. Although Huntington refused the suggestion, as he had earlier refused Goulding's appeal for reinstatement, Cole's embarrassment was profound. This and other incidents of staff discord undermined Cole's confidence in his ability to continue to administer the library. In addition he had been troubled, as he reported to Huntington, by "somewhat impaired eyesight," and he wished for "more time to carry out some cherished plans of writing on topics which greatly interest me, together with the desire to have more time at my disposal for home life."[12] From a man who had devoted his life to bibliography and was nearing his seventy-fourth birthday, the request seemed perfectly reasonable. Finally, Cole was disappointed that work on his favorite project, the bibliographical catalog of English books printed before 1641, had been dropped with no hope for its resumption, because staff attention was completely absorbed by the arrival of new books.

In his farewell letter to the staff Cole reflected on what the library had meant to him and what he hoped for its future.

> I scarcely need say that the work this library is carrying out will always be of the greatest interest to me. It is my intention to devote my remaining days to the advocacy and advancement of bibliographical research and of comparative bibliography. I shall watch your individual careers with intense interest and trust you may each

and all meet with the highest success attainable in the profession you have chosen for your lifework.[13]

As a final act of service Cole prepared a 215-page report for Huntington and the trustees, tracing the growth and development of the library during his tenure. In ringing phrases, Cole emphasized the research potential of the library.

> It should in my opinion be the fixed and invariable policy of the Huntington Library not only to meet most freely and liberally the needs and requirements of all scholarly students . . . but of itself to become a fountainhead for the advancement and dissemination of knowledge through the publication of special catalogues of its treasures. . . . It would be the greatest mistake in the world if, after having brought together the finest and most valuable library of its kind in existence, there should exist contentment with the simple routine of cataloguing and administration as practiced by libraries in general. With a staff trained to do bibliographical work of the most thorough and exacting nature, such a lapse into the methods of the past would be nothing less than a calamity.[14]

Huntington had no wish to make major changes in the administration of the library and on 1 October 1924 appointed Assistant Librarian Chester March Cate, who had been a staff member since 1915, to take over Cole's responsibilities. In a self-effacing memorandum to the staff Cate stressed the importance of working together on common goals.

> I sincerely hope, that the transfer of the destiny of the library into younger and less experienced hands may not be the cause of any great change in the daily routine of our Library work. I have no innovations to introduce and, at present at least, no changes in mind in the personnel of the staff. I shall enter upon my new duties with no strong feeling of personal sufficiency. There is no member of the staff who is not better versed in some phase of the work than I am . . . and it is your individual friendship and joint cooperation on which I base all my hopes for my own success and the internal welfare of the Huntington Library.[15]

Cate's term as librarian lasted only seven months. On 21 May 1925, the Los Angeles newspapers reported his death by suicide. Huntington asked Bliss to serve as acting librarian and in August of the following year formally appointed him to the position of librarian.

With Huntington now permanently in residence in California, Rosenbach had to resort to doing a good deal of business with him by mail. That winter the sales that offered the most interesting possibilities were those of the libraries of two distinguished collectors of English literature, William H. Arnold and Beverly Chew. Although Huntington gave Drake a few bids for the Arnold sale, he worked through Rosenbach for all the important items. For $3,600, a price he told Huntington was very cheap, Rosenbach obtained lot 626, a letter from Michaelius dated 8 August 1628 and thought to be the earliest known document written in New York. Other Arnold items falling to Rosenbach included a group of 146 letters from Hawthorne to his publisher William Ticknor, the manuscript for Robert Burns's poem "Queen Mary's Lament," and General Grant's letter book covering the period March and April 1865. The most talked about item in the sale was without question the 160-page manuscript of Stevenson's *Kidnapped*. Rosenbach was ready with Huntington's bid of $5,500, an amount, he thought, large enough to discourage the competition. As the bidding progressed, however, Rosenbach found himself in an unexpectedly heated exchange with J. P. Morgan's formidable librarian, Belle da Costa Greene. Greene went higher and higher until the Doctor, determined to have the item at almost any cost, heard Anthony Bade, the Anderson's suave auctioneer, bang the gavel down on his bid of $10,000 and announce, "Sold to Dr. R."[16] Would Huntington object to a $4,500 increase over his bid limit? It was an index of Huntington's state of mind that winter that he authorized payment for what Rosenbach called "the most important Stevenson manuscript in private hands" without any argument.

The next important event of the season was the sale of the library of Beverly Chew. A New York banker and one of the early members of the Grolier Club, Chew had devoted his life to collecting. He had sold his large American literature collection to Jacob C. Chamberlain in 1900 and his English literature to Huntington in 1912. After that he started all over again, finding many attractive buys in the Huntington duplicate sales. It became a matter of some pride for collectors in the 1920s to claim owner-ship of books with a circuitous Chew-Huntington-Chew provenance. Among the many highlights of the Chew sale were the Wyatt-Lefferts-Winans-Whistler copy of the first edition of Milton's *Paradise Lost* (1667), with the first title page and in the original sheep binding, a jewel that brought $5,600; the first edition of the three parts of Defoe's *Robinson Crusoe* (1719–20), sold for $5,350; and Blake's *Songs of Innocence and Experience* (1789–94), a small octavo in old calf with fifty-four colored plates that went for $5,500. In total the December sale brought the estate $145,366, a substantial return for 474 lots. The high prices realized were a tribute to Chew, one of the most respected collectors of his generation. Rosenbach attended the sale but, with only a few commissions from Huntington, bought conservatively.

Within the highly competitive book auction world, the Anderson Galleries and the American Art Association had become bitter rivals. The Anderson had staged a coup in 1911 with the Robert Hoe sales but usual-ly found itself far outdistanced in total annual revenues by the older and better-known AAA. When Kennerley took over the Anderson in 1915 he decided that if he couldn't match the AAA ormulu candelabrum for ormu-lu candelabrum and peachbloom vase for peachbloom vase, at least he would give them lively competition in the sale of rare books. By handling book consignments with care, printing accurate and attractive catalogs, and offering buyers extended terms for payment, sometimes up to twelve months, Kennerley attracted some of the top collectors and dealers of the day. Kennerley's success was partly a matter of personal style—a mixture of bonhomie and showmanship. At the Anderson he attracted wealthy cus-tomers with exhibitions of avant-garde paintings and photographs followed by elegant black-tie dinner parties. If collectors like Huntington helped put money in the Anderson till, the writers, artists, and musicians who attend-ed the sales and the parties—people like A. Edward Newton, Amy Lowell, Christopher Morley, Jerome Kern, and Alfred Stieglitz—put it on the map. Huntington didn't attend the soirees or need the word of outsiders to con-vince him that the Anderson was the place to buy and sell books. In response to Kennerley's request for a letter of recommendation he wrote enthusiastically:

It gives me pleasure to say that I have had business dealings with Mr. Mitchell Kennerley for many years, having had, at the Anderson Galleries of which he is President, twelve sales of duplicates from my library, and being about to have another. My dealings with Mr. Kennerley, both personally and in a business way have always been most pleasant. I am sure that anyone having undertaken business connections of whatsoever nature will appreciate, as I have, the careful consideration of the business man, and the courteous treatment of the gentleman, which Mr. Kennerley will certainly give.[17]

After Huntington moved back to California, Kennerley kept him up-to-date on the auction-room gossip, particularly anything to do with the rivalry between the Anderson and the AAA. In the spring of 1923 he reported gleefully that the AAA people had spent $750,000 on a new building on Fifty-seventh Street, just three blocks away from the Anderson, but that it "was too much for them."[18] Further, the AAA administrative structure, he said, had recently turned everything upside down. The new owner, the breezy millionaire Cortlandt Field Bishop, had dismissed former director Thomas Kirby and his son and forced them to sign an agreement to stay out of the auction business for ten years. After that he placed former staff members Otto Bernet, Hiram Parke, and Arthur Swann in charge. Kennerley considered Parke and Bernet dull and unimaginative, hardly worth his consideration, but toward Swann, who did know books, he demonstrated a waspish ill will. First he blackballed Swann's application for membership in the Grolier Club and then, at the first opportunity, saw to it that he lost his job with the AAA. Kennerley didn't reveal the depth of his distaste for Swann in correspondence with Huntington but rather confined himself to remarks on business—how well his own was going and how poorly the AAA was doing in its overpriced palace on Fifty-seventh Street. Huntington enjoyed hearing about this kind of competitive thrust and parry since it reminded him of his own achievements in his early days in railroading. There was never any question about Huntington's loyalty to the Anderson Galleries. Kirby received a blunt "no" the one time he tried to talk Huntington into selling his duplicates at the AAA. For fifteen years the Anderson provided Huntington with an efficient conduit for the books he wanted to buy or sell. It served a crucial role in the development of his library.

Following Arabella's death Huntington settled his affairs in New York as rapidly as possible. With little regret he left the somber mansion on Fifty-seventh Street never to return.[19] The California ranch had always been home and Huntington returned to it now with a sense of pleasure mixed with a sense of urgency. There were several projects that needed his immediate attention. First, he wanted to create a suitable memorial for Arabella. To help with that task he asked Rosenbach to furnish drawings and photographs that might suggest a design for a temple-like mausoleum. In mid-December 1924 he wrote:

> I am planning to build as a mausoleum a small marble structure above the spot where we have laid Mrs. Huntington to rest, and where in time I expect to be, in the shape of a marble temple. I should like to have you get for me some books that will show designs for this. I do not mean merely architectural books, but those that may possibly give reproductions from temples already built, or those of old Greece and Rome. I expect to build one with a diameter of about 25 feet. Knowing your versatility, I think you are able to do this for me better [than] any one else I know.[20]

Next he commissioned Duveen to supply a variety of paintings, porcelain, furniture, and sculpture that would form what he planned to call the Arabella Huntington Memorial Art Collection. Beyond that, Huntington was determined to continue to add to the library as appropriate books and manuscripts came to his attention. In the fall of 1924 the most appealing offer, a large collection of incunabula, came from Dr. Otto H. F. Vollbehr.

Shortly after he returned to California in October, Huntington met Vollbehr, a German national, who not only shared his enthusiasm for incunabula but happened to have a large stock for sale. One authority suggested that Vollbehr worked his way into Huntington's circle by ingratiating himself with a group of Los Angeles bankers who were on close terms with the collector.[21] However the introduction was made, Vollbehr, one of the most intriguing personalities of the book world of the 1920s, quickly used it to his advantage. In November 1924 he sold Huntington 392 incunabula, chiefly Spanish and Portuguese imprints, for $170,000. This success was enough to send him scurrying back to Europe for more of the same. In January 1925 he wrote Bliss about a collection of four thousand incunabula in his possession, of which at least three thousand would be, he claimed, an excellent purchase for the Huntington library. "You will stand amazed," he wrote, "when you see my treasures." Bliss, who had started to worry about the direction these costly negotiations were taking, told Vollbehr that if he had other chances to dispose of his books to go ahead and do so. Vollbehr replied testily that he could sell books every day but that "the buyer must satisfy me."[22] Vollbehr's stated aim, as he explained it to Huntington, was to

> make the collection of incunabula in the Huntington Library as important, if possible more important and more numerous than those contained in any of the World's Great Libraries. With your cooperation, it would be my ambition to make your collection of incunabula more important and more numerous even than that of the British Museum.

This was the right line to take with Huntington, who was never more eager than when he saw himself gaining ground on the British Museum. In March 1925 he paid Vollbehr $770,000 in a combination of cash and Pacific Electric bonds for 1,740 more incunabula. After this second large purchase Huntington made one of his "out of the market" decisions and told Vollbehr he was not interested in any more incunabula at present.[23] Vollbehr read the words "not interested" with gloom but took "at present" to mean that all was not lost. In November 1925 he set up his base of operations at the luxurious Vista Del Arroyo Hotel in Pasadena, just a few miles from Huntington's home. From that site he dispatched a flurry of offers to Huntington and Bliss.

In early December, identified as "one of the leading philologists, bibliophiles and scholars of the world," Vollbehr gave an interview to a reporter from the *Los Angeles Times*. "The American people," he declared, "and the entire world owe an undying debt of gratitude to Henry E. Huntington . . . for the monumental service to the spread of culture which he is effecting by the collection of the Huntington Library."[24] In February Huntington bought a third cache of incunabula from Vollbehr, bringing the total purchased from that agent to 2,385 titles. Vollbehr always preferred to be known as a collector rather than a dealer and in the interview maintained that he and Huntington "were exchanging incunabula when one collector has two of a type and the other none." Later that year he wrote to Bliss, "To prove to you I am not a dealer trying to make money, I refused an offer . . . from a well-known international dealer at the purchase price plus 10%." In March 1926 Vollbehr offered Huntington one more collection of incunabula, 1,333 titles in all, available for $640,000 including a special thirty percent discount. In acquiring these books, Vollbehr told Bliss, he had not only spent a great deal of time but had made vast personal financial sacrifices. Then, in an abrupt change of tone, he closed, "In offering you this collection at such a low price kindly give me an answer yes or no. I reserve the privilege to withdraw this offer after 48 hours." Not to be browbeaten by such imperious behavior, Huntington turned the offer down. Vollbehr's days of selling books to Huntington were over, but that didn't stop the flow of letters. In June 1926 he wrote Bliss saying he had just acquired "the dearest book in the world," the Gutenberg Bible in three volumes from the Benedictine cloister of St. Paul in Carinthia. "But," he went on petulantly, "I make you no offer. In the first place you have treated me badly and secondly you flatly refused my last offer." Vollbehr then suggested that there had been a "change of feeling" toward him at the Huntington library and accused Bliss of listening to innuendos from "envious souls and meddlers." Bliss simply answered, "Between American history and English literature incunabula will be a small factor for some time with us."[25]

It took six months to settle up all the accounts, and right to the end Vollbehr continued to identify himself as a collector. In October 1926, after receiving a final payment, he wrote Huntington, "This makes a happy ending of all our transactions, which though you succeeded in screwing me down appallingly in some of my prices, were always conducted in a spirit of mutual courtesy as is becoming to good book collectors."[26] Vollbehr did eventually find a customer for the Gutenberg Bible. In July 1930 the United States Congress unanimously passed and President Herbert Hoover, himself a book collector, signed an act appropriating $1,500,000 for the purchase of Vollbehr's three thousand incunabula for the Library of Congress, including the St. Paul copy of the Gutenberg Bible.

At times Huntington's rush to buy incunabula during the last four years of his life seemed utterly chaotic. He took whole collections at a gulp without careful consideration of the importance of specific items. In his eagerness to build the library up to and beyond the level of the British Museum, it almost seemed as if he would buy any pre-1501 printing. Along with a scattering of truly outstanding items Huntington bought a large number of unimpressive religious tracts, deservedly obscure scientific treatises, and pedestrian poetic effusions. Dealers like Vollbehr and Rosenbach, taking advantage of Huntington's new enthusiasm, found it relatively easy to sell him manufactured "collections."

In February Rosenbach traveled to San Marino with a portfolio of reproductions of Greek and Roman temples in answer to the collector's request for help in planning a mausoleum. While he was there, he got Huntington's bids for the next Britwell sale and for $84,000 sold him another assortment of rarities: a William Bradford printing of Sir Matthew Hale's *Some Necessary and Important Considerations* (1736), Tennyson's *The Lover's Tale* (1833), two Indian treaties signed in Falmouth, Massachusetts, in 1776 and 1777; a Wynkyn de Worde printing of *The Floure of the Commaundementes* (1521); and fifty-three assorted incunabula. Back in Philadelphia, Rosenbach weighed the conflicting Britwell bids from Huntington, Folger, and Pforzheimer, with preference usually going to Huntington. At the sale, with Huntington bids in his pocket, Rosenbach was in complete control. In the end he took 438 lots for a total of £47,201. Writing from the Carlton Hotel in London, Rosenbach sent his usual cheerful report: "I secured for you nearly every lot at very reasonable prices. I do not think there was a single bid from America as I arranged all that before I left, so there was no competition from our side of the water." In a letter to Bliss, Rosenbach commented that Christie-Miller had been very disappointed with the results of the sale as some of his rarest volumes had gone at sacrifice prices.[27]

With the Britwell sales behind him Rosenbach moved on to other business. He bought a Kilmarnock Burns, an 1865 *Alice in Wonderland*, attended the sale of books sponsored by the Royal Society, and visited Thirlestaine House to examine another display of Phillipps manuscripts. All of this was more or less run-of-the-mill Rosenbach business. What really made the 1925 trip memorable was a chance to examine the Robert Holford library at Dorchester House in London. During the middle years of the nineteenth century Holford, a wealthy and ambitious collector in the pattern of Huth, Christie-Miller, and Lord Vernon, had formed a remarkable library of incunabula, French illustrated books of the eighteenth century, early printings of the Greek and Roman classics, Americana, and rare editions of Shakespeare, Milton, and Spenser. After Holford's death in 1892 the estate descended to his son Sir George L. Holford, a member of the Life Guards and equerry to various members of the royal family. Sir George preferred orchids to books and was happy to consider selling part of the library in order to support his taste for exotic plants.

Rosenbach had seen many fine collections but this one topped them all. Working quickly he made pencil notes on 133 titles—all of which looked eminently salable—among them four blockbooks, three Caxtons, a Jenson Cicero (1470), the four Shakespeare folios and twenty-one quartos, including an uncut *Troilus and Cressida* (1609), one of four known copies of the second edition of *Venus and Adonis* (1594), a presentation copy of Captain John Smith's *Generall Historie of Virginia* (1624), Wynkyn de Worde's printing of Dame Juliana Berners's *Book of Hawking, Hunting and Heraldry* (1496), and the first edition of Dante's *Divina Commedia* (1472). All he needed was $534,000, the amount he and Holford had agreed on as the selling price. With this mouth-watering collection Rosenbach felt sure he could produce well over a million dollars in sales. It would be the coup of his career. Six days after he returned to the United States he wired Huntington:

> DO YOU EXPECT TO COME EAST VERY SHORTLY IF NOT CAN YOU SEE ME ABOUT MOST IMPORTANT MATTER OFFERED SOME MARVELOUS SHAKESPEAREANA FROM GREATEST PRIVATE COLLECTION IN EUROPE QUICK ACTION NECESSARY PLEASE WIRE.[28]

Bringing along his usual trunkful of odds and ends, Rosenbach arrived in Pasadena on 11 June. The contents of the trunk cost Huntington $61,000 but that was only bait. The real business of the day was the Holford books. It was a collection, Rosenbach told him, he couldn't pass up, a once-in-a-lifetime

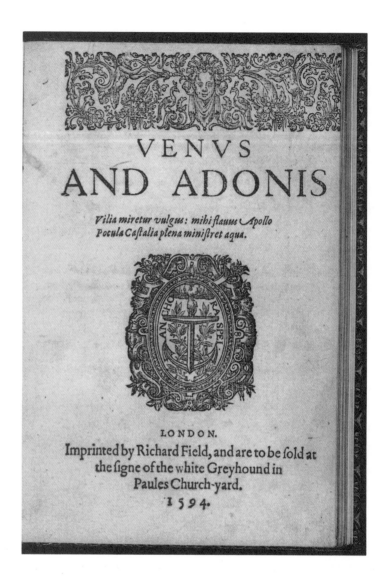

Fig. 45
The Holford copy
of *Venus and Adonis*
was acquired by
Huntington through
Rosenbach in 1925.
Huntington had
obtained the
Britwell copy of the
rarer 1599 edition
in 1919 for a record
price.

opportunity. Huntington agreed. He took the *Venus and Adonis,* Smith's *Virginia*, the Foligno Dante, *The Book of Hawking*, the Jenson Cicero, and twenty-six other Holford items plus eighty-three incunabula from another source for $350,000. That meant Rosenbach only needed $185,000 to settle the transaction with Holford. Would Huntington help out by coming up with the difference? Always ready to support Rosenbach in a just cause, Huntington accepted the dealer's six-month note at five percent interest and cabled $534,000 to London. Even by Rosenbach's standards this was a landmark deal. With sales to Huntington in 1925 reaching just over $1,220,000, both dealer and collector might have agreed, it was a landmark year.

Although Rosenbach controlled the big sales to Huntington over the spring and summer of 1925, a number of other individuals marketed their wares to him at a more modest level. From Jack London's widow he acquired manuscripts of some of his major works for $25,000—*White Fang, Martin Eden, The Iron Heel, The Valley of the Moon,* and others, along with a large file of London's correspondence. A similar collection made up of Ambrose Bierce letters and manuscripts came from Bierce's publisher, the

COMINCIA LA COMEDIA DI
dante alleghieri di fiorenze nella q̃le tracta
delle pene et punitioni de uitii et demeriti
et premii delle uirtu: Capitolo primo della
p̃ma parte de quefto libro loquale fechiama
inferno : nel quale lautore fa prohemio ad
tucto eltractato del libro:·

EL mezo delcamin dinrã uita
mi trouai puna felua ofcura
che la diricta uia era fmarrita
Et quanto adir q̃lera cofa dura
efta felua feluagia afpra eforte
che nel penfier renoua la paura
Tante amara che pocho piu morte
    ma pertractar del ben chio uitrouai
    diro dellatre cofe chi uo fcorte
I non fo ben ridir come uentrai
    tantera pien difonno infuquil punto
    che la uerace uia abandonai
Ma poi che fui appie dum colle gionto
    ladoue terminaua quella ualle
    che mauea dipaura el cor compuncto
Guardai inalto et uir de le fuoe fpalle
    ueftite gia deraggi del pianeta
    che mena dricto altrui perogni calle
Allor fu la paura un pocho cheta
    che nellaco del cor mera durata
    la nocte chio paffi contanta pieta

Fig. 46
The elegant first edition of *The Divine Comedy* (Foligno, 1472), the Holford copy, sold to Huntington by A. S. W. Rosenbach. Huntington's collection of incunabula, with over five thousand titles, was the largest in the United States until it was surpassed by that of the Library of Congress after World War II.

Figs. 47 and 48

Captain John Smith's note to the Society of Cordwainers, London *(right)*, in a large-paper copy of his *Generall Historie of Virginia, New-England, and the Summer Isles* (1624), acquired through Rosenbach. The presentation binding *(above)* depicts the arms of James I.

To

The Worshipfull the Master Wardens
& Societie of the Cordwyners of
yᵉ Cittie of London.

Worthie Gentlemen

Not only in regard of your Courtisie &
Loue, But also of yᵉ Continuall vse I haue had
of yoᵘʳ Labours, & the hope you may make some
vse of mine I salute yᵒᵘ with this Cronologicall
discourse, whereof yᵒᵘ may vnderstand with what infi-
nite Difficulties & Dangers these Plantations first began,
with their yearlie proceedings, & the plaine description
& Condition of those Countries; How many of your Com-
panie haue bin Adventurers, whose Names are omitted or not
nominated in the Alphabett I know not, therefore I intreate
yᵒᵘ better to informe me, that I may hereafter imprint yᵒᵘ
amongst the Rest, But of this I am sure for want of
shooes among the Oyster Bankes wee tore our hatts & Clothes
& those being worne, wee tied Barkes of trees about our
ffeete to keepe them from being Cutt by the shelles amongst
which wee must goe or starue, yett how many thousand of
shooes hath bin transported to these plantations, how many
soldiers Marriners & Saylers haue bin & are likely to be
encreased thereby, what vent yoᵘʳ Comodities haue had &
still haue, & how many shipps & men of all ffaculties haue
bin & are yearlie imployed I leaue to yoᵘʳ owne Judgments,
& yett by reason of ill managing, the Returnes haue neither
answered the generall Expectation, nor my desire, the Causes
thereof yᵒᵘ may readie at Large in this Booke for your better
satisfaction, & I pray yᵒᵘ take it not in ill part that I
present the same to yᵒᵘ in this manuscript Epistle soe
Late, for both it & I my self haue bin soe ouertired by
attendances that this worke of mine doth seeme
to be Super-annuated before its Birth, notwithstanding
Lett me intreat yᵒᵘ to giue it Lodging in your Hall freelie
to be perused for euer, in memorie of yoᵘʳ Noblenesse
towards mee, & my Loue to God, my Countrie, your Societie,
& those plantations, Euer resting

Your's to vse.

John Smith.

Neale Company of Washington, D.C. To support his Civil War interests, Huntington paid Stan Henkels, the Philadelphia auctioneer, $6,000 for some 260 letters, notes, and military documents, all relating to the career and campaigns of Confederate General J. E. B. Stuart. Further documentation on early American history came from the en bloc purchase of the contents of two catalogs issued by L. Kashnor of the Museum Book Store in London. This brought Huntington 850 maps covering the French and Indian and Revolutionary wars and a collection of some seven hundred pamphlets and other documents dealing with the period from 1700 to the beginning of the War of 1812 (Museum Book Store catalogs nos. 93 and 96; contents obtained for £5,000 and £2,000, respectively). The most significant purchase from Kashnor consisted of a portion of the papers of the Temple, Grenville, and Brydges families, familiarly known as the Stowe manuscripts, identified by the name of the country house where the papers had been deposited.[29] This archive included court rolls, charters, deeds, and seals going back to the twelfth century, as well as account books, letters, and legal documents from the fifteenth through the eighteenth centuries. Huntington took the archive for £24,000.

Winding up the year, Huntington acquired a collection of some three hundred letters from Robert Morris, the financier of the Revolutionary War, through Thomas Madigan, an autograph dealer in New York City. Madigan told Huntington that his $7,500 asking price was "very reasonable." Huntington and Bliss agreed. A month later Bliss praised Madigan for the purchase of some letters at the Thomas sale in Philadelphia. "I am indeed pleased with your work," Bliss exclaimed, in a rare bit of flattery.

> It may interest you to know that this is the first time we have ever entrusted bids for material of this class to a man who deals in nothing else. I am always interested in buying materials at what you yourself consider to be reasonable prices. Simply because I am buying for the Huntington Library is no reason why I should be asked to pay a figure out of all proportion to what the item should regularly sell for.[30]

With new orders going to Madigan, Maggs Brothers, and the Museum Book Store, the Huntington ledgers show a gradual turn away from the Rosenbach

Company. The change can be attributed in large measure to Bliss. He had never trusted Rosenbach, and now that he had the power to do so he began to place orders with a variety of other dealers.

During this time, Huntington became more preoccupied with family matters and with his own health. After the death of his son and his wife Huntington found himself without familiar moorings. In addition, old friends were slipping away. The death of his lawyer, W. E. "Billy" Dunn, was particularly hard to take. In the years they worked together, sharing the same office in the Los Angeles Railway Company building, there had always been trust and camaraderie. That was over.

During the spring and summer of 1925, with time on his hands, Huntington spent several hours each week in the downtown offices of the railway company.[31] He liked to keep track of the lines he had started fifteen years earlier and was proud that he had been able to maintain a five-cent fare while other municipal rail services had increased their rates to six and even ten cents a ride. He was also proud of his streetcar men and maintained that he had, on his own initiative, provided them with regular raises without ever giving in to union demands.[32] He had been independent and strong.

Recently, however, it had become more difficult to maintain some aspects of that stolid independence. For one thing his personal health had become a concern. Up to the age of sixty-five he had been robust but in recent years had suffered from various incapacitating illnesses, some that confined him to bed for several weeks. In early October 1925 his personal physician, Dr. E. A. Bryant, scheduled a trip for Huntington to the Lankenau Hospital in Philadelphia for a battery of examinations. The specialists found cancer of the prostate and decided to operate at once. Dr. John Deaver of the Medical College of the University of Pennsylvania performed the surgery in the morning of 18 October and after Huntington regained consciousness in the afternoon pronounced the operation a success. Huntington recovered slowly but in two weeks was able to walk on his own and shortly after that even managed to visit Rosenbach at his shop on Walnut Street. This of course included some book business, with Huntington spending $100,000 for another assortment of incunabula. It was a month before Huntington felt well enough to make the trip back to California—which he did just before

Thanksgiving, traveling in his private car on the Southern Pacific. In spite of constant medical attention and a flood of encouraging notes and books from family and friends, his recovery was discouragingly slow. He wrote Rosenbach, "I have received a copy of the Life and Times of Laurence Sterne, and appreciate very much your sending this to me. I know I shall enjoy it and it comes at an opportune time as I am reading considerably and am tiring of the light fiction everyone is thrusting upon me."[33] Bliss wrote to the Pasadena book dealer Alice Millard on 4 March to report that Huntington had gotten up and dressed that day—the first time he had felt well enough to do so since October.[34] In April Huntington wrote to Kennerley that although he was "gaining steadily," he was not "up and about yet" because the wound had not completely healed.[35] It would be well into the summer before Huntington regained his usual vigor.

With Huntington mending slowly Bliss took on even more responsibility for book selection. In early January he sent Rosenbach a notice that could not have been received with any enthusiasm.

> I think it only fair to warn you that as regards incunabula I have adopted a somewhat different policy in purchases for the library. We have five thousand of such books already, so I am not going to base our purchases in the future simply on material we do not already possess nor on such as is already not in America but rather on something special about the item, mainly on whether or not we already have something by the same press or in the same type. Consequently, for that reason it will be much better for consideration of your future offers in early printed books if you list the price of each book. We can then check your lists and accept or reject what we wish with much less difficulty.[36]

The days of buying the big "collections," it seemed, were over. From now on, items would stand or fall on their own merit. At the moment Rosenbach was too busy buying the Melk Abbey copy of the Gutenberg Bible for Mrs. Edward S. Harkness to be concerned, and besides he felt his personal relationship with Huntington would surmount any roadblocks thrown up by librarian Bliss. When Rosenbach traveled to Pasadena in late February to pick up commissions for the next Britwell sale he was able to confirm his optimistic view of matters. Although there was no room for him to stay in the San Marino house, since family members and Duveen had already absorbed the guest space, he managed to sell Huntington a tidy $184,800 miscellany. Among the purchases were forty-seven incunabula, the Naples Horae collection from the library of W. A. White, a number of early Aberdeen and Glasgow imprints, and eleven early English manuscripts. In June Huntington bought $84,800 worth of incunabula from Rosenbach and in late October, when the Doctor visited San Marino once again, another assortment for $73,205.[37] So much for Bliss and his rules.

The day before the seventeenth Britwell sale was to begin in London Rosenbach learned that both of his sisters had died of influenza in Philadelphia. Completely overcome, he was unable to attend the first sessions of the sale. With apologies, he turned Huntington's bids over to Seymour de Ricci, the noted bibliographer. The list of bids was shorter than in previous years, with total purchases coming to £23,000, about half the amount spent in 1925. Rosenbach wrote that the books had gone for "reasonable prices" and that "there were no really spectacular bids in the whole lot."[38] Even with that, some of the prices seemed unreasonable to Bliss. He sent back a number of books, including Timothy Bright's rare treatise on stenography, *Characterie* (1588), because, he argued, the charge of £510 was more than ten percent above the library's bid. In May, Bliss extended his tight-fisted approach to all bids submitted for the upcoming John L. Clawson sale, probably the most important event of the 1925–26 New York auction season. Clawson, a businessman from Buffalo, New York, owned a remarkable library covering the period 1550–1660 made up of Shakespeare quartos, Milton first editions, morality plays, and Elizabethan poetry—most of it purchased after the war through the Rosenbach Company. Bliss sent a short note to Rosenbach in response to a suggested list of bids supplied by the Philadelphia dealer: "Mr. Huntington considers many of these too high." The point, Bliss told Rosenbach, was not to exceed the set limits, in any circumstances.[39] After the sale he snapped back saying the rigid limits had held him so much in check that he had only been able to buy ten lots out of thirty-seven wanted. "You must realize," he told Huntington, "much water has passed under the bridge since the Huth sale of 1912— The group of new collectors [Owen D. Young, Carl Pforzheimer, and Frank Bemis], realizing that the Clawson sale was probably the last opportunity to secure fine English books, was willing to pay good prices for them."[40] With a not entirely subtle reference to the Huth prices—ancient history—followed by a mention of new collectors—willing to pay good prices—Rosenbach cleared the way for change. There would be a few more sales, but essentially Huntington and Rosenbach had come to a crossroads. Huntington and Bliss decided to economize and Rosenbach found new customers more than willing to pay his prices.

Chapter 12

"THE REWARD OF ALL THE WORK
I HAVE EVER DONE"
1926–1927

The future of the library concerned not only
Huntington and his immediate family but a number
of his friends and associates as well. By means of the
trust indenture drawn up in September 1919,
Huntington had transferred land, buildings, and
"objects of artistic, historic and literary interest" to a board of trustees—
although he would retain control during his lifetime—for the stated purpose
of creating and maintaining "A free public library, art gallery, museum and
park."[1] Although this was a good start it failed to provide specific continuing
support of a kind that such an institution would require to make its mark. It
was the need for continuing support that had long concerned the astronomer
and intellectual gadfly George Ellery Hale. Over the years Hale had tried to
win Huntington's approval for a number of schemes, some practical, some
fanciful, related to the future of the library. Of course it should be located in
Pasadena, destined, according to Hale, to be the "Athens of the West," and
administratively it should be patterned on the scientific institutions with
which Hale was familiar, with funding for a director, a permanent research
staff, and visiting fellows. Further, it should sponsor expeditions to the Near
East, develop a museum of artifacts, and initiate an elaborate series of schol-

arly publications. The possibilities, in Hale's sometimes overactive imagination, were limitless. As a member of the newly formed board of trustees in 1919 he was in a position to push his ideas.

With the new library building still under construction and the move from New York in progress, Huntington had little time in the fall of 1919 to listen to Hale's futuristic plans. This was discouraging but Hale, schooled in dealing with realities when large amounts of money were involved, knew how to wait for the right moment. He never lost his enthusiasm for what he saw as the library's unequaled potential to serve as the core of an important West Coast research initiative. In early 1925 he wrote up a proposal based on notions that had been simmering in his mind for several years. The library would include a permanent research staff, a fund for fellowships, a distinguished scholar to be appointed as research director, and an active publications program. Hale submitted this plan to his fellow trustee George Patton, who then read it to an appreciative Huntington.[2] Hale refined the text once more, this time coming up with a five-page document that laid out an administrative structure for the library and elaborated on the theme that "books, manuscripts, and works of art are instruments of research." On 14 October 1925 Huntington read and approved the text, henceforth identified by Hale as the "Huntington Scheme" but formally entitled "The Future Development of the Huntington Library and Art Gallery."[3]

This was progress but it was a paper plan and a paper plan only. To have any significance it needed legal substance and a large infusion of money. On 8 February 1926, the trustees revised the original indenture. Where the institution had been defined originally as a "free public library, art gallery, museum and botanical garden," the new text identified it more specifically as a free public *research* library. Further, the objective of the institution, as now stated, was

> to disseminate and contribute to the advancement of useful information and knowledge: to prosecute and encourage study and research in original sources of history, literature, art, science and kindred subjects and to provide Research Associates and Fellows, consisting of scholars of exceptional ability engaged in special study and research in such subjects, and generally to conduct an institution of educational value to the public.[4]

FIG. 49
Max Farrand, the
first director of
research, with the
manuscript of
Benjamin Franklin's
Autobiography open
to a page blurred
with ink spilled by
Franklin.

The second and more important problem, proper funding, would be more difficult to solve. In order to help establish the case for an adequate budget Hale decided to use outside pressure. The position of research director stood waiting to be filled, and it seemed to Hale that once the right candidate could be identified, that person would be able to make the case for support better than anyone else. What Hale needed was a distinguished Anglo-American scholar with a solid research record and tested administrative ability. By great good fortune Dr. Max Farrand, former professor of American history at Stanford and Yale universities and recently appointed educational officer for the Commonwealth Fund, was scheduled to visit a group of Commonwealth fellows in Pasadena in January 1926. Farrand already knew Robert Millikan, president of the California Institute of Technology, and through Millikan met Hale. It took Hale only a short time to size up Farrand, a highly reputable scholar and a proven administrator, as the ideal candidate for the position of director.

After Farrand returned east events began to move rapidly. In the early spring the trustees asked him to come to the library as the first research associate, a position that was clearly a preliminary step toward the directorship. Farrand had immediate responsibilities with the Commonwealth Fund but said he would come for two months beginning in November. In the meantime, at Hale's request, he wrote a lengthy letter to Huntington explaining something of his own research interests and the needs of research scholars in general. It was well received, and by the time Farrand arrived in Pasadena the trustees and Huntington had agreed that he was the right man for the job. Farrand, with prompting from Hale and the other trustees, laid out the terms under which he would feel comfortable accepting the appointment. Many of these—a well-funded research staff, money for visiting fellows, a program of publications—were in fact the same as those initially proposed by Hale.

After a careful reading of Farrand's draft, Huntington asked to see a budget. This was a crucial moment in the negotiations that had been going on between Hale and Huntington for several years. Farrand had prepared both a minimum and maximum estimate covering salaries for a number of resident scholars, assistant professors, instructors, visiting research associates, and fellows. As Farrand remembered the conversation that took place on the day he presented his figures, Huntington wanted to know what it would all cost.

> I asked "Minimum or maximum?" He said, "Maximum, of course," and I said "$340,000." He said "Is that every year?" and I said it was. He asked whether it was in addition to what he was already doing and I said it was. He asked if I realized that meant the income on seven million; I said I did. And immediately and without hesitation he said "You may have it."

When Farrand asked Huntington about his interest in research the collector replied, "I don't know what it is all about. I have confidence in my trustees, who I think are an extraordinary group of men, and they tell me you are the best person to do the job. I like you and I am going to do whatever you tell me to do." Sensing that this was an opportunity that might never come again, Farrand plunged ahead. What was really needed, he told Huntington, if the institution was to achieve distinction in the years ahead, was ten million more. Huntington must have paused a moment or two before he answered.

"I don't know whether I have it," he said, and went on to enumerate what he felt he must do for his children and their families. Then he added, "If there are sufficient funds you shall have it."[5] In answer to one final question, he promised to change his will to take care of the institutional needs as he and Farrand had agreed.

In January 1927 Huntington approved an annual budget of $348,000 for research and publication and $190,000 for buildings and grounds. This was what Farrand had been waiting for. On 5 February 1927 he accepted the trustee's offer of the position of director of research at a salary of $12,000, with a separate annual research budget of nearly $400,000. On leaving the board meeting where he had approved the final figures, Huntington is reported to have said to Patton, "I never had any idea of doing anything of this kind."[6] To get the process started, Huntington transferred $1,200,000 into the endowment fund in January and February 1927 and $3,100,000 more in April. If that process had continued the endowment might easily have reached the $7,000,000 total that he and Farrand had discussed. On 25 April, however, the day before he left for Philadelphia for a second operation, Huntington wrote a codicil to his will withdrawing all further benefits to the library and stating that his recent gifts had been sufficient to assure it a healthy future. It was a serious blow to Hale and Farrand, but with an existing endowment of $10,500,000, producing an annual interest income of $530,000, they could still, as Hale put it, "do very well."[7]

After the trustees approved Farrand's appointment at their February meeting, they passed another motion, almost as significant, opening the library on a limited basis to the general public. As early as 1916 a few scholars had been permitted to use books in the New York library, but it was a privilege granted only rarely. After the move to California in 1920, and with a reading room designed for the purpose, the number of visiting researchers grew steadily. Although there had been much interest, the library and the grounds had never been open to the public. This changed on Friday, 18 March 1927, when 146 people, all holding free admission tickets secured in advance, walked through the entrance doors to view the books and paintings on exhibit. Bliss was pleased with the occasion and reported, "I did not anticipate any trouble and there was none. The visitors as a whole seemed intelligent, were very quiet, and examined the items of the exhibition with apparent interest."[8]

FIG. 50
Originally built to accommodate visiting scholars, the library's reading room was soon available to them only in the mornings; it doubled as the public exhibition hall in the afternoons.

The library continued to be open every Friday from 2:00 to 5:00 to the first two hundred people who applied for tickets and enclosed the required self-addressed stamped envelope. Between 18 March and the end of December, 1927, five thousand people entered the grounds and scrutinized the carefully planned exhibitions.[9]

In 1926, the Bibliographical Society of London brought out its long-awaited *Short-Title Catalogue of Books Printed in England, Scotland, Ireland and of English Books Printed Abroad 1475–1640* (known as the *STC),* under the able editorial direction of Alfred W. Pollard and Gilbert R. Redgrave. The catalog identified 26,143 items that the editors had located in libraries or private collections in England or America. Cole had associated himself with the project from the beginning and following his retirement had devoted much of his time to reading and correcting the proof sheets. In all, Cole found that the Huntington library owned 8,726 of the entries, or slightly more than a third of the total. Within that number, 668 entries were in the Huntington library only. Cole could well be proud of these figures, as he had been the chief advocate for securing pre-1641 books and had made their acquisition a top priority during his nine years as chief librarian. Modestly, he gave much of the credit to Brigham, whose three trips to England between 1921 and 1923 added some 2,700 pre-1641 entries to those already held in San Marino.[10] If they had not realized it before, bibliographers, librarians, and collectors were now made aware that Huntington's collection, with three times as many STC entries as any other American library, and ranked internationally only behind the British Museum and the Bodleian Library, was indeed a remarkable international research archive.

As the Huntington collections grew in stature, opportunities for sharing bibliographic information presented themselves. Cole was enthusiastic about the possibilities of the photostat machine and urged Huntington to set up the equipment that would enable the library to copy text and exchange it with other institutions and private collectors.[11] Once this was done Huntington and William A. White made an agreement to exchange photostats of twenty-five rare titles. A number of other collectors made similar agreements with Huntington. In the case of Edward E. Ayer, the noted collector of materials on North American Indians, the right to copy from one collection to another took the form of a gentleman's agreement. Ayer spent his winters in Pasadena and over the years developed a warm personal friendship with Huntington and his library staff. In late March 1923 he wrote to Huntington explaining his ideas about cooperation.

> I have been thinking some time that I would like to have everything arranged so that for all time to come, if your great library wanted to copy *anything* in my department of the Newberry that you and your successors would be perfectly free to do so. I am giving you a list of things (manuscripts, pencil drawings, photographs, oil portraits etc.) I think you may want; . . . anything that I have missed that the great Huntington Library shall *ever* find in my library that will enhance the value of theirs, they shall be at liberty to copy. . . . Of course Mr. Huntington, you and I are doing what *we can* to help educate *any and all* the people of our beloved country.

After thanking Ayer for his generosity Huntington replied,

We are working along the same lines and to the same ends; I shall always be glad to be of any service to you and your interests in supplying copies of anything you may need, or information of any nature whatsoever. Your sympathy and cooperation in what I am attempting here is most helpful, and I wish that all of the libraries might work together in the same way.[12]

Word of the important holdings in the Huntington Library began to circulate shortly after the move to California. In 1920 Cole published a paper with the Historical Society of Southern California describing the library and two years later expanded the same topic for the *Library Journal*.[13] In 1927 George Ellery Hale brought the library to national attention with a long illustrated article, "The Huntington Library and Art Gallery and the New Plan of Research," published in *Scribner's*.[14] Newspapers of course had long provided the public with coverage of Huntington's purchases.

By the end of 1926, with the development of the library as a research institution well underway and with attention focused on it by the *STC*, Huntington saw his private collection turned into a national and even an international research resource. In part this was a consequence of the ambitious plans of Hale and Farrand. But a change in Huntington's collecting patterns in the last year and a half of his life was even more significant for the library's future role in scholarly research. He turned largely away from books, except those produced in the first fifty years of printing, and toward original manuscripts and documents. These great collections of papers, perhaps even more than the rarities and treasures that drew Huntington initially, would ultimately be indispensable to scholars.

In 1926 he participated in only two public sales, spending $75,000 in London (Britwell) and $25,000 in New York (Clawson), a pale reflection of his earlier adventures in the auction markets. At the close of 1926 he bought in rapid succession three collections of eighteenth-century materials: the Chevalier Destouches papers on French-American cooperation during the Revolution, the Rufus King letters on American-British foreign policy and the Henry Stevens pamphlets on European politics.

His most important purchases in 1926 came as a result of negotiations with Maggs Brothers, a well-known London firm with roots going back to the middle of the nineteenth century. Huntington had ordered Americana from Maggs catalogs for a number of years and found their service of the highest quality. In January, Maurice Ettinghausen, a sophisticated linguist and Maggs representative, offered Huntington a collection of some one thousand documents on sixteenth-century Peru, many of them dealing with the uprising of 1548 and the capture of Gonzalo Pizarro by Pedro de la Gasca. Although a bit out of Huntington's usual scope, the Pizarro papers did support his interest in the early settlement of the Americas, a specialty that Wagner had helped to define several years earlier. Huntington's next purchase from Maggs, and one decidedly closer to his traditional Anglo-American enthusiasms, came with his acquisition of four hundred letters written by Admiral Richard Howe, all dealing with eighteenth-century British naval affairs. Following his success with the Pizarro manuscripts and the Howe letters, Ettinghausen produced a truly outstanding archive, fifty thousand letters, seals, charters, deeds, land grants, court rolls, and household books known as the Hastings-Huntingdon papers, a record that traced the history of the earls of Huntingdon from the twelfth through the eighteenth centuries. Among the riches in this collection there were letters concerning the Gunpowder Plot, Sir Walter Raleigh's expeditions, and the colonization of America. One remarkable document, a grant to the Marquis of Dorset, was signed by Sir Thomas More, Cardinal Wolsey, and King Henry VIII. Priced at $307,000 and acquired in January 1927, just four months before his death, the Hastings-Huntingdon papers were Huntington's last major purchase.

When Rosenbach asked Huntington about bids for the 1927 Britwell sale, he hardly expected the curt answer that came back by wire:

SUDDENLY OUT OF THE MARKET STOP TRIP FOR BRITWELL ABSOLUTELY USELESS STOP HOPE CATCHES YOU IN TIME STOP NO PURCHASES WHATEVER.[15]

The wire arrived in Philadelphia the day following Rosenbach's departure. When he got to California he found Huntington in low spirits and too preoccupied to talk about books. There was nothing to do but enjoy the sunshine, gossip with Hapgood, quibble with Bliss, and return home. Huntington found that he needed all his dwindling energy to keep up with plans for the library reorganization and to maintain control over the arrangements for the

Charles R.

Right trusty and right wellbeloued Cousin, wee greete you well. The late disorder in o[u]r realme of Scotland begun vpon p[re]tence of Religion, but now apparring to haue been raised by factious spiritts, and fomented by some few ill and traiterously affected p[ar]ticular p[er]sons, whose ayme hath been by troubling the peace of that o[u]r kingdome to worke their owne p[ri]uate ends, and indeed to shake of all Monarchicall gouernment, though wee haue often assured them, that wee resolue to maintaine constantly, the religion established by the Lawes of that kingdome is now growne to that height, and dangerous consequence that under those sinister p[re]tences they haue so farre seduced o[u]r people there, as great and considerable forces, are raised and assembled, in such sort, as wee haue reason to take into consideration the defence and safety of this our realme of England. And therefore vpon due and mature consultation, w[i]th the Lordes of our Councell, wee haue resolued to repaire in o[u]r royall p[er]son to the Northerne partes of this o[u]r realme, there by the helpe of Almighty God and the assistance of o[u]r good subiects, to make resistance against any Invasion that may happen. And to the end that this Expedition may bee as effectuall as wee desire, to the glory of God, the honor and safety of us, and of this o[u]r said kingdome of England. Wee haue directed, that a considerable Army both of horse and foote shalbe forthw[i]th leavyed out of all the Shires, to attend us in this action, wherein wee nothing doubt but the affection, fidelity and courage of our people shall well appeare. In the meane time, wee haue thought fitt hereby to giue you notice of this o[u]r resolution and of this estate of o[u]r affaires, and doe hereby to require you to attend o[u]r royall p[er]son, and Standard at o[u]r City of Yorke by the first day of Aprill, next ensuing, in such equipage, and w[i]th such forces, as y[ou]r birth, yo[u]r honor, and yo[u]r interest, in the publiq safety doe oblige you vnto, and as wee doe and haue reason to expect from you; And these o[u]r L[ett]res shalbe as sufficient and effectuall a warrant and discharge vnto you for putting yo[u]r selfe, and likewise such as shall attend you, into armes, and order as aforesaid, as if you were authorised thereunto vnder o[u]r great seale of England. And wee doe require you to certify us vnder yo[u]r hand w[i]thin fifteene daies, what assistance wee shall expect from you herein, and to direct the same to one of o[u]r principall Secretaries of State. / Giuen vnder o[u]r Signett at o[u]r Pallace of Westminster the six; and twentith day of Ianuary in the ffowrteenth yeare of o[u]r raigne

Ex Warwick

Arabella Huntington Memorial Art Collection. Now it was Duveen who had Huntington's ear. What art objects, Huntington asked, would be most appropriate to honor his late wife, to reflect her tastes and interests? Duveen, with three boxcars of French furniture, porcelain, and sculpture waiting on an Alhambra rail siding, three miles from San Marino, had the answer. The Memorial would contain only the finest—tapestries by François Boucher, a Louis XV writing table, a collection of elegant snuff boxes, eight Italian bronzes, a Louis XVI clock, Sèvres porcelain, and marble busts by Etienne-Maurice Falconet and Jean-Antoine Houdon. In late January Huntington spent $2,500,000 on Duveen's stock, nearly emptying the boxcars. Two weeks after completing the transaction with Duveen he turned down a request from George Watson Cole, who had asked him to consider a modest gift to the New York Public Library in support of one of their important bibliographic projects. In a polite but firm letter Huntington explained:

> I fully appreciate the value of the work [completion of Sabin's "Dictionary"] and heartily agree with you in the matter, but as you know my whole interest is centered in California and I feel that all the financial support, which I have, to offer at the present time, is required here at home in the Huntington Library and Art Gallery to carry on the work which we have planned.[16]

With his health problems increasing, Huntington made plans to return to Philadelphia to consult once more with Dr. Deaver. He wrote Rosenbach:

> I have decided to come on to Philadelphia with Dr. Bryant to find out why the wound does not heal satisfactorily and am leaving this coming Friday. I have made no plans but undoubtedly shall see you and your brother while I am in your native town. I am feeling very well and felt that this is the time to come on, especially as I do not want to be in the East during the hot weather.[17]

On Friday, 5 May 1927, Dr. Deaver performed cancer surgery for the second time. Huntington seemed to make a good recovery in the first few days after the operation and was able to visit with Rosenbach and Duveen and various other business associates. On 15 May, however, he had a relapse. Rosenbach wrote Bliss:

Fig. 51 (opposite)
A letter from Charles I to the Earl of Huntingdon (26 January 1639), acquired with the Hastings-Huntingdon papers.

> For your private information Mr. Huntington is really in a seri-
> ous state. He does not respond to treatment . . . and Dr. Bryant
> is with him all the time. Mrs. Metcalf [Huntington's daughter] is
> here and also Mr. and Mrs. Holladay [Huntington's sister and
> brother-in-law].[18]

On 23 May Huntington lapsed into a coma and on the 25th, late in the morning, he died. Rosenbach wired the news to San Marino.

With family members in attendance, a black-draped, flag-bearing Southern Pacific engine carried the ebony casket in a private car back to California. On the day of the burial, Tuesday, 31 May, Mayor George E. Cryer of Los Angeles ordered the flag on top of city hall to be flown at half mast. Throughout the city and county all Pacific Electric and Los Angeles Railway cars stopped for one minute. Following private services, burial took place on the north end of the ranch, close to the site of a marble mausoleum then being constructed as a tomb for both Mr. and Mrs. Huntington.[19]

Condolences and tributes came to the family from all over the country. Newspapers eulogized the collector and his accomplishments, many with phrases similar to those used by the *Los Angeles Times:* "Huntington Monument Unmatched in World."[20]

Huntington's life was directed from the first by the principles of hard work and thrift, virtues that served him well in business and in collecting. Beyond that, he was independent and competitive, characteristics fostered early as he worked on the railroad for Uncle Collis. Once established, with a fortune of his own, he showed utter disregard for many of the conventional attitudes and practices of the wealthy of his day. He had no yacht and owned no string of race horses. He had no interest in gaining political power for himself or his friends, and he made no effort to enter society or to force society to recognize his accomplishments.

He was fixed in many of his ideas. Books in foreign languages were useless, he was convinced in the early years; paintings should show elegant rather than simple people; women should not serve in the workplace; union organizers were in league with the devil. On this last point he was emphatic. A Huntington rail employee who joined the union was promptly fired. Neither was he generous with his immediate staff. The house servants, library workers, gardeners, and gatekeepers were all paid at the bottom of the wage scale. It was simply a matter of thrift.

A practical man of business—that was the way he would have defined himself. Sentiment was a quality he neither displayed nor approved of. He had little interest in philanthropy of the kind preferred by other wealthy men of his day—setting up charities, establishing scholarships, providing free health care for the destitute. If people would work and save as he had, none of these provisions for the poor would be necessary. Although he was no snob, he believed in supporting Anglo-American culture at the highest level for those sophisticated enough to appreciate the finer things. He felt that he could best accomplish that objective by gathering a large library and an important collection of paintings and sculpture. But fine libraries and galleries took decades, even centuries, to form, and he didn't have that much time. The way of the traditional book collector, browsing in bookshops, studying bibliographies, and buying item by item, was not for him. He realized early that to get what he wanted he would need to break the rules, buy opportunistically, consolidate existing holdings, and annihilate the competition. He had used these approaches successfully in business and had no reason to believe they would not work in developing a distinguished library. In addition, his vast fortune would enable him to buy what he wanted. Impatient and somewhat imperious by nature, Huntington made his mark on the book world as early as 1911. If "they" bid $49,000 for a Gutenberg Bible, he had Smith on hand to bid $50,000. If a collection could be secured en bloc, he had Rosenbach on hand to complete the purchase. Huntington was not satisfied with merely owning a good library; it had to be outstanding and to rank with the distinguished collections in the world. Did the British Museum hold more Shakespeare quartos than Huntington? How many more? Of all the books printed in England before 1641, what was his position as compared with Oxford, Cambridge, and the British Museum? Was it possible to catch up? Was any American library close to him in the total number of incunabula held? These questions drove Huntington, his library staff, and his favorite book dealers to greater and greater efforts. That an American library, even more startling a California library, could match the strength of the great libraries of England was a matter of continuing pride.

Huntington was first and last a shrewd and successful businessman. At the age of sixty he left the railroad business and took up with equal seriousness the business of forming an important library, art collection, and botanical garden. As with his business concerns, his goals and ambitions developed and expanded; he never rested in one place without looking ahead to the next. He started, rather uncertainly, buying elaborately bound, finely illustrated limited editions, then moved on to entire libraries of English and American history and literature and completed the cycle by acquiring a number of manuscript collections. In the process he was aided by well-chosen associates, the trained bibliographers Cole, Bliss, Schad, Brigham, and Wagner; the knowledgeable and aggressive agents Smith, Sessler, Kennerley, and Rosenbach; and the trusted advisers Hale and Farrand. It was Huntington himself however who set the boundaries of the collections, established price limits, and ultimately made the decisions to buy or not to buy. He wanted to form an important library and do it quickly, but he did not stop there: of course the collection would be admired but would it be used? Who would use it? How would it be administered? What kind of financial support would be required? Huntington grappled with these questions for years without coming to a satisfactory answer. Finally, under the influence of Hale and Farrand, he decided to support the concept of a research library, a decision only slightly modified by a last-minute change to his will.

There are many things to admire about Huntington's approach to book collecting. His domination of the market from 1911 to 1926 can only be compared to that exercised by the voracious English collectors of the nineteenth century, Richard Heber, S. R. Christie-Miller, and Thomas Phillipps. He set about the task with enthusiasm and courage, drew on the experience of others, recognized the importance of quality, and later, planned for the eventual use of the materials by those most able to profit from them. Was Huntington, as the newspapers frequently claimed, the greatest collector the world has ever known? It may be enough to respond that his sweeping collecting style was remarkable for its day and that it produced a library that is one of the world's preeminent research centers. Huntington himself wanted no fame other than that bestowed by the library. "It is," he said,"the reward of all the work I have ever done and the realization of much happiness."[21]

Auctions in which substantial purchases were made

1908

| Nov 17–18 | Poor, Henry W. (pt 1) |
| Dec 7–9 | Poor, Henry W. (pt 2) |

1909

Jan 12–14	Poor, Henry W. (pt 3)
Feb 23–25	Poor, Henry W. (pt 4)
Apr 5–7	Poor, Henry W. (pt 5)

1910

| Apr 12–14 | Hollingsworth, Amor |

1911

Jan 19–20	Stedman, Edmund C. (pt 2)
Apr 24–28	Hoe, Robert (pt 1, A–K)
May 1–5	Hoe, Robert (pt 1, L–Z)
Nov 15–24	Huth, Henry (pt 1)

1912

Jan 8–12	Hoe, Robert (pt 2, A–K)
Jan 15–19	Hoe, Robert (pt 2, L–Z)
Apr 15–19	Hoe, Robert (pt 3, A–K)
Apr 22–26	Hoe, Robert (pt 3, L–Z)
May 9–10	Lossing, Benson (pt 1)
Jun 5–14	Huth, Henry (pt 2)
Nov 11–15	Hoe, Robert (pt 4, A–L)
Nov 18–22	Hoe, Robert (pt 4, L–Z)

1913

Feb 17–19	Borden, Mathew
Mar 24–28	Crane, Edward
Jun 2–12	Huth, Henry (pt 3)
Oct 30–31	Thacther, John Boyd (pt 1)

1914

Jan 8–9	Thacher, John Boyd (pt 2)
Jan 14–16	Lambert, Major William H. (pt 2)
Feb 25–27	Lambert, Major William H. (pt 2)
Apr 16–17	Nelson, William
Jun 25–26	Pembroke, Earl of
Jul 7–10	Huth, Henry (pt 4)
Jul 15–17	Arthur, T. G. (pt 1)
Jul 21	Arthur, T. G. (pt 2)
Nov 23–25	Stevenson, Robert Louis (pt 1)
Dec 15–18	Joline, Adrian H. (pt 1)

1915

Jan 18–22	Joline, Adrian H. (pt 2)
Apr 6–9	Ives, Brayton
Oct 19–22	Joline, Adrian H. (pt 7)

Oct 25–29	Burton, John (pt 1)
Nov 3–4	Thatcher, John Boyd (pt 6)
Nov 17–19	Burton, John (pt 4)
Nov 22–23	Nelson, William
Nov 22–24	Joline, Adrian H. (pt 8)

1916

Jan 12–14	Burton, John (pt 5)
Mar 6–7	Burton, John (pt 6)
Apr 25–27	Coggeshall, Edwin W. (pt 1)
May 15–17	Coggeshall, Edwin W. (pt 2)
Jul 4–7	Huth, Henry (pt 5)
Aug 15–17	Britwell Court
Nov 10	Crimmins, John D.
Nov 20	Jones, H. V.

1917

Jan 18–19	Clawson, J. L.
Mar 5–6	Learmont, J. B. (pt 1)
Mar 26	Clawson, J. L.
Jul 11–18	Huth, Henry (pt 6)
Dec 12–13	Groves, Charles J.
Dec 21–23	Shinn, Charles Howard

1918

Jan 3	Samson, William H.
Jan 7–8	Learmont, J. B. (pt 3)
Jan 9–11	Learmont, J. B. (pt 4)
Feb 13–14	Anderson Galleries
Feb 19–20	Caplin, Stephen
Feb 26–Mar 1	Robinson, Mark P.
Mar 5–7	Crimmins, John D.
Apr 29–May 1	Robinson, Mark P.
May 13–16	Hagen, Winston H.
Jul 1–9	Hugh, Henry (pt 7)
Oct 28–30	Anderson Galleries
Nov 21–22	Dodd, Robert H.
Dec 2–3	Jones H. V. (A–H)

1919

Jan 6–9	Church, William P.
Jan 13–14	Dodd, Robert H. (pt 2)
Jan 15–16	Young, James Carleton
Jan 29–30	Jones, H. V. (H–P)
Feb 3–5	Young, James Carleton (pt 2)
Feb 17–19	Halsey, Frederic R.
Feb 24–27	Crawford, John W. Roy

Mar 4–5	Jones, H. V. (P–Z with Addenda)
Mar 10–11	Anderson Galleries
Mar 20–21	Mostyn, Lord
May 13–14	Anderson Galleries
Jun 3	Thompson, Sir Henry Yates
Jun 30–Jul 3	Britwell Court
Jul 8–11	Huth Henry (pt 8)
Oct 15–25	Wendell, Evert Jansen
Nov 17–18	Du Bois, Loren Griswold
Nov 17–18	De Puy, Henry F. (pt 1)
Dec 15–16	Britwell Court

1920

Jan 12–16	DeVinne, Theodore Low
Jan 22–23	Newdigate–Newdegate, Sir Francis
Jan 26–27	De Puy, Henry F. (pt 2)
Feb 6–11	Anderson Galleries
Feb 17–18	American Art Association
Mar 15–17	Forman, H. Buxton (pt 1)
Mar 22–25	Wallace, Walter Thomas
Apr 16	Mostyn, Lord
Apr 19–20	De Puy, Henry F. (pt 3)
Apr 23	Stetson, John B.
Apr 26–28	Forman, H. Buxton (pt 2)
Apr 28–May 1	Holden, Edwin B.
May 5–6	Robinson, Charles L. F. (pt 2)
May 5–7	Britwell Court
May 24–25	Smith, George D. (pt 1)
Jun 14–15	Britwell Court
Jun 22–25	Huth, Henry (pt 9)
Nov 8–9	Dunlap, Boutwell
Nov 11–12	Smith, George D. (pt 2)
Nov 22–23	Edgar, Herman Le roy (pt 1)
Nov 29–30	Clawson, John L.
Dec 13–14	O'Brien, Dr. Frank P. (pt 2)

1921

Jan 10–12	Chamberlin, Emerson
Jan 10–12	Brickner, Mrs. W. M.
Jan 31–Feb 2	Britwell Court
Feb 14–16	Chamberlin, Emerson
Mar 4	Romm , Charles
Mar 10–11	Britwell Court
Apr 18–19	Andrews, William Loring
May 25–Jun 3	Brooke, Sir J. A.
Nov 1–2	Rhode Island Historical Society
Nov 28–29	Anderson Galleries
Dec 6–7	American Art Association

1922

Feb 6–7	Van Duzer, Henry Sayre
Feb 6–10	Britwell Court

Feb 8	Coates, Sir Edward F.
Apr 10	Butler, Edward K.
Oct 26	Hoes, Captain Roswell Randall
Nov 15	Severance, Frank H.
Nov 16	Sheehan, Dr. R.
Nov 20–22	Sturges, Henry Cady (pt 1)

1923

Jan 15–16	Sturges, Henry Cady (pt 3)
Feb 5–6	Anderson Galleries
Feb 28–Mar 2	Bement, Clarence S.
Mar 8–9	Winters, William H.
Mar 12–16	Britwell Court
Mar 20–22	Powis, Earl of
May 2	Norton, Charles Eliott
Jul 2	Carysfort, Earl of
Nov 12–14	Quinn, John (pt 1 A–C)
Nov 20	Welles, Gideon
Nov 20–21	Sotheby (Kendall–Holme)
Dec 10–12	Quinn, John (pt 2 D–H)

1924

Jan 4	Welles, Gideon (pt 2)
Jan 14–16	Quinn, John (pt 3 I–M)
Jan 21	House, H. F.
Feb 11–13	Quinn, John (pt 4 M–S)
Mar 17–19	Quinn, John (pt 5 S–Z)
Mar 31–Apr 4	Britwell Court
Apr 7–9	Britwell Court
Apr 14–15	Northbourne, Lord
Apr 28–29	Wakeman, Mrs. Alice L.
Jul 24–25	Sotheby, Col. H. G.
Nov 10–11	Arnold, William Harris

1925

Mar 17–19	Duff, E. Gordon (pt 2)
Mar 23–26	Britwell Court
Mar 31–Apr 4	Britwell Court
May 4	Royal Society
Nov 23–25	Cromwell, Lord

1926

Mar 15–18	Britwell Court
Mar 22–24	Britwell Court
May 20–21	Clawson, John L. (pt 1)
May 24–25	Clawson, John L. (pt 2)
Jul 21–22	Henkele, Stan
Nov 11	C. F. Gunther
Dec 1	American Art Association

1927

Jan 7	Isham, Ralph
Jan 10	Anderson Art Galleries

Libraries purchased – a selected list

1904	Charles A. Morrogh library	Fine printing
1904	John A. Morschhauser library	Fine printing, illustration
1907	Schneider library (Juliet Brown owner)	Incunabula, printing history
1911	E. D. Church library	Americana and English literature
1912	Beverly Chew library	Sixteenth- and seventeenth-century English poetry
1913	Grenville Kane library	George Washington
1913	John Quinn library	Literary manuscripts
1914	Duke of Devonshire library	Kemble-Devonshire plays and Devonshire Caxtons
1914	Ward Hill Lamon library	Abraham Lincoln
1915	Frederick R. Halsey library	American and English history
1915	George D. Smith library	Early European printing
1916	Augustin Macdonald library	Californiana
1916	Britwell Court library	Americana
1917	Bridgewater library	English literature and history
1918	William K. Bixby library	Literary and historical manuscripts
1919	G. W. Michelmore library	Railroading
1922	Charles Gunther library	Incunabula
1922	Henry R. Wagner library	Californiana
1922	Judd Stewart library	Abraham Lincoln
1922	Walter Lewisson library	George Washington
1922	John Nicholson library	Civil War history
1922	Robert A. Brock library	Southern history
1922	James T. Fields papers	American literature, letters
1923	Simon Gratz library	Early American imprints
1922	George Barr McCutcheon library	American literary manuscripts
1923	James Abercromby papers	Colonial history
1923	Loudoun papers	Colonial history
1923	James Ellsworth library	Incunabula
1923	Battle Abbey papers	English history
1923	Wilberforce Eames library	American printing
1923	Sir Thomas Phillipps library	Incunabula
1923	A. S. W. Rosenbach library	Incunabula
1924	Otto H. F. Vollbehr library	Incunabula
1925	Jack London library	Manuscripts and letters
1925	Stowe manuscripts	English history
1926	Chevalier Destouches papers	American colonial period
1926	Rufus King letters	American British foreign policy
1926	Pizarro papers	Sixteenth-century Peru
1926	Richard Howe papers	Eighteenth-century British Navy
1926	Hastings-Huntingdon papers	English history

Abbreviations Used in the Notes

People

LB	Leslie Bliss
GWC	George Watson Cole
HEH	Henry E. Huntington
BQ	Bernard Quaritch
ASWR	Abraham Simon Wolf Rosenbach
ROS	Robert O. Schad
GDS	George D. Smith

Newspapers

LAE	*Los Angeles Examiner*
LAH	*Los Angeles Herald*
LAT	*Los Angeles Times*
NYT	*New York Times*

Henry Huntington Library

HIA GC	Huntington Institutional Archives – General Correspondence – uncataloged
HIA GC Bi	Huntington Institutional Archives – General Correspondence – Biographical Project – uncataloged
HEH C	Henry E. Huntington Collection – cataloged

Chapter 1 — ONEONTA AND BEYOND (1850–1900)

1. John Drinkwater, "A Memory of George D. Smith," *The Bookman* 53 (January 1921): 308.

2. *NYT*, 25 April 1911.

3. A passport issued to HEH, 16 April 1913, by the Department of State describes him as follows: Age–63, Forehead–high, Eyes–blue, Height–5' 10 ½", Complexion–fair, Hair–bald, Nose–straight, Mouth–large, Chin–prominent, Face–oval. HEH C.

4. Huntington's immediate family was made up of an older sister, Mary Leonora, and two older brothers, Howard, who died as a teenager, and George, who died at the age of five. He also had a younger brother, Willard, and two younger sisters, Harriet, who died at the age of two, and Caroline, later Mrs. Edmund Burke Holladay.

5. Caroline Holladay, "Recollection," 14 January 1929. HIA GC Bi.

6. HEH to Harriet Huntington, 10 July 1871. HEH C.

7. Oscar Lewis, *The Big Four* (New York: Knopf, 1938), 214.

8. HEH to Harriet Huntington, 1 July 1872. HEH C.

9. N. V. Franchot to ROS, 4 May 1929. HIA GC Bi.

10. HEH to Harriet Huntington, 20 October 1881. HEH C.

11. Quoted in ROS, "Henry E. Huntington: The Founder and the Library," *Huntington Library Bulletin* 1 (May 1931): 6.

12. HEH to Harriet Huntington, 7 June 1892. HEH C.

13. Robert E. Cowan, *Booksellers of Early San Francisco* (Los Angeles: Ward Ritchie Press, 1953), 58.

14. William Doxey to HEH, 7 May and 21 July 1898. HIA GC

15. Note on William Doxey letterhead, n.d. HIA GC.

16. Marian Huntington to ROS, 1 February 1930. HIA GC Bi.

17. Kevin Starr, *Inventing the Dream* (New York: Oxford, 1985), 64.

18. *LAT*, 8 April 1906.

19. Glenn Dumke, "Early Transportation in the Los Angeles Area," *Quarterly of the Historical Society of Southern California* 19 (September 1940): 131.

20. HEH letter quoted in *LAT*, 8 April 1906.

21. Clara Huntington to ROS, 19 April 1929. HIA GC Bi.

Chapter 2 — A Few Shelves of Sumptuous Books (1900–1910)

1. Myron Hunt to George Hapgood, 8 May 1928. HIA GC Bi.

2. "Aaron Mendoza: 1888–1960," *AB Bookman's Weekly* 25 (1960): 1,607.

3. Isaac Mendoza to ROS, 18 October 1930. HIA GC Bi.

4. Ibid.

5. *Catalogue of the Illustrated Works and First Editions in the Library of Charles Morrogh* (New York: Privately printed, 1902).

6. Isaac Mendoza to ROS, 18 October 1930. HIA GC Bi.

7. Ibid.

8. On the billing a few titles are marked "to Howard" (Howard Huntington) and "to Marian" (Marian Huntington). HIA GC.

9. HEH to Dodd, Mead, 9 May 1905. HIA GC.

10. HEH quoted in *LAH*, 19 November 1905.

11. Harris Newmark, *Sixty Years in Southern California* (New York: Knickerbocker, 1916), 620.

12. *LAT,* 4 October 1906.

13. It was at this dinner that Huntington found himself seated next to the noted astronomer George Ellery Hale. The talk turned to books. Huntington asked Hale if he thought the rare book collection stored in New York should be brought to California. Hale made a strong case for California. See Helen Wright, *Explorer of the Universe: A Biography of George Ellery Hale* (New York: Dutton, 1966), 372–73.

14. HEH quoted in *LAT,* 8 April 1906.

15. James Canfield to Henry Carpenter, 2 October 1906. HIA GC.

16. Handwritten notes attached to the "Catalog of the Schneider Library" indicate that Huntington sold the German language materials immediately as not appropriate to the scope of his collections. HIA GC.

17. N. Chapin to HEH, 2 March and 15 March 1907. HIA GC.

18. *NYT*, 12 November 1908.

19. See Wesley Towner, *The Elegant Auctioneers* (New York: Hill and Wang, 1970), 255–58. Towner includes a highly colored account of Huntington and Smith's midnight visits to the Anderson stockroom to view the Henry Poor books.

20. *NYT,* 22 November 1908.

21. Ruth Park claimed that in the winter of 1907 Sessler started Huntington on his career as a rare book collector. This claim seems dubious as HEH had by that time already purchased several important libraries. See Ruth Park, "A Great Romantic," *Publisher's Weekly*

116 (1929): 2,400–2,401.

22. Charles Sessler to HEH, 16 February and 25 March 1909. HIA GC.

23. Mabel Zahn to Roland Frye, 5 April 1974. HIA GC Bi.

24. HEH to Charles Sessler, 2 June 1909. HIA GC.

25. HEH quoted in *NYT*, 30 April 1911.

26. HEH quoted in *LAT*, 26 April 1910.

Chapter 3 — From Church to Hoe to Huth (1911–1912)

1. W. N. C. Carlton, "Henry Edwards Huntington, 1850–1927, an Appreciation," *American Collector* 4 (August 1927): 3.

2. *NYT*, 9 April 1911.

3. *Nation* 87 (September 1908): 205.

4. GWC, comp., *A Catalogue of Books Relating to the Discovery and Early History of North and South America Forming a Part of the Library of E. D. Church* (New York: Dodd, Mead, 1907).

5. *American Historical Review* 13 (October 1908): 177.

6. *NYT*, 16 April 1911.

7. HEH quoted by ROS in "The Founder and the Library," *Huntington Library Bulletin* 1 (May 1931): 13.

8. *NYT*, 8 April 1911.

9. Luther Livingston to HEH, 8 April 1911. HIA GC.

10. Emory S. Turner to HEH, 10 April 1911. HIA GC.

11. Beverly Chew, "Foreword," *The Library of Robert Hoe* (New York: Anderson Auction Company, 1911).

12. *NYT*, 13 April 1911.

13. *NYT*, 25 April 1911.

14. The term "illuminated books" was used by Blake to describe his work in a prospectus, "To the Public," issued 10 October 1793. Detailed information on the Huntington Library Blake holdings and acquisitions can be found in *The Works of William Blake in the Huntington Collections: A Complete Catalogue,* comp. Robert N. Essick (San Marino, Calif.: Huntington Library, 1985).

15. Walter Hill quoted in the *NYT*, 28 April 1911.

16. Belle da Costa Greene quoted in the *NYT*, 30 April 1911.

17. *NYT*, 30 April 1911.

18. Several of the major participants in the sale are depicted in a cartoon, "The Bloodless Battle, or Books of the Bibliophiles," *New York Herald Tribune,* 14 January 1912. Included

were caricatures of Arthur Hoe, A. S. W. Rosenbach, M. Eissmann, Major E. S. Turner, Bernard Quaritch, Lathrop Harper, Arthur Swann, George D. Smith, and Dr. G. Martini.

19. The *NYT*, 29 April 1912, reported that Hoe had purchased the item from the London dealer Bernard Quaritch for $3,000 in 1889.

20. The *San Francisco Star*, 28 April 1911, reported: "The sum would have given one hundred working men and their families more than an average income for an entire year."

21. Marvin Johnson to HEH, 11 June 1911. HIA GC.

22. C. E. Graham to Mr. Courtney, 28 April 1912. HIA GC.

23. Epes Randolph to HEH, 2 May 1911, and HEH's reply of 8 May. HIA GC.

24. *Catalogue of the Huth Collection of Printed Books and Illuminated Manuscripts* (London: Sotheby, Wilkinson, and Hodge, 1911).

25. HEH to BQ, 27 October 1911. HIA GC.

26. Dr. Rosenbach's profit from the sale of *Thel* is noted by Edwin Wolf and John Fleming in *Rosenbach: A Biography* (Cleveland: World, 1960), 74.

27. Thomas Barbour, Recollections (typescript, n.d.). HIA GC Bi. According to the *Annals of the Hobby Club of New York City 1912–1920* (New York: Privately printed, 1920), Huntington served as one of two vice presidents from 1911 to 1920 and was a member of the board of governors during the same period.

28. Ibid.

29. Charles Sessler to HEH, 31 January 1911. HIA GC.

30. HEH to BQ, 17 May 1912, and HEH's reply of 29 May. HIA GC.

31. BQ to HEH, 4 June 1912. HIA GC. An account of Harry Elkins Widener's collecting interests is given in Wolf and Fleming, *Rosenbach*, 55–58.

32. BQ to HEH, 10 July 1912. HIA GC.

33. Beverly Chew, quoted in Robert Nikirk, "Two American Book Collectors of the Nineteenth Century: William Loring Andrews and Beverly Chew," in *Book Selling and Book Buying* (Chicago: American Library Association, 1978), 111. Chew is quoted in full as saying, "I really didn't want to sell, so mentioned a price that I doubted if anyone would pay."

34. GWC, "The Henry E. Huntington Library 1915–1924" (typescript, n.d.), George Watson Cole Papers, American Antiquarian Society.

Chapter 4 — FOLLOWING THE AUCTION MARKET (1913–1914)

1. Turner convinced the Hoe family that they should place the library with the Anderson Auction Company after he showed them a scathing review in the *Athenaeum*, 24 March 1900, claiming that the American Art Association catalog for the John Daly sale (March 1900) was a shoddy piece of work (see Towner, *Elegant Auctioneers*, 264–65).

2. GDS to HEH, 3 February, 10 February, 25 February 1913; 12 March 1914; and 6 March 1913. HIA GC.

3. The bulk of Kane's library eventually went to Princeton University.

4. John Quinn, quoted in B. L. Reid, *The Man from New York* (New York: Oxford, 1968), 123. Quinn's comment is difficult to understand as the Huntington library was not organized as a public institution until 1919.

5. *NYT,* 8 June 1913.

6. HEH to Caroline Holladay, 13 July 1913. HEH C.

7. HEH to Caroline Holladay, 20 July 1913. HEH C.

8. Huntington's purchase of the Devonshire Shakespeare collection forced Marsden J. Perry to give up his goal of building a great Shakespeare library. Perry is reputed to have said to friends that if he could not have the Devonshire quartos he would give up collecting (see Wolf and Fleming, *Rosenbach,* 114–15).

9. *Times,* London, 19 and 20 March 1914.

10. *NYT,* 21 March 1914.

11. C. E. Graham to HEH, 16 March 1914. HIA GC.

12. "Huntington, C. A. Montague Barlow and George D. Smith Agreement"; signed 19 January 1914 by C. E. Graham for Huntington, C. A. Montague Barlow for the Duke of Devonshire, and George D. Smith (typescript). HIA GC.

13. G. Miles to HEH, 19 March 1914. HIA GC.

14. Under the headline "Huntington takes Devonshire Books," the *NYT* of 19 March 1914 reported that George D. Smith obtained the collection for between $1,000,000 and $1,200,000. The article also mentioned Smith's inflated price of $1,300,000, supposedly paid for the Chew library in 1912. The accurate total for the Chew collection was $750,000.

15. *NYT,* 4 January 1914.

16. *NYT,* 23 March 1914.

17. GDS to HEH, 2 July 1914. HIA GC. Smith's guess on the Whitey-Brown papers was close; it sold for $3,800.

18. GDS to HEH, 12 March and 2 April 1914. HIA GC.

19. Dring to HEH, 27 March 1914. HIA GC.

20. GDS to HEH, 26 June 1914. HIA GC.

21. *NYT,* 26 June 1914.

22. *NYT,* 8 July 1914.

23. *Times,* London, 9 July 1914.

24. Dring to HEH, 24 September 1914. HIA GC.

25. Dring to HEH, 10 February 1915. HIA GC.

26. *New York Sun,* 18 July 1914.

27. *NYT,* 19 July 1914.

28. GDS to HEH, 7 April 1916. HIA GC. A full description of the Shakespeare bookcase is given in the *NYT,* 19 March 1916, Magazine Section. In a letter of 22 July 1919 to GDS, Folger still expressed interest in the bookcase. HIA GC. A billing statement of 4 March 1916 shows the original selling price as $6,000. HIA GC.

29. *NYT,* 25 July 1914.

30. *NYT,* 12 July 1914.

31. "Man Who Saved Theodore Roosevelt from Death Rescues Mrs. Henry E. Huntington from War Zone," *NYT,* 27 September 1914.

Chapter 5 — The Passion Becomes a Plan (1915–1916)

1. Harold Carew, "Toiler in the Vineyard of Books," *Touring Topics* 21 (February 1929): 48.

2. HEH quoted in *LAT,* 12 February 1915.

3. Mrs. Widener also gave Harvard University funds for a rare book library building named in memory of her son, Harry Elkins Widener.

4. Major auction houses mounted 72 sales January–May 1914 and 96 in the same period in 1915. See George L. McKay, comp., *American Book Auction Catalogues 1713–1934: A Union List* (New York: New York Public Library, 1937).

5. GWC to HEH, 19 July 1915, and HEH's reply of 27 July. HIA GC.

6. GWC, "The Henry E. Huntington Library 1915–24," Cole Papers, American Antiquarian Society.

7. Lodewyk Bendikson, "Remarks by Dr. Lodewyk Bendikson at a dinner honoring him on his retirement from the Huntington Library" (typescript, 30 June 1943). HIA GC Bi.

8. Margaret F. Maxwell, *Shaping a Library: William L. Clements As a Collector* (Amsterdam: N. Israel, 1973), 102.

9. GDS to HEH, 7 April 1916, and HEH's reply of 19 April. HIA GC.

10. On 7 July 1922 HEH supplied a warm letter of recommendation for Kennerley beginning, "My dealings with Mr. Kennerley, both personally and in a business way, have always been most pleasant." HIA GC.

11. The Henry E. Huntington duplicate sales proceeded as follows: 29–31 March 1916, 230 of 1,141 lots from Huntington; 21–22 November 1916, 890 lots; 24–25 January 1917, 308 lots; 26–28 February 1917, 519 of 1,107 lots from Huntington; 10 December 1917, 493 lots; 11 December 1917, 330 lots; 4–6 February 1918, 1,035 lots; 24–26 April 1918, 598 lots; 6–7 November 1918, 636 lots; 6 March 1919, 241 lots; 28–29 January

1920, 614 lots; 11–12 March 1920, 408 lots; 8–10 January 1923, 1,014 lots; 2 December 1924, 446 lots; and 12–13 January 1925, 434 lots.

12. GDS, "To My Customers," in *Monuments of Early Printing in Germany, the Low Countries, Italy, France, and England 1460–1500* (New York: George D. Smith, 1916), n.p.

13. Smith, with his usual disregard for the facts, gave the sale price of the incunabula as $115,000, as announced in the *NYT,* 28 March 1916.

14. HEH to Robert Cowan, 3 April 1916, and Cowan's reply of 24 April. HIA GC.

15. Henry R. Wagner quoted by Alan Jutzi in "Western Americana in Los Angeles Libraries," in John Bidwell, ed., *A Bibliophile's Los Angeles* (Los Angeles: W. A. Clark Memorial Library, UCLA, 1985), 124. Jutzi quotes a letter of 1916 from Wagner to Robert E. Cowan: "There are rumors here that Macdonald has sold his collection to that shark H. E. Huntington."

16. Robert Cowan to HEH, 28 April 1916, and HEH's reply of 9 May. HIA GC.

17. *Times,* London, 15 August 1916.

18. Seymour de Ricci, *English Collectors of Books and Manuscripts* (New York: Macmillan, 1930), 105; 111–12.

19. BQ to HEH, 15 July 1916. HIA GC.

20. GDS to HEH, 31 July 1916. HIA GC.

21. GWC to BQ, 21 July 1916. HIA GC.

22. HEH to GDS, 1 September 1916. HIA GC.

23. Quoted in *NYT,* 16 August 1916.

24. Dring to HEH, 15 August 1916. HIA GC.

25. GDS to HEH, 7 July 1916. HIA GC.

26. William L. Clements to Clarence Brigham, 30 November 1916. HIA GC.

27. HEH to Dring at Quaritch, 16 June 1916, and Dring's reply of 10 July. HIA GC.

28. GDS to HEH, 11 April 1916, and HEH's reply of 19 April. HIA GC.

29. GDS to HEH, 9 May 1916. HIA GC.

30. GDS to HEH, 6 May 1916. HIA GC.

31. GDS to HEH, 13 July 1916, and HEH's reply of 25 July. HIA GC.

32. GDS to HEH, 31 July 1916. HIA GC.

33. HEH to GDS, 29 January 1918. HIA GC.

34. Mitchell Kennerley to HEH, 22 November 1916. HIA GC.

35. HEH quoted in *LAT,* 12 February 1915.

36. HEH quoted in *LAT,* 10 April 1916.

Chapter 6 — A Magnificent Scale (1917–1918)

1. J. Payne Collier, *A Catalogue Bibliographical and Critical of Early English Literature Forming a Portion of the Library at Bridgewater House, the Property of Rt. Hon. Lord Francis Egerton, M.P.* (London, 1837).

2. Sotheby and Company, *The Bridgewater Library* (London: Sotheby, 1917).

3. *The Complete Works of Geoffrey Chaucer,* ed. W. W. Skeat (Oxford: Clarendon, 1930), xiii.

4. *Catalogue of the Larpent Plays in the Henry E. Huntington Library* (San Marino, Calif.: Huntington Library, 1939).

5. Signed contract with Sotheby's for Bridgewater books and manuscripts, 21 February 1917. HIA GC.

6. GDS to HEH, 4 April 1917. HIA GC.

7. *NYT,* 18 May and 21 May 1917.

8. *NYT,* 27 May 1917.

9. Mitchell Kennerley, *Extraordinary Collection of Americana* (New York: Anderson Auction Company, 1917).

10. HEH to Mitchell Kennerley, 2 February 1917. HIA GC.

11. Mitchell Kennerley to HEH, 23 May 1917. HIA GC

12. Wolf and Fleming, *Rosenbach,* 107; 106.

13. *LAT,* 7 September 1918.

14. GWC, "Report" (typescript, 1918), Cole Papers, American Antiquarian Society.

15. Bendikson, "Remarks," 2. HIA GC Bi.

16. Ibid.

17. Robert Dodd to HEH, 20 November 1917, and HEH's reply of 26 November 1917. HIA GC.

18. Ernest Dressel North to HEH, 11 March 1919, and HEH's reply of 14 March. HIA GC.

19. George H. Sargent in the *Boston Evening Transcript,* 10 April 1918.

20. Beverly Chew, "Foreword," in *Catalogue of the Library of the Late Winston H. Hagen* (New York: Anderson Galleries, 1919), 5.

21. HEH to GDS, 25 September 1918. HIA GC.

22. HEH to C. E. Graham, 30 September 1918. Apparently it was a regular practice for Huntington to loan Smith money. A note in the Huntington Institutional Archives verifies the loan of $20,000 in 1916. HIA GC.

23. *LAT,* 7 September 1918.

24. Ernest Batchelder, a close friend of George Ellery Hale, is quoted by Helen Wright (*Explorer,* 379), as claiming that Archer was violently opposed to moving the collection to

California. In a summary report prepared after Huntington's death, Cole referred to the move of books to California as "the greatest mistake Mr. Huntington ever made" (GWC, "The Huntington Library 1915–1924," Cole Papers, American Antiquarian Society).

25. *LAT,* 24 January 1914.

Chapter 7 — So Little Time (1919)

1. Charles Dorr, "Literary Treasures of Herschel V. Jones," *Art World* 4 (November 1918): 33.

2. GDS to HEH, 18 November 1918. HIA GC.

3. Herschel V. Jones to HEH, 24 February 1919. HIA GC.

4. H. Jones to L. Bendikson, 10 January, 2 May, 16 May, 2 June 1919. HIA GC.

5. *Times*, London, 31 January 1919.

6. Seymour de Ricci had both the Medwall and the Wager titles printed in facsimile for the Huntington Library in 1920.

7. LB to HEH, 7 May 1919. HIA GC.

8. HEH to GDS, 1 July 1919, and GDS's letters of 9 July and 29 August. HIA GC.

9. HEH to C. E. Graham, 13 September 1919. HIA GC.

10. GEH to HEH, April 1914; and HEH's reply of 5 October. HIA GC

11. HEH to GEH, 22 April 1916. HIA GC.

12. Henry E. Huntington Library. Trust Indenture. 1919. HIA GC. The original indenture was amended several times over the next six years—June 1920, October 1921, February 1922, February 1926, and April 1927.

13. Henry Folger to HEH, 30 June 1922. HIA GC.

14. ASWR to HEH, 1 August 1919. HIA GC.

15. Handwritten note on ASWR billing of 1 August 1919 shows original cost to Rosenbach of entire Perry Library was $163,500. HIA GC.

16. HEH to GWC, 21 August 1919, and GWC's reply of 16 September. HIA GC.

17. HEH to GDS, 4 December 1919. HIA GC.

18. Dring to HEH, 24 October 1919, and HEH's reply (written by Cole), 12 November. HIA GC.

19. Sotheby and Company, *Catalogue of a Further Selection of Rare and Valuable Works* (London: Sotheby, 1919).

20. E. Millicent Sowerby, *Rare People and Rare Books* (Williamsburg, Va.: Bookpress, 1987), 81–83.

21. GDS quoted in *NYT*, 17 December 1919.

22. *NYT*, 18 December 1919.

23. A. W. Pollard, "English Books," *The Observer* 21 (December 1919): 9.

24. William A. White to HEH, 5 December 1919, and HEH's reply of 16 December. HIA GC. Huntington of course changed his mind about the form in which he would grant public access to the library.

25. HEH quoted in *LAE*, 2 August 1919.

Chapter 8 — THE BOOKS MOVE WEST (1920)

1. GDS to HEH, 5 January 1920. In this cable Smith asked Huntington for a loan of £5,000. HIA GC.

2. *NYT,* 5 March 1920.

3. Charles F. Heartman, "George D. Smith, 1870–1920: Gentleman Bookseller," *American Book Collector* 23 (May–June 1973).

4. John Drinkwater, "A Memory of George D. Smith," *The Bookman* 53 (January 1921): 308.

5. Mitchell Kennerley quoted in Mathew Bruccoli, *Mitchell Kennerley* (New York: Harcourt, 1986), 133.

6. Heartman, "George D. Smith," 45.

7. GWC to HEH, 11 March 1920, and HEH's reply of 16 March. HIA GC.

8. Thomas E. Kirby to HEH, 5 March 1920. HIA GC.

9. Mitchell Kennerley to HEH, 12 April 1920. HIA GC.

10. C. E. Graham to HEH, 12 April 1923. HIA GC.

11. Leslie Bliss, interview, with background on the New York library and its staff in the early years, 1915–20 (typescript, 3 January 1968). HIA GC Bi.

12. LB to HEH, 17 March 1920. HIA GC.

13. ROS to HEH, 18 November 1921. HIA GC.

14. Carl Cannon, *American Book Collectors and Collecting* (New York: H. W. Wilson, 1941), 151–52.

15. A full discussion of the Wallace sale was printed in the *New York Evening Post,* 3 April 1920.

16. A. E. Newton quoted by Maxwell Luria in "Lowell and Newton: A Literary Friendship," *Harvard Library Bulletin* 29 (January 1981): 11.

17. Handwritten note on Wallace billing from LB to HEH: "Entire Library said to have sold for $100,000 less than it should." HIA GC.

18. LB to HEH, 30 April 1920. HIA GC.

19. ASWR to HEH, 20 April 1920. HIA GC.

20. LB to HEH, 2 April 1920. HIA GC.

21. LB to HEH, 6 April 1920. HIA GC.

22. *LAT*, 25 March 1920.

23. GWC to HEH, 12 June 1920. HIA GC.

24. GWC to HEH, 25 October 1920. HIA GC.

25. HEH to GWC, 16 December 1920. HIA GC.

26. New York University Citation (New York, 1927). HIA GC.

27. HEH to Caroline Holladay, 18 December 1920. HIA GC.

28. GWC, "The Henry E. Huntington Library 1915–1924," Cole Papers, American Antiquarian Society.

29. HEH to Caroline Holladay, 18 December 1920. HIA GC.

30. HEH to Russell Benedict, 17 November 1920. HIA GC.

31. LB to HEH, 9 December 1920. HIA GC.

32. Francis Ferguson to HEH, 18 August 1920. HIA GC.

33. Clarence Brigham to HEH, 17 April 1920. HIA GC.

34. Clarence Brigham to GWC, 27 July 1920. HIA GC.

35. Clarence Brigham to HEH, 17 August 1920; 19 January and 13 August 1921. HIA GC.

36. Chester Cate to Clarence Brigham, 23 July 1921. HIA GC.

37. Clarence Brigham to GWC, 28 November 1921; GWC's letter of 10 November 1922. HIA GC.

38. HEH to Clarence Brigham, 21 December 1923, and Clarence Brigham's reply of 7 January 1924. HIA GC.

39. LB to Clarence Brigham, 10 February 1924. HIA GC.

40. Clarence Brigham, in *To Doctor R.: Essays Here Collected and Published in Honor of the Seventieth Birthday of Dr. A. S. W. Rosenbach* (Philadelphia, 1946), 52.

Chapter 9 — Incunabula and Manuscripts (1921–1922)

1. ASWR to HEH, 27 May 1921. HIA GC.

2. HEH to Robert Jaffray, 14 April 1921. HIA GC.

3. HEH to GWC, 23 June 1921. HIA GC.

4. See Mitchell Kennerley to HEH, 24 December 1921. HIA GC.

5. HEH quoted in *LAT,* 9 January 1922.

6. HEH quoted in letter, ROS to LB, 24 January 1922. HIA GC.

7. *Emicardulfe,* by E. C., esquier (1595); *Fidessa,* by B. Griffin (1596); *Laura* by R. Tofte (1597); and *Cynthia,* by R. Barnfield (1595).

8. *Times*, London, 11 March 1922.

9. ASWR to HEH, 15 March 1922 (indicating that Christie-Miller expected £200,000 and realized only £80,259); and HEH's reply of 21 March. HIA GC.

10. Walter Benjamin to GWC (typescript, n.d.). HIA GC.

11. ASWR to HEH, 23 November 1922. HIA GC.

12. Henry R. Wagner, *Collecting: Especially Books* (Los Angeles: Ward Ritchie Press, 1968), 20.

13. HEH to H. Wagner, 7 April 1922. HIA GC.

14. Wagner, *Collecting,* 21.

15. Henry Wagner to HEH, 22 September 1923. HIA GC.

16. LB to H. Wagner, 20 November 1923. HIA GC.

17. Wagner, *Collecting,* 20.

18. Ruth Axe to the author, 15 May 1991.

19. LB to H. Wagner, 26 March 1924. HIA GC.

20. H. Wagner to LB, 20 June 1925, and LB's reply of 2 July. HIA GC.

21. Wagner, *Collecting,* 20. On Huntington's death he wrote a warm tribute saying "America has lost one of its outstanding citizens. Indeed it would not, perhaps, be too much to say that in future years he will be looked back upon as one of the greatest philanthropists of any time"; see *California Historical Society Quarterly* 6 (June 1927): 200.

22. Walter Lewisson to Charles Prussing, 11 February 1922. HIA GC.

23. HEH to Prussing, 5 January 1922. HIA GC.

24. Lewisson to LB, 18 May 1922. HIA GC.

25. Lewisson to ROS, 6 January 1922. HIA GC.

26. Mrs. J. P. Nicholson to HEH, 24 April 1922; and to ROS, 22 January 1923. HIA GC.

27. ROS to HEH, "The R. A. Brock Library" (typescript, n.d.); and ROS to HEH, 13 October 1922. HIA GC.

28. *Richmond News Leader,* 15 November 1922.

29. Elizabeth Brock to HEH, 10 November 1922, and HEH's reply of 21 November. HIA GC.

30. HEH to ROS, 14 October 1922. HIA GC.

31. LB to ROS, 24 October 1922. HIA GC.

32. LB to ASWR, 10 November 1922 and 7 February 1923; ASWR's reply of 15 February. HIA GC.

33. ASWR to HEH, 22 November 1922. HIA GC.

34. Account of Rosenbach arrangements on *Pericles* in Wolf and Fleming, *Rosenbach,* 162.

35. ASWR to HEH, 27 November and 29 November 1922. HIA GC.

36. ASWR to HEH, 6 December and 4 December 1922. HIA GC.

37. ASWR to HEH, 15 January 1923. HIA GC.

38. LB to ASWR, 25 January 1923, and ASWR's replies, to LB, 19 February, and HEH, 6 February. HIA GC.

39. Mitchell Kennerley to HEH, 15 November 1922. HIA GC.

40. Alice Millard to HEH, 22 November 1922, and LB's reply of 29 November. HIA GC.

41. LB to James Drake, 7 May 1921. HIA GC.

42. In a letter dated 14 July 1926, Bliss asked Drake not to send "limited" first editions, since at $15 and $20 "they are becoming too expensive." HIA GC.

Chapter 10 — WORKING WITH ROSENBACH (1923)

1. "A Note by John Quinn," in *The Library of John Quinn* (New York: Anderson Galleries, 1923).

2. James Drake to HEH, 4 December 1923. HIA GC.

3. B. L. Reid, *The Man from New York* (New York: Oxford, 1968), 604–5.

4. HEH to ASWR, 19 November 1923. HIA GC.

5. Drake to LB, 12 November 1924. HIA GC.

6. LB to Edward Eberstadt, 26 April 1923, and Eberstadt's reply of 2 May. HIA GC.

7. Nicknames of other dealers of the era, as assigned by Charles Heartman, were: Whitman "I revolutionize the game" Bennett; Barnett J. "What difference does it make?" Beyer; Alfred J. "Give it to me" Boden; Ernest E. "Only I know how to sell books" Dawson; R. H. "Gentleman" Dodd; James F. "the one and only" Drake; P. K. "Enough said" Foley; pathetic Robert E. Fridenberg; Alfred E. Goldsmith (who could have been among the biggest); Chas. E. "Yankee" Goodspeed; George "No enemy" Grasberger; Byrne Hackett (who never settled down to brass tacks); Lathrop C. "Pre-occupied" Harper (if anybody should tell him about the troubles of the book business he will say "But you should have to worry over real estate"); Elmer V. Heise (who never misses an auction sale); suave George E. Hellman; Walter M. "Sensitive and sentimental" Hill; Merle "High Spot" (I wish I had never done it) Johnson; "Jew" (no disrespect) Dr. Rosenbach; Joseph F. "Grand old man" Sabin; Alvin J. "Kike" Scheuer (who notwithstanding his large purchases and prompt payments was disliked by everybody); Charles "Dandy" Sessler; the greatest of all of them, the never-equalled "Bull-dog" George D. "Try to take it away from me" Smith; Bill "Cincinnati" Smith; Oscar "Afraid" Wegelin; Edgar E. "Harvard" Wells (too much of an idealist); Doctor Gabriel "Rutgers" Wells (two souls, but always cash to buy with).

Among the collectors identified by Heartman were William Randolph "slow pay" Hearst; "magnificent" A. Edward Newton; H. R. "Yale" Wagner; and Henry H. "Must have everything in a hurry" Huntington. See Charles Heartman, *Twenty-Five Years in the Auction Business and What Now?* (Privately printed, 1938).

8. Eberstadt to LB, 7 May 1923. HIA GC.

9. Lathrop Harper to HEH, 11 January 1924. HIA GC.

10. Harper to HEH, 10 March 1923. HIA GC.

11. LB to Harper, 26 April 1923, and Harper's response of 10 May. HIA GC.

12. Edward Fowles, *Memories of the Duveen Brothers* (London: Times Books, 1976), 149.

13. Joseph Duveen to HEH, 18 December 1923, and HEH's response of 19 December. HIA GC.

14. LB to Walter Lewisson, 21 June 1923. HIA GC.

15. HEH to GWC, 3 June 1923. HIA GC.

16. HEH to GWC, 21 July 1923. HIA GC.

17. HEH to Mitchell Kennerley, 29 October 1923. HIA GC.

18. During 1923 ASWR also sold $45,000 worth of books to Mrs. Huntington (balance sheet in Huntington papers, Rosenbach Museum).

19. Herschel V. Jones to HEH, 1 May 1922; and Jones to LB, 23 November: "The price is $10,000." Then, LB to Jones, 28 November: "Was the price $7,500?" Finally, Jones to LB, 10 December 1925: "There was a smile on my face as I noted the wording of your sentence in your letter of the 28 regarding the price of $7,500 for "The Pirate." It cost me $11,000 but I have a good income tax this year and would not mind a little loss but I do not want to sell it for less than $8,000. I know this is a difference of only $500 but there is a principle in this case. I do not want to sell for less than $8,000." HIA GC.

20. ROS to LB, 5 August 1922. HIA GC.

21. H. V. Jones, *Later Library of Herschel V. Jones* (New York: Anderson Galleries, 1923).

22. ASWR to HEH, 5 February 1923. HIA GC.

23. In the midst of one of his periods of serious illness HEH wrote to Jones, 25 April 1925: "I missed seeing you in California and will forgive you, but not again." HIA GC.

24. LB to ASWR, 24 January 1923. HIA GC.

25. ASWR to HEH, 9 February and 17 February 1923; HEH's reply of 23 February. HIA GC.

26. ASWR to HEH, 19 March 1923. HIA GC.

27. C. E. Graham to HEH: "Have cabled Rosenbach as directed amount of draft proceeds not available for ten days in meantime have atal pighead [borrowed $75,000, as decoded from Huntington Railroad Code Book]to make up the difference." HIA GC.

28. ASWR to HEH, 27 September and 24 November 1923. HIA GC.

29. Wolf and Fleming, *Rosenbach*, 186.

30. Rosenbach paid Fenwick $22,816 for the documents and sold them to HEH for $150,000. See Leslie Morris, *Rosenbach Abroad* (Philadelphia: Rosenbach Museum, 1988), 39.

31. HEH to Walter Wyman, 20 April 1924. HIA GC.

32. Rosenbach bought the Thomas-Stanford incunabula for $34,000 and sold them to HEH for $82,500 (Wolf and Fleming, *Rosenbach*, 206).

33. Ibid., 207.

34. George Hapgood to ASWR, 4 February 1925. HIA GC.

35. ASWR to GWC, 2 November 1923, and GWC's reply of 10 November. HIA GC.

36. ASWR to HEH, 21 June 1923. HIA GC.

37. *NYT,* 16 December 1923.

38. HEH to ASWR, 3 October 1923; and ASWR's further report of 27 May 1924. HIA GC.

39. *NYT,* 16 December 1923.

Chapter 11 — An Outstanding Endowment (1924–1925)

1. The original board members were W. E. Dunn, George Ellery Hale, Archer Huntington, George S. Patton, and Henry M. Robinson.

2. State of California. Senate Concurrent Resolution Number 27, Relative to the Establishment of the Huntington Foundation (15 May 1923). HIA GC.

3. HEH to Mitchell Kennerley, 29 December 1922. HIA GC.

4. *LAT*, 13 October 1923.

5. Wright, *Explorer*, 384.

6. HEH to Charles Sessler, 23 December 1924. HIA GC.

7. ASWR to HEH, 5 February 1924.

8. HEH to ASWR, 20 February 1924, and ASWR's reply of 23 February. HIA GC.

9. *Catalogue of a Further Selection of Rare and Valuable Works in Early English Poetry* (London: Sotheby and Company, 1924), 4.

10. ASWR to HEH, 7 April 1924. HIA GC.

11. Letters between Dring and HEH of 1 July 1924, 14 July, and 1 August. HIA GC.

12. Letters between GWC and HEH, 7 January 1924 and 1 June. HIA GC.

13. GWC to staff, 23 September 1924. HIA GC.

14. GWC, "Report of the Librarian" (typescript, 1924). HIA GC. Cole asked for and received a lifetime title of Librarian Emeritus and retirement on half pay. GWC to HEH, 2 June 1924. HIA GC.

15. Chester Cate to staff, 23 September 1924. HIA GC.

16. ASWR to HEH, 12 November 1924. HIA GC.

17. HEH, To Whom it May Concern, 7 July 1922. HIA GC.

18. Mitchell Kennerley to HEH, 2 April 1923. HIA GC.

19. When the house was demolished in 1926 Archer gave the furnishings to the Yale University Art Gallery and the important paintings to the Metropolitan Museum in New York. See Isabelle Hyman, "The Huntington Mansion in New York," *Syracuse University Library Association Courier* 25 (1990): 7.

20. HEH to ASWR, 18 December 1924. HIA GC.

21. Maurice L. Ettinghausen, *Rare Books and Royal Collectors* (New York: Simon and Schuster, 1966), 162.

22. LB to Otto Vollbehr, 19 December 1924, and Otto Vollbehr's reply of 19 January 1925. HIA GC.

23. Otto Vollbehr to HEH, 26 January 1925; HEH to Vollbehr of 13 April 1925. HIA GC.

24. *LAT*, 2 December 1925.

25. Letters between Otto Vollbehr and LB of 2 March 1926, 9 June, and 10 July. HIA GC.

26. Otto Vollbehr to HEH, 2 October 1926. HIA GC.

27. ASWR to HEH, 7 April 1925. HIA GC. On the same day Rosenbach wrote to Bliss: "Mr. Christie-Miller was disappointed at the results of the sale, as there were in this lot many of the rarist and most important volumes in his collection." HIA GC.

28. ASWR to HEH, 25 May 1925. HIA GC.

29. Frank Marcham to LB, 9 May 1939. HIA GC.

30. Frank Madigan to HEH, 6 August 1925; LB's reply of 6 September. HIA GC.

31. Emma Quigley (typescript of interview, 21 April 1967). Quigley, the office manager for Huntington and Dunn, reported that Huntington often brought his lunch, usually a cheese sandwich and an apple, in a tin box. HIA GC Bi.

32. *LAT*, 13 October 1923.

33. HEH to ASWR, 20 December 1925. HIA GC.

34. LB to Alice Millard, 4 March 1926. HIA GC.

35. HEH to Mitchell Kennerley, 3 April 1926. HIA GC.

36. LB to ASWR, 12 January 1926. HIA GC.

37. HEH to ASWR, 5 November 1926. HIA GC.

38. ASWR to HEH, 14 May 1926. HIA GC.

39. LB to ASWR, 5 May and 14 May 1926. HIA GC.

40. ASWR to HEH, 27 May 1926. HIA GC.

Chapter 12 — "The Reward of all the Work I Have Ever Done" (1926–1927)

1. Henry E. Huntington Library, trust indenture, 1919.

2. George Patton to George Ellery Hale, 2 September 1925. HIA GC.

3. On 14 October 1925—following the words "I approve the adoption of the above policy for the Huntington Library and Art Gallery"—HEH signed a typescript document entitled "The Future Development of the Huntington Library and Art Gallery." HIA GC. It was also published in *Huntington Library Quarterly* 11 (May 1948): 296–300.

4. Henry E. Huntington Library, trust indenture, 1926.

5. Max Farrand, "Recollections of HEH" (typescript, 8 February 1933). HIA GC Bi.

6. Ray Allen Billington, "The Genesis of the Research Institution," *Huntington Library Quarterly* (1969): 369.

7. G. E. Hale to Farrand, 30 May 1927. HIA GC.

8. LB to G. E. Hale, 10 March 1927. HIA GC.

9. Henry E. Huntington Library, *Annual Report* (1927).

10. GWC, "The Henry E. Huntington Library 1915–1924," Cole Papers, American Antiquarian Society.

11. GWC, "The Photostat in Bibliographical and Research Work," *Publications of the Bibliographical Society of America,* no. 1 (1922): 14.

12. Edward Ayer to HEH, 25 March 1923, and HEH's reply of 12 April. HIA GC.

13. GWC, "The Henry Huntington Library," in *Annual Publication of the Historical Society of Southern California* (1920); see also "The Huntington Library," in *Library Journal* 47 (15 September 1922).

14. George Ellery Hale, "The Huntington Library: A New Plan of Research," *Scribner's* 82 (27 July 1927).

15. HEH to ASWR, 17 February 1927. HIA GC.

16. HEH to GWC, 10 February 1927. HIA GC.

17. HEH to ASWR, 26 April 1927. HIA GC.

18. ASWR to LB, 17 May 1927. HIA GC.

19. Mr. and Mrs. Huntington's bodies were moved to the mausoleum 1 October 1929; Diana Wilson, *The Mausoleum of Henry and Arabella Huntington* (San Marino, Calif.: Huntington Library, 1989).

20. *LAT,* 29 May 1927.

21. *LAT,* 9 January 1922.

Books and articles

Allen, Frederick Lewis. *The Big Change*. New York: Harper, 1938.

———. *Only Yesterday*. New York: Blue Ribbon, 1931.

Annals of the Hobby Club of New York City 1912–1920. New York: Privately printed, 1920.

Behrman, S. N. *Duveen*. New York: Random House, 1952.

Bidwell, John. "Four Founders of Rare Book Libraries." In *A Bibliophile's Los Angeles*, edited by John Bidwell. Los Angeles: William Andrews Clark Memorial Library, UCLA, 1985.

Billington, Ray A. "The Genesis of the Research Institution." *Huntington Library Quarterly* 32 (1969): 351–72.

Bliss, Leslie E. "The Research Facilities of the Huntington Library." *Huntington Library Quarterly* 3 (1939): 131–35.

"The Bloodless Battles for Books of the Bibliophiles." *New York Herald Tribune*, 14 January 1912, sec. 3, p. 4.

Bowen, Dorothy. "Huntington and His Hobby." *Saturday Review of Literature* 26 (October 1943): 19–20.

Boyer, David. "Huntington Library." *National Geographic Magazine* 113 (February 1958): 251–76.

Bruccoli, Matthew. *The Fortunes of Mitchell Kennerley, Bookman*. New York: Harcourt Brace Jovanovich, 1986.

Burton, Katherine. *Henry E. Huntington*. Norton, Mass.: Periwinkle Press, 1939.

Cannon, Carl. *American Book Collectors*. New York: H. W. Wilson, 1941.

Carlton, W. N. C. "Henry Edwards Huntington." *American Collector* 4 (August 1927): 165–67.

Cole, George Watson. "The Henry E. Huntington Library." In *Annual Publication of the Historical Society of Southern California*. Los Angeles: Historical Society of Southern California, 1920.

———. "The Huntington Library." *Library Journal* 47 (15 September 1922): 745–50.

———. "Book Collectors as Benefactors of Public Libraries." *Papers of the Bibliographical Society of America*, no. 3 (1915): 47–110.

Cowan, Robert E. *Booksellers of Early San Francisco*. Los Angeles: Ward Ritchie Press, 1953.

Crump, Spencer. *Henry Huntington and the Pacific Electric*. Los Angeles: Trans Anglo Books, 1970.

Davies, Godfrey. "The Huntington Library as a Research Center 1925–1927." *Huntington Library Quarterly* 11 (May 1948): 293–95. (Includes transcript of "The Future Development of the Huntington Library and Art Gallery," which Huntington signed on 14 October 1925.)

De Ricci, Seymour. *English Collectors of Books and Manuscripts*. New York: Macmillan, 1930.

Dickinson, Donald C. "Mr. Huntington and Mr. Smith." *The Book Collector* 37 (Autumn 1988): 367–93.

———. *George Watson Cole*. Metuchen, N.J.: Scarecrow Press, 1990.

———. "Mr. Huntington and Mr. Brigham." *The Book Collector* 42 (1993): 241-57.

Duveen, James Henry. *Secrets of an Art Dealer*. New York: Dutton, 1938.

Essick, Robert N. *The Works of William Blake in the Huntington Collections*. San Marino, Calif.: Huntington Library, 1985.

Ettinghausen, Maurice. *Rare Books and Royal Collectors*. New York: Simon and Schuster, 1966.

Evans, Cerinda. *Collis Porter Huntington*. Newport News, Va.: Mariners' Museum, 1954.

Farrand, Max. "To Mr. Huntington and the Trustees of the Henry E. Huntington Library and Art Gallery." *Huntington Library Quarterly* 11 (May 1948): 300–306.

Farrar, John. "World's Greatest Private Library." *The World Magazine* (24 October 1920).

Fowles, Edward. *Memories of the Duveen Brothers*. London: Times Books, 1976.

Friedricks, William B. "Henry E. Huntington and Real Estate Development in Southern California 1898–1917." *Southern California Quarterly* 71 (Winter 1989): 327–40.

———. "A Metropolitan Entrepreneur Par Excellence: Henry E. Huntington and the Growth of Southern California, 1898–1927." *Business History Review* 63 (Summer 1989): 329–55.

———. *Henry E. Huntington and the Creation of Southern California*. Columbus, Oh.: Ohio State University Press, 1992.

Hale, George Ellery. "The Huntington Library and Art Gallery." *Scribner's Magazine* 82 (27 July 1927): 31–43.

Hall, Wilbur. "Treasures of Time." *The World's Work* 44 (July 1922): 319–23.

Harlan, Robert D. *At the Sign of the Lark*. San Francisco: Book Club of California, 1983.

Heartman, Charles F. *Twenty-five Years in the Auction Business, and What Now?* Privately Printed, 1938.

——. "George D. Smith, 1870–1920, Gentleman Bookseller." *American Book Collector* 23 (May–June 1973): 3–26. (Originally published as a Yuletide Greeting from the Book Farm, Beauvoir Community, Miss., 1945.)

Hertrich, William. *The Huntington Botanical Gardens 1905–1949.* San Marino, Calif.: Huntington Library, 1949.

Hyman, Isabelle. "The Huntington Mansion in New York." *Courier* (Syracuse University Library Associates) 25 (Fall 1990): 3–29.

Lavender, David. *The Great Persuader.* Garden City, N.J.: Doubleday, 1970.

Lewis, Oscar. *The Big Four.* New York: Knopf, 1938.

McKay, George L. *American Book Auction Catalogues, 1713–1934.* New York: New York Public Library, 1937.

McWilliams, Carey. *Southern California Country.* New York: Duell, Sloan, Pearce, 1946.

Maher, James T. *The Twilight of Splendor.* Boston: Little Brown, 1975.

Marcosson, Isaac. *A Little-Known Master of Millions.* Boston: E. Rollins, 1914.

Maxwell, Margaret F. *Shaping a Library: William L. Clements as a Collector.* Amsterdam: Israel, 1973.

Morris, Leslie A. *Rosenbach Abroad.* Philadelphia: Rosenbach Museum and Library, 1988.

Newmark, Harris. *Sixty Years in Southern California.* New York: Knickerbocker Press, 1916.

Newton, A. Edward. *The Amenities of Book Collecting.* Boston: Atlantic Monthly Press, 1918.

Nikirk, Robert. "Two American Book Collectors of the Nineteenth Century: William Loring Andrews and Beverly Chew." In *Book Selling and Book Buying.* Chicago: American Library Association, 1978.

Olmert, Michael. "Truth and Beauty Are Still in Flower at the Huntington." *Smithsonian Magazine* 12 (December 1981): 64–72.

Pomeroy, Elizabeth. *The Huntington.* London: P. Wilson, 1983.

Pomfret, John E. *The Henry E. Huntington Library and Art Gallery.* San Marino, Calif.: Huntington Library, 1969.

Reid, B. L. *The Man from New York.* New York: Oxford, 1968.

Rosenbach, A. S. W. *Books and Bidders.* Boston: Little Brown, 1927.

Rouse, Parke. "The Huntington." *Westways* 70 (December 1978): 44–47.

Schad, Robert O. "Henry Edwards Huntington—The Founder and the Library." *Huntington Library Bulletin* 1 (May 1931): 3–32.

——. "A Quarter Century at the Huntington Library." *Quarterly Newsletter of the Book Collectors of California* (Fall 1952): 75–80.

Sherburn, George. "Huntington Library Collections," *Huntington Library Bulletin* 1 (May 1931): 33–106.

Spurgeon, Selena A. *Henry Edwards Huntington: His Life and His Collections.* San Marino, Calif.: Huntington Library, 1992.

Sowerby, E. Millicent. *Rare People and Rare Books.* Williamsburg, Va.: Bookpress, 1987.

Starr, Kevin. *Americans and the California Dream 1850–1915.* New York: Oxford, 1986.

——. *Inventing the Dream.* New York: Oxford, 1985.

——. *Material Dreams.* New York: Oxford, 1990.

Thorpe, James. *Gifts of Genius.* San Marino, Calif.: Huntington Library, 1980.

——. "The Founder and His Library." *Huntington Library Quarterly* 32 (August 1969): 291–308.

Towner, Wesley. *The Elegant Auctioneers.* New York: Hill and Wang, 1970.

Wagner, Henry R. *Bullion to Books.* Los Angeles: Zamorano Club, 1942.

——. *Collecting: Especially Books.* Los Angeles: Ward Ritchie Press, 1968.

Wark, Robert R. "Arabella Huntington and the Beginnings of the Art Gallery." *Huntington Library Quarterly* 32 (August 1969): 309–31.

Wilson, Diana G. *The Mausoleum of Henry and Arabella Huntington.* San Marino, Calif.: Huntington Library, 1989.

Watkins, Louise. *Henry Edwards Huntington.* Gardena, Calif.: Spanish American Institute Press, 1928.

Wolf, Edwin, and John F. Fleming. *Rosenbach, a Biography.* Cleveland: World Publishing, 1960.

Wright, Helen. *Explorer of the Universe: A Biography of George Ellery Hale.* New York: Dutton, 1966.

Wright, Louis B. *Of Books and Men.* Columbia: University of South Carolina Press, 1976.

——. "Huntington and Folger, Book Collectors With a Purpose," *Atlantic Monthly* 209 (April 1962): 70–74.

Unpublished material

Barbour, Thomas. Recollection of HEH. HIA GC Bi.

Bendikson, Lodewyk. Remarks by Dr. Lodewyk Bendikson at Dinner Honoring Him on his Retirement from the Huntington Library, 30 June 1943. HIA GC Bi.

Bliss, Leslie. Interview. 3 January 1968. HIA GC Bi.

Carpenter, Edwin. "The Huntingtons at Home." Tape recording, n.d. Property of the author.

Cole, George Watson. "Report of the Librarian." October 1924. HIA GC.

——. "Book Collectors with Reference to the Library of Henry Edwards Huntington." 22 January 1929. HIA GC.

——. "The Henry E. Huntington Library 1915–1924," n.d. George Watson Cole Papers, American Antiquarian Society.

Farrand, Max. Recollection of HEH. 8 February 1933. HIA GC Bi.

Gomez, Alfonso. Interview. 11 April 1968. HIA GC Bi.

Hale, George Ellery. Recollection of HEH. 8 February 1933. HIA GC Bi.

Harper, Henry. Recollection of HEH. 25 June 1937. HIA GC.

Henry E. Huntington Library and Art Gallery. Annual Reports, 1927–

——. The Founders Choice: An Exhibition for the Fiftieth Anniversary of the Founding of the Huntington Library 1919–1969. The Founders Choice is a recreation of an exhibit of thirty-five choice items that Mr. Huntington arranged in his home in New York in 1919 for a visit of the Authors Club. San Marino, Calif.: The Huntington Library, 1969.

——. Check List or Brief Catalogue of the Library of Henry E. Huntington. English Literature to 1640. New York: Privately printed. Issued in parts 1919–1920.

——. Trust Indenture. 30 August 1919. HIA GC.

——. Last Will and Testament. 26 May 1927. HIA GC

Holladay, Caroline. Recollection of Harriet Saunders Huntington. 14 January 1929. HIA GC.

——. Recollection of HEH. 16 March 1929. HIA GC.

Hunt, Myron. Interview. 1 February 1930. HIA GC Bi.

Miles, G. E. Recollection of HEH, n.d. HIA GC Bi.

Quigley, Emma. Interview. 21 April 1967. HIA GC Bi.

Schad, Robert O. "Founder's Day Address." 27 February 1930. HIA GC Bi.

Walker, A. O. Interview. 23 March 1960. HIA GC Bi.

Manuscript collections

George Watson Cole Papers. American Antiquarian Society, Worcester, Massachusetts. The collection includes diaries, correspondence, cash ledgers, photographs, reminiscences, essays and appreciations. The collection consists of 66 boxes of manuscripts and 92 bound octavo volumes.

Henry E. Huntington Papers. Henry E. Huntington, Library and Art Gallery, San Marino, California. The collection is divided into a cataloged and an uncataloged section. The cataloged portion, some 23,000 items, consists of personal and business corresponce; specific items are identified in the Manuscript Card Catalog. This material is referred to as the HEH Collection. The uncataloged portion consists of a wide variety of materials including book lists (16/1–5), book bills (25/1–6), marked auction catalogs (46/1–9), clippings (38/2), a biographical file of recollections and interviews concerning the life of Henry E. Huntington (19/1–5), and letters from book dealers, fellow collectors, librarians, and friends. A detailed listing of the contents of the uncataloged materials is provided in a "Summary Report and Inventory Sheet of the HEH Collection."

Abraham Simon Wolf Rosenbach Papers. Abraham Simon Wolf Rosenbach Museum. Philadelphia, Pennsylvania. Includes some 150 letters exchanged between Henry E. Huntington and A. S. W. Rosenbach, 1909–27.

Note

Records that disclose details about Huntington's personal life and his reactions to the people and events of his day are sparse, even among the large quantity of his papers, cataloged and uncataloged, in the Huntington Library. Huntington never made speeches, was reluctant to grant interviews, and wrote no articles for publication. His letters were typically businesslike and to the point. The author found the materials contained in the uncataloged Biographical File (19/1–5) particularly useful. On 4 June 1928, the board of trustees authorized the collection of "biographical materials relating to the life and interests of the Founder for preservation and later use." Robert O. Schad, curator of rare books, was designated as curator of the Biographical File. Between 1928 and 1933 Schad gathered letters and recollections from family members and friends. The Huntington Library Annual Reports from 1927 to 1933 carry accounts of the growth of this archive. The project was abandoned in 1934 when Caroline Holliday, executrix of Huntington's will, told Schad that she did not feel the time was ripe for any continued biographical effort. Of particular interest to those concerned with Huntington as a book collector are letters and recollections from Mrs. Edward Ayer, Thomas Barbour, Max Farrand, George Ellery Hale, Henry Harper, Myron Hunt, Isaac Mendoza, G. E. Miles, and Otheman Stevens.

Abbreviations

HEH   Henry Edwards Huntington
HL   Henry E. Huntington Library and Art Gallery
MS.   manuscript
MSS.   manuscripts
(ill.)   an illustration and/or its caption
(nn)   not named, i.e. person or subject is referred to without being named
NYL   HEH's library in New York City

RICHARD﹢TOTTEL